Kevin Cahill, Lene Johar

Considering Class

Transnational and Transatlantic American Studies

edited by

Mita Banerjee (Siegen)
Kornelia Freitag (Bochum)
Walter Grünzweig (Dortmund)
Randi Gunzenhäuser (Dortmund)
Rüdiger Kunow (Potsdam)
Wilfried Raussert (Bielefeld)
Michael Wala (Bochum)

Volume 4

LIT

Kevin Cahill, Lene Johannessen (Eds.)

CONSIDERING CLASS

Essays on the Discourse of the American Dream

LIT

Cover Picture: Former Walmart Employees in Saguenay, Quebec, May, 2005
Photo: Jeannot Levesque/AP/Scanpix

We would like to thank the Faculty of Arts and the Department of English at the
University of Bergen for their financial support. We are also grateful to Walter
Grünzweig for his editorial assistance.

Bibliographic information published by the Deutsche Nationalbibliothek
The Deutsche Nationalbibliothek lists this publication in the Deutsche
Nationalbibliografie; detailed bibliographic data are available in the Internet at
http://dnb.d-nb.de.

ISBN 978-3-8258-0259-2

A catalogue record for this book is available from the British Library

© LIT VERLAG Dr. W. Hopf Berlin 2007
Auslieferung/Verlagskontakt:
Fresnostr. 2   48159 Münster
Tel. +49 (0)251–620320   Fax +49 (0)251–231972
e-Mail: lit@lit-verlag.de   http://www.lit-verlag.de

Distributed in the UK by: Global Book Marketing, 99B Wallis Rd, London, E9 5LN
Phone: +44 (0) 20 8533 5800 – Fax: +44 (0) 1600 775 663
http://www.centralbooks.co.uk/acatalog/search.html

Distributed in North America by:

Transaction Publishers
New Brunswick (U.S.A.) and London (U.K.)

Transaction Publishers
Rutgers University
35 Berrue Circle
Piscataway, NJ 08854

Phone: +1 (732) 445 - 2280
Fax: + 1 (732) 445 - 3138
for orders (U. S. only):
toll free (888) 999 - 6778
e-mail:
orders@transactionspub.com

Contents

Introduction

In the chapter on socialism and unionism in the United States in his acclaimed *American Exceptionalism: A Double Edged Sword* Seymour Martin Lipset writes as follows: "The United States has stood out among the industrial nations of the world in frustrating all efforts to create a mass socialist or labor party. The fact has occasioned a considerable literature seeking to explain this aspect of American exceptionalism [....]"[1]

The present collection of essays also tries to address this riddle, and does so from a trans-disciplinary perspective that provides a number of different partial answers. The collection is also transnational, not just in terms of where the authors themselves come from, but more significantly in that several of the essays bring the implications of disparate ethnic and national origins and imaginaries within the U.S. to bear on the economical, cultural, and social configurations of class. This transnationalism adds further to the puzzle, which this volume as a whole is concentrated on, namely the exceptional nature of American exceptionalism.

As others have noted before, while a nation's narrative of its genesis and trajectory is unique, the conviction that the uniqueness in itself is unique, is truly exceptional.[2] The trajectory of this culturological self-perception is long and complex, but all through US history the claim to simultaneous universality and uniqueness is both constitutive of and constituted by it. The dialectics could be said to gravitate around a new economy that marks the Unites States' coming into being in the world, an economy that launches a particular manifestation of liberal democracy and market capitalism framed by a frontier mentality that is inherently without boundaries.[3] The point has been made many times in the past, but it bears repeating: America named an idea that long preceded its actual coming into being as the nation we know it as. Djelal Kadir thus argues that 'America' signifies an interesting tension between the 'new land' that is 'clear', 'bright', 'shining', 'ever young', 'ever fair' and 'Nowhereland', a utopia, a place that is no place.[4] The idea as it merged with an actual place marked the origin of a very real imaginary that held out the promise of progress and unbridled pursuit of aspiration and potential happiness, a promise that extended into the world as an irresistible and advanced version of modernity. Free from older conceptions of divine law, and from the obligations of order handed down

---

[1] Seymour Martin Lipset, *American Exceptionalism: A Double Edged Sword* (New York: W.W. Norton, 1996) 77.

[2] See eg. Djelal Kadir, ""Introduction: America and Its Studies," *PMLA*, 118:1, 2003, 9-24.

[3] Economy is used here in the sense Charles Taylor discusses it in his essay "Modern Social Imaginaries, as an interlocking set of activities of production, exchange, and consumption, which form a system with its own laws and dynamic ... the economic now defines a way in which we are linked together, a sphere of coexistence that could in principle suffice to itself." Charles Taylor, "Modern Social Imaginaries," *Public Culture*, 14:1, 2002, 105.

[4] Djelal Kadir, quoted in Sophia A. McClennen, "Inter-American studies or Imperial American studies?," *Comparative American Studies*, 3:4, 2005, 397.

by centuries of traditions and civic laws, this imaginary presents itself as an economy that relies on the reason and rationality inherent in all human beings. The American imaginary thus draws into its fold spaces far away, and it both feeds on and is fed by that part of other imaginaries elsewhere that dream of aspiration's free reign.

What is not being said here, however, is that that very promise is also the promise of failure, as Scott Sandage demonstrates so well in his *Born Losers: A History of Failure in the America.*[5] His discussion of "failure" goes a long way towards explaining the ideological-cultural reasons for why class and its discourses have suffered in the history of the U.S. Somewhere along the way the "pursuit" of happiness becomes programmatic, and happiness measured in terms of a material success mostly unhinged from the early Puritans' introspection and search for inward signs of salvation. As Sandage puts it, "Self-reliance and self-criticism went hand in hand," and the shame of failing in business and enterprise "echoed the abasement rituals and testimonies of American Protestantism."[6]

From a very early point, then, what would become American national culture valued economic success as the outward sign of moral and personal accomplishment. The eminent Ralph Waldo Emerson, whose words at Henry Thoreau's funeral Sandage begins his book with, saw the lack of ambition in his deceased friend as "a fault in [Thoreau]" and would later note that "There is always a reason, in the man, for his good or bad fortune, and so in making money."[7] In what James Morone calls a "moral economy," a "spirited form of capitalism,"[8] it is inevitable that for the individual an alliance with the working class is the same as breaking with the culturological covenant, an admission to failure in a "nation that worships success."[9]

The contributions in *Considering Class: Essays on the Discourse of the American Dream* in particular focus on the (dys)functional position of class in American socio-political and cultural reality and imagination. It is of course open to debate whether the category of class is any more stable and thus more resistant to being relativized than other categories, or significantly more resilient to post-capitalism's absorption and appropriation of critical outsides. There is increasing recognition, however, that class remains a category with the potential to transcend the rifts and divisions that run along lines of race, ethnicity and gender, and with the potential to reconfigure the current American political landscape.

---

[5] It is appropriate here that Sandage chooses "America" rather than "the United States" in his title, since only the former embodies those ideas of the imaginary that emphasize the universal appeal to aspiration and a particular form of ambition.
[6] Scott Sandage, *Born Losers: A History of Failure in America* (Cambridge: Harvard UP, 2005) 47.
[7] Sandage, 46.
[8] James Morone, "Good for Nothing." Book review. *London Review of Books*, 27:10, 2005.
[9] Sandage, 3.

Class and the Culture of Exceptionalism

From various perspectives the essays in this section all inquire into the consequences of the American idiosyncrasy of its claim to a "unique uniqueness." The main emphasis of Omar Swartz's "Power, Praxis, and Equity in the Struggle for Working Class Dignity" is on how American exceptionalism has all but neutralized class-consciousness among the large working class population that exists and generally rendered the discourse of economic equality in public debates a non-entity. Using the Supreme Court ruling in "In re Debs" (1895) as his prime focus, Swartz demonstrates how this ruling, by arguing that the railroad workers functioned as an invited "mob," denounced the right of unions to protest. The precedence this ruling set would account for numerous instances of federal intervention in labor conflicts that would prove fatal to a sustained development of union practices we find in other industrial nations.

If American exceptionalism in large part accounts for the disempowerment and denigration of class-based movements, it also explains why individuals shy away from being categorized as anything less than "middle." In "The Elephant in the Room: Culture, Cohesion, and Context in the American Middle Class," Marina Moskowitz takes as her point of departure a no less idiosyncratic feature of American culturological self-understanding, namely the fact that the vast majority of the population classifies itself as belonging to the middle class. In order to account for this, she argues, we must employ a definition of the category which also includes factors such as aspiration, organization of daily life, and sense of commonality with others. Precisely because these factors are impossible to quantify, the category "middle-class" becomes essential as a category based in shared culture. Moskowitz focuses mostly on the early 20th century, both because this is the time of the proliferation of the middle-class in the US, and because the simultaneous emergence of the social sciences gave rise to a corresponding interest and research in this particular societal segment. She thus sets out to examine the ways in which these early explorations of the middle-class as social and cultural phenomena also refracted an emphasis on culture and inclusiveness rather than economy and exclusiveness: "By considering class in these ways, we can begin to understand how and why so many Americans wish to come together under the umbrella of the middle class." (16)

One curiosity of American exceptionalism is of course how the immense number of immigrants from across the globe has tended to embrace the imaginary, the new "moral economy." In the 19th century the majority of immigrants came from Europe, and very many from countries where the structures of industrial labor movements had already been in existence for years. And yet, only occasionally were these experiences successfully brought to bear on the new social and economic environments. When they were, they often went in tandem with political positions and actions against oppression in the mother country.

To adequately account for this, Malini Cadambi and Evan Matthew Daniel argue in "(Re)Examining Class: Transnational Workers and Nationalist Struggles in the late 19th Century United States," that we need to synthesize materialist and post-modern concepts of class. In their analysis of Indian agricultural workers and Cuban cigar makers in the US in the late 19th century the authors maintain that, "both groups constructed collective identities based on their class positions as well as their notions of nationality as colonial subjects." (47) This approach addresses the question of the relation between globalization processes and the steady de-symbolization of the concept of class by concretely presenting two case studies where early manifestations of the transnational economic system become evident. Cadambi and Daniel's argument not only pertains to the U.S., it is also highly relevant to the situation of work migrants in the new EU and elsewhere. What is the potential of class as category of identification to forge politically transnational ties that can both work locally and globally? This question is increasingly important to ask, but one that, not unexpectedly, remains largely unexamined.

The Discourse of Class

Any consideration of the absence of a robust discourse of class in the US will eventually run up against the culturological bulwark that constitutes and is constituted by the "American Dream." This is perhaps nowhere more evident than in the many representations of social and economical inequality found in literature and film. However, while issues relating to class, and particularly to the middle-class, have been explored in a variety of aesthetic, cultural and historical contexts, few manage to maintain their focus on class as a primary concern. In movies the complexity of class often dissolves into vortexes of the suburb, of gender, ethnicity, race etc.

In literature we see the fluctuations in interpretation varying with the culturological and aesthetic concerns of any given period, and these concerns have for some time now emphasized the "ever-elusive revolutionary subject" always sought after in for instance American Studies.[10] That subject has increasingly been looked for in other, marginalized and/or sub-cultural strata of the American societal fabric. The essays in this section re-direct attention to class in textual and film representations by re-reading and reinstating class as the lens through which the narratives are told and explored.

Masood Raja uses E. L. Doctorow's *Ragtime* to engage critically what he sees as the neo-liberal economy's appropriation of the political left's traditional positions under the heading of individual freedom in its many-faceted manifestations. In "Doctorow's *Ragtime:* Inserting Class in a Literary Discussion" Raja

---

[10] Winfried Fluck, "Theories of American Culture," conference lecture, "Transatlantic American Studies: Transcultural Visions of Identities in Images and Texts," Humboldt-Universität zu Berlin, February, 2005.

reads this acclaimed and allegedly radical text from a critical standpoint that brings out the shortcomings of readings that fail to factor in the changes wrought by neo-liberal globalization. In this reading the story of the main protagonist becomes a rather bleak one: "[He] moves through the earlier redemptive myths of American exceptionalism and reaches the ultimate and the most enduring one – the myth of the sacred marketplace." (113) Differently from for instance Linda Hutcheon, then, who maintains a criticism of the novel based in categories of solidarity and social mobility, Raja redirects focus to the forces of accommodation and appropriation which the text, perhaps against its will, end up refracting.

Rosalie Baum takes a similar perspective in her "Defining Working-Class Realities in Chicago and Rocksburg, PA: 'Partial Descriptions,'" where she examines two literary works that come to class in very different ways. Reading Frank Norris's short story "A Deal in Wheat" (1902) against the pseudonymous K. C. Constantine's *Grievance* (2000) she discusses the complexities involved in labelling and representing such a multifaceted category as working class literature. The rich nuances that saturate *Grievance* crisscross ethnic differences, a feature that is largely absent from the naturalist approach taken by Norris:

> The struggle that Norris portrayed in 1902 between capitalist-speculators on one side and farmers and urban workers on the other becomes, in Constantine's twenty-first century world, a complex system with capitalists, government, charitable foundations, politicians, and law enforcement on one side and workers on the other. (80)

Baum's essay thus brings class into the canon debate, and expands the revisions undertaken in the past decades to also problematize the relationship between the parameters of identity, ethnicity and class. "Working-Class Studies," she argues, "must not evolve in an oppositional position to the traditional or dominant culture: it must be incorporated into a 'common culture.'" (84)

Nowhere does the consciousness and discourse of class tend to lose out as completely to interpretative categories such as race, ethnicity as in discussions of popular culture and media. In "Gendered Dreams and the Hollywood Cross-Class Romance" Wuming Zhao decodes and retells the many and poignant discourses pertaining to class in a series of movies she subsumes under the heading of "Cinderella stories." Cross-class romantic love in Hollywood products such as *Sabrina* (1954), *My Fair Lady* (1964), *Love Story* (1970), *Working Girl* (1988), *Pretty Woman* (1990) are not only, as in the standard conception and interpretation, tales of the American Dream. Instead, Zhao argues, they should be regarded as versions of the Cinderella narrative. What this narrative paradigm offers is a discursive synthesis of two competing themes, namely the romanticizing of the domestic woman and woman as aspiring "American" individual. Against the backdrop of the emergence of feminist ideologies, the Cinderella paradigm also becomes "a popular site for women to negotiate their roles and goals in the realization of their own dream of success." (129) In this description, class is a dominant category where the national mantra of individualism finds a site for female aspiration and realization.

The communicative potential and power of both literature and film to undermine or consolidate culturally and politically received attitudes regarding social and economic mobility cannot be underestimated. The eschewing of class in public discourse has a long and complicated history, starting, as has been noted above, with the very inception of the American project as a project centering on material success as a measure of moral and ethical integrity and triumph. A crucial link between elected officials and organizations representing "the politically mobilized classes" is the rhetorical means by which the former are able to reach out to the latter in order to manipulate or reassure them accordingly. (89) In their essay "Class Presidents" political scientists Jason C. Myers and Stephen R. Routh's focus on non-major presidential addresses (i.e. excluding State of Union addresses, major foreign and domestic addresses and international summit meeting remarks and speeches) from Harry Truman to Bill Clinton. The speeches Myers and Routh examine are of interest here, not only because they were directed to organizations representing distinct class interests, but also because they were given only after the particular president was safely in office. There is more to their political content, therefore, than can be accounted for purely in terms of an attempt to generate voter participation. While they build on already existing research into presidential communications, Myers and Routh examine these speeches in terms of the distinction between owners and employees, rather than through the more usual lenses of blue collar and white collar. In their view, this permits a better representation of the role of class in these speeches since it yields an account of the interests and actions of capital as well as those of labor.

Class and Institutions

Marx famously wrote in his *Theses on Feuerbach* that the "philosophers have only interpreted the world in various ways, the point, however, is to change it." Ken Oldfield's and Tom Nesbit's papers may not have the revolutionary scope Marx had in mind, but both do connect up with his spirit in at least one important sense, namely, in the way each focuses on the prospects of concrete policy and institutional changes (whether revolution should be construed as the ultimate policy and institutional change is perhaps worth contemplating elsewhere). Philosopher Albert Borgmann has warned of the way in which social theory "remains inconclusive until it hits the catalytic layer of tangible reality."[11] The relevance of Oldfield's and Nesbit's papers to the overall thrust of this collection, then, is in large measure ascribable to the ways in which they take up the burden of exploring two faces of that reality.

---

[11] Albert Borgmann, "Theory, Reality, Practice," *Inquiry*, 38:1-2, 1995, 148.

The title of Oldfield's paper is "Achieving Social Class Diversity Throughout the Workforce: A Case Study of TIAA-CREF." In its own words, TIAA-CREF is "a group of companies [that] offers educators, researchers, their families, and the public a range of products and services to help them save for retirement and other goals." (156) While Oldfield notes that TIAA-CREF can be justly proud of the way in which its hiring practices show a genuine concern for diversity regarding race and gender, his analysis of the TIAA-CREF board of directors shows how this concern is conspicuously absent when it comes to considering socioeconomic background.[12] Oldfield, however, does not argue that TIAA-CREF is merely giving cynical lip service to diversity, while knowingly excluding those coming from what he calls "humble origins." (116) Rather, his point is that it is an indication of the extent to which social class is simply not on the radar screen of American political consciousness that even an explicit wish for diversity can so easily fail to take it into account. He concludes by arguing that taking social class into account for the makeup of its board of directors would make TIAA-CREF a genuine leader in the diversity movement.

Many of the same considerations hold true of Tom Nesbit's paper "Social Class and Adult Education." Despite the longevity of the myth that anyone can make it in America, it is by now practically a truism that class and education are highly determinative for the individual's prospects in the United States. As Nesbit makes clear, moreover, class structures are commonly mimicked in the educational system, thus thwarting education's potential to augment social mobility. But while there has been some research on the relation between social class and participation in education, relatively little work has examined the ways in which class bears on educational issues such as course content, classroom environment, pedagogy, and learning styles, all of which have been studied far more extensively in connection with race and gender. Nesbit's paper looks at how class and education meet in the specific arena of adult education, which he understands broadly to include not only such things as literacy programs and so-called continuing education, but also training centers, and private companies. He makes clear the relevance of this focus in the following passage:

> [A]dult education is now firmly established as central to the smooth functioning of economic systems and societies. As such concepts as lifelong learning and the knowledge society gain prominence, education and training become key vehicles for preparing people to be adaptable to economic changes in society. Even though the aim of adult education is generally to ameliorate the social disadvantages that class and background produce, nowadays adult education often serves to merely exacerbate those disadvantages. (136)

---

[12] It is perhaps worth noting that questions of genuine diversity in an institution such as TIAA-CREFF seem particularly pressing at the moment given the growing potential for influencing corporate policy that resides in the way working people invest their pension funds. See William Greider, "The New Colossus," *The Nation*, 280:8, 2005, 13-18.

Given the intimate relation between dominant modes of production on the one hand, and the functions and methods of adult education on the other, Nesbit thinks that a proper critique of adult education must include a class perspective so as to bring to light ways in which it can fulfil its true promise: not to reproduce social structures and relations but to change them.

Narratives of Class

As mentioned above, the papers by Oldfield and Nesbit respond to the need for concreteness in their emphasis on policy and institutions. But of course this is not the only inflection that can be given to the idea of concreteness. For just as assuredly as the worth of intellectual work can, and to some degree must be measured by the way in which it holds out a prospect of bettering peoples' lives, so this work must remain sterile if it forgets that it is always the lives of individuals whose experiences will be shaped by the way they encounter policies and institutions. Accordingly, while the two essays introduced here certainly contain lessons that go far beyond any expression of "mere subjectivity." they do come to the topic from a far more personal angle than do the other essays in the collection. More specifically, each of the authors explores the complexities arising when class is not only the reality that an academic researcher is looking at but one of the main formative structures of where he or she is coming from.

One could say that "The Stories We Tell" by Irvin Peckham is "typical" for the genre of working-class academic narratives, simply because Peckham is a white, working-class male. And this would be true as far as it goes. But one would also want to be cautious here, since it is far from Peckham's intention merely to give one more expression of, and so one more endorsement of, a whole genre of literature without further ado. Quite the contrary, his narrative is meant to confess, as it were, to what one might have suspected all along were it not so obvious: that for all of the difficulties that working-class academics have in adjusting to the middle-class culture of the academy, part of their original motivation for doing so was to escape the working class and join the middle class. While it is no part of Peckham's intention to undermine the research of working class scholars (whether or not that research happens to be on class), his calling our attention to this motivation not only places it alongside what are surely other motivations, it gives us a truer picture of current debates on class by getting a truer picture of many of those participating in those debates.

Peckham tells a sad story from his early childhood of the Wicks, a poor family who moved into his rural working class community. The Wicks children were badly teased in school because of their poverty and Peckham relates to us his memory of Rose, the oldest Wicks child, trying to protect her younger siblings: "They were gone in a few weeks." (178) We might say that Rose Wicks and her siblings have returned to have their say in Vivian Adair's essay "U.S. Poverty Class/Working Class Divides: The Missing Story of Ourselves." Without denying the struggles and contributions of the working class, including the struggles and contributions of working class academics, Adair's paper is a forceful portrayal of the personal, professional, and societal consequences of overlooking the very real distinction between working class and poverty class (a distinction, it should be noted, that Peckham's tale about the Wicks is intended to acknowledge), most notably in the academy. Part of Adair's point is simple: focusing so much on what can surely be the difficulties of being working class in America is akin to ignoring the fact that while new shoes are greatly preferable to old shoes, old shoes are infinitely preferable to no shoes. Drawing in part on her own experience as a student and researcher, Adair makes the additional argument that the conflation of working and poverty classes in the academy has reproduced a set of factors that are particularly disastrous for poverty class women.

In brief, we might sum up Adair's argument in the following way. The study of class in the academy is frequently infused with what we might call a set of working class values. Unwittingly or not, however, this often plays into the hands of those who would like to brand poor women as examples of "what is wrong with America," and thus as a social problem to be dealt with in terms of a patriarchal conservative political agenda. Yet this agenda includes economic and social policies that in the end are not only injurious to poverty class women but also to all those who are either struggling to get out of poverty or to stay out of poverty. Therefore, overlooking the distinction between poverty class and working class tends to obscure those areas of commonality which might form a true basis of solidarity between them.

Kevin Cahill and Lene Johannessen

PART I

CLASS AND THE CULTURE OF EXCEPTIONALISM

The Elephant in the Room: Culture, Cohesion, and Context in the American Middle Class

Marina Moskowitz (University of Glasgow)

The American middle class is both large and invisible. Large, unquestionably, because over the generations since the 1940s an overwhelming majority of Americans have claimed membership in the middle class. Invisible, because what meaningful spectrum can be divided in such a way that its "middle" constitutes the vast majority of its whole? The polling statistics that document the breadth of the middle class in the United States also seem to uphold the limits to which class is a useful category in delineating American society. Still, perhaps this elephant in the room in fact demands that we consider what class means to this broad middle, rather than ignoring, or even dismissing, its monolithic presence.[1]

In 1940, *Fortune* magazine published, and publicised, a poll in which seventy-nine per cent of their representative sample identified themselves as belonging to the middle class. In more recent surveys, upwards of ninety percent have considered themselves to constitute this expanding group.[2] Debates arise over the validity of self-identification as a means of classification along socioeconomic lines; for example, Robert Lynd, co-author of the landmark survey of American society, *Middletown*, cautioned against "subjective self-rating" as the basis for class delineation, but nonetheless cited the *Fortune* statistics as fodder for social scientists.[3] In his 1935 study of the American middle class, Alfred Bingham defends self-evaluation as the criterion for categorisation, writing:

> We are what we think we are. And if the bulk of the people, in a modern capitalist country like the United States, thinking of themselves as being of the mid-

---

[1] My use of the term "elephant in the room" refers specifically to the middle class, and its dominant, but often unconsidered, presence in American society. For a broader discussion of the category of class itself as the "elephant in the room," an unexplored terrain in social and cultural analysis of the United States, see bell hooks, *Where We Stand: Class Matters* (New York: Routledge, 2000).

[2] "The Fortune Survey," *Fortune*, 21, February, 1940, 14; J. Anthony Lukas cites a 1991 survey in which ninety-three per cent of Americans polled perceive of themselves as members of the middle class; see *Big Trouble: A Murder in a Small Western Town Sets Off a Struggle for the Soul of America* (New York: Simon and Schuster, 1997), 13. For further background on *Fortune* and its place in twentieth-century American culture, see Kevin Reilly, "Corporate Stories: *Fortune* Magazine and the Making of a Modern Managerial Culture," Ph.D. Diss., University of Massachusetts-Amherst, 2004; for a discussion of the place of social surveys in American culture, see Sarah Igo, "America Surveyed: The Making of a Social Scientific Public, 1920-1960," Ph.D. Diss., Princeton University, 2001.

[3] Robert S. Lynd, Lecture Notes, "Role of the Middle Class in Contemporary Social Change," John Reed Society, Harvard University, 3 November 1947, p. 5, Container 2, Reel 1, File: Lectures, outlines, notes, Robert and Helen Merrell Lynd Papers, Manuscript Division, Library of Congress, Washington, DC. (Subsequent references to this archival collection will be designated "LP," with appropriate container and file location.)

dle class, having interests between those of "capital" and "labor," then there is such a middle class or middle group of classes.[4]

In this essay, I am less interested in whether or not self-identification results in "valid" patterns of class status recognised by traditional theorists and social analysts, than in what the term middle class represents to those who claim membership in it. Certainly, the prevalence of this assertion of middle-class identity is revealing in terms of social experience and as such has provided the impetus for varied studies of the middle class, from Lynd's post-war lectures on the topic, to John Gilkeson's 1986 community study of Providence, Rhode Island, in the nineteenth and early twentieth centuries, to Jeffrey Hornstein's recent study of realtors and the meaning of property in twentieth-century America.[5]

If the *Fortune* survey was the bellwether for a twentieth-century trend of middle-class affiliation, it can also be seen as the culmination of a generation spent representing the middling sorts, particularly in the realm of print culture. Over the course of the early twentieth century, a broad cross-section of American authors, writing for literary, popular, and academic audiences, set out to describe the American middle class. They often saw themselves as part of this central group, existing, in socioeconomic terms, between those who financed the nation's industrial productivity and those who tended the production lines. Indeed, Sherwood Anderson, author of the acclaimed *Winesburg, Ohio* (1919), wrote in a letter to his future wife that, "[s]urely in this situation, capital on one side and labor on the other, there should be a place for the artist who wants merely to be open-eyed, to receive impressions and make his pictures, wanting to serve only the central inner story and not one side or the other."[6]

The social relationships of the industrial era had been a growing concern in the United States, particularly in the years following the Civil War. Many Americans held ambivalent views about the course of industrialization, on the one hand benefiting from the seemingly secure footing for the national economy and material comforts, while on the other, hoping to contain its physical presence and social influence. The widening gap between the richest and poorest strata of the country, and their access to political influence, economic security, and consumer goods, was increasingly apparent to the reformers of what is now known as the Progressive Era. Characterized broadly as an "age of reform" or "search for order" by historians, the first generation of the twentieth century saw a rise in the civic concern of the managerial classes.[7] They sought to apply

---

[4] Alfred Bingham, *Insurgent America: Revolt of the Middle Classes* (New York: Harper and Brothers, 1935) 47.

[5] Robert Lynd, Lecture Notes, 5; John S. Gilkeson, Jr., *Middle-Class Providence, 1820-1940* (Princeton: Princeton University Press, 1986); Jeffrey Hornstein, *A Nation of Realtors: A Cultural History of the Twentieth-Century American Middle Class* (Durham: Duke University Press, 2005).

[6] Charles E. Modlin, ed., *Sherwood Anderson's Love Letters to Eleanor Copenhaver* (Athens: University of Georgia Press, 1989) 37.

[7] I take these terms from two classic works on the Progressive Era: Richard Hofstadter, *The Age of Reform* (New York: Vintage, 1955) and Robert Wiebe, *The Search for Order, 1877-1920* (New York:

the mediating and managerial roles they had learned in industrial settings to everyday life. Starting in the last quarter of the nineteenth century and continuing into the twentieth, middle class reformers and statisticians studied budgets, costs of living, housing, and domestic relationships, particularly of the American working classes.

In their initial aim of documenting the society that they hoped to improve, progressive reformers' work was underpinned by the burgeoning work of the social sciences. Early studies, such as Helen Campbell's *Prisoners of Poverty* (1887), Walter Wyckoff's *The Workers* (1897), and Robert Chapin's *The Standard of Living of Workingmen's Families in New York* (1909), concentrated on the working class, but by the 1910s and 1920s, studies of middle-class living standards and household budgets were common in sources ranging from Robert and Helen Merrell Lynd's classic text, *Middletown*, to women's magazines.[8] Social scientists began using the methods of observation and analysis that they had developed while studying other nations, cultures, and classes for projects closer to home. Anthropologists, sociologists, and economists grew more likely to turn their trained eyes on groups similar to themselves, sometimes at very close range, such as Jessica Peixotto's groundbreaking study *Getting and Spending at the Professional Standard of Living*, which focused on academics at her own institution, the University of California at Berkeley.[9] It is perhaps not surprising that as the middle class grew, it would also become the object of academic study, but this trend did raise a challenge for those completing the research; as Lynd said, tacitly assuming the middle-class status of his peers, "in

---

Hill & Wang, 1967). For additional background on the Progressive Era, see Steven J. Diner, *A Very Different Age: Americans of the Progressive Era* (New York: Hill and Wang, 1998) and Nell Irvin Painter, *Standing at Armageddon: The United States, 1877-1919* (New York: W.W. Norton, 1987).

[8] Helen Campbell, *Prisoners of Poverty: Women Wage Workers, Their Trades and Their Lives* (1887; rpt. Westport, CT: Greenwood Press, 1970); Walter Wyckoff, *The Workers: An Experiment in Reality* (New York: Charles Scribner's Sons, 1897); Robert Chapin, *The Standard of Living of Workingmen's Families in New York* (New York: Charities Publication Committee, 1909); Robert S. Lynd and Helen Merrell Lynd, *Middletown: A Study in Modern American Culture* (New York: Harcourt, Brace and Co., 1929). Daniel Horowitz traces the expansion of scope in the study of household budgets from the working class to the middle class in *The Morality of Spending: Attitudes Toward the Consumer Society in America, 1875-1940* (Baltimore: Johns Hopkins University Press, 1985). For historiography of the burgeoning social sciences, see Dorothy Ross, *The Origins of American Social Science* (Cambridge: Cambridge University Press, 1991); Maurine Greenwald and Margo Anderson, eds., *Pittsburgh Surveyed: Social Science and Social Reform in the Early Twentieth Century* (Pittsburgh: University of Pittsburgh Press, 1996); Martin Bulmer, Kevin Bales, and Kathryn Kish Sklar, eds., *The Social Survey in Historical Perspective, 1880-1940* (Cambridge: Cambridge University Press, 1991); and Igo, "America Surveyed."

[9] Jessica B. Peixotto, *Getting and Spending at the Professional Standard of Living: A Study of the Costs of Living an Academic Life* (New York: Macmillan, 1927) vii. Similar studies of other universities include: Yandell Henderson and Maurice Davie, eds., *Incomes and Living Costs of a University Faculty* (New Haven: Yale University Press, 1928) and John H. McNeely, *Salaries in Land-grant Universities and Colleges* (Washington DC: Government Printing Office, 1932). See also Horowitz, *The Morality of Spending*, 138-48.

trying to think about [the] middle class objectively – all of us have to try to achieve a stance outside ourselves."[10]

Analyses and representations of the middle class were not confined to academic journals and textbooks, but were mirrored in popular forms of print culture as well, whether articles on the family budget in domestic magazines, prescriptive literature such as household management or etiquette manuals, or in fiction. The early twentieth century also witnessed a huge boom in the American publishing industry, which produced copious numbers of magazine stories and novels depicting middle-class life. This "social fiction" followed the lives of male and female clerks, managers, professionals, and their families through their daily routines.[11] Authors who had trained as journalists to observe and report, much as their counterparts in the social sciences had, joined with those of the realist literary tradition to create what one contemporary critic called "the literature of national introspection."[12]

All of these texts helped to identify and unite the middle class at the beginning of the twentieth century; at the beginning of the twenty-first, they encourage a recasting of class as a category of social experience rather than measurable status. Writing what Anderson called "the central inner story," these authors describe the experience of class status from within rather than limn it from without. Thus, a backwards glance at these authors provides a useful model. Reading the varied literature of the early twentieth century, three themes emerge: class was understood as a cultural designation, beyond a strictly economic one; class could be cohesive rather than stratifying; and class was understood on a national scale, as much as in local communities. By considering class in these ways, we can begin to understand how and why so many Americans wish to come together under the umbrella of the middle class. In order to make sense of this group, the category of class must be considered in terms beyond its link to measurable socioeconomic conditions, just as recent cultural history and theory have reconsidered the categories of race and gender beyond the biological or physiognomic characteristics that originally defined them.[13] Looking at

---

[10] Lynd, Lecture notes, 3.

[11] I have borrowed the useful term "social fiction" from the historian and bibliographer Archibald Hanna; his *Mirror for the Nation: An Annotated Bibliography of American Social Fiction, 1901-1950* (New York: Garland, 1985) is an invaluable tool for locating fiction documenting the middle class. For additional background on the publishing industry, the middle class, and the culture of books and reading, see David Minter, *A Cultural History of the American Novel* (New York: Cambridge University Press, 1994); Joan Shelley Rubin, *The Making of Middlebrow Culture* (Chapel Hill: University of North Carolina Press, 1992); James L.W. West, III, *American Authors and the Literary Marketplace* (Philadelphia: University of Pennsylvania Press, 1988).

[12] Clipping, Maxwell Lerner, review of *Middletown*, Container 12, File: Middletown Reviews, LP.

[13] See, for example, Joan Wallach Scott, *Gender and the Politics of History* (New York: Columbia University Press, 1988); Denise Riley, *"Am I That Name?": Feminism and the Category of "Women" in History* (Minneapolis: University of Minnesota Press, 1988); Gail Bederman, *Manliness & Civilization: A Cultural History of Gender and Race in the United States, 1880-1917* (Chicago: University of Chicago Press, 1995); Mark C. Carnes and Clyde Griffen, *Meanings for Manhood: Constructions of Masculinity in Victorian America* (Chicago: University of Chicago Press, 1990);

class as a social and cultural construct as well as a financial or political one, we may begin to capture not only how class is defined but also how it is experienced.

While class is certainly a socioeconomic categorisation, writings of the early twentieth century look beyond measurable financial criteria to describe the affinities of groups united by class status. Of course, economic attainment is a factor, but not an exclusive one; in particular, annual income based on wages or salary is a limited measure for assigning class status. As sociologist Robert Chapin, an expert on the different living standards of Americans, wrote, "It goes without saying that the standard of living attained does not depend simply upon income."[14] In seeking a more useful measure, some critics looked to occupational groupings as a basis for class status. For example, in *Middletown* the Lynds drew one primary class distinction between what they termed the working class and the business class:

> Members of the first group, by and large, address their activities in getting their living primarily to things, utilizing material tools in the making of things and the performance of services, while the members of the second group address their activities predominantly to people in the selling or promoting of things, services, and ideas. [15]

Still, while the working class and business class were categorised by their modes of work, these terms were in essence a shorthand reference to two different systems of organising daily life.

The authors were as concerned with how income was spent as how it was earned. Lynd himself discussed the limitations of both income and occupation as "a sure basis for class identity in our society." [16] In his view, varied and variable costs of living required a more refined measure than income, while occupational designations encompassed too broad a range of earnings and experience. Shared income level could also mask diversity in consumer choice that might betray significant differences in the ways in which daily life was carried out. In descriptions of household contents and décor, the Lynds showed how different priorities between families of the same income level might be encapsulated in their material surroundings:

Michael Omi and Howard Winant, *Racial Formation in the United States: From the 1960s to the 1990s* (New York: Routledge, 1994); Matthew Frye Jacobson, *Whiteness of a Different Color: European Immigration and the Alchemy of Race* (Cambridge: Harvard University Press, 1998).

[14] Robert C. Chapin, "The Influence of Income on Standards of Life," *American Journal of Sociology*, 14:5, March, 1909, 638.

[15] Lynd and Lynd, 22. The organisation of *Middletown* is the first clue to the place that work experience occupied in the Lynds' estimation. Although "Getting a Living" was the starting point for the book, it was only one of six major categories of daily life experience that defined the community; the others were: Making a Home, Training the Young, Using Leisure, Engaging in Religious Practices, and Engaging in Community Activities.

[16] Lynd, Lecture Notes, 7.

> There is less likely to be a radio than in the more prosperous working class home, but one may come upon a copy of Whistler's portrait of his mother or a water-color landscape and a set of Dickens or Irving in a worn binding; the rugs are often more threadbare than those in the living room of a foreman, but textbooks of a missionary society or of a study section of the Woman's Club are lying on the mission library table. [17]

Here, the Lynds seem to pit the technology and home furnishings of the working class against the cultural expressions and continuing education of the business class as priorities for expenditure. The Lynds' emphasis on books in particular as material and intellectual markers of the business class suggests that they saw their readers as members of this numerically small but culturally significant group, in which the authors themselves were placed by means of their occupational status, among other possible traits.

The authors of such studies could see themselves reflected not just in their projected audience, but even in their subjects. As noted above, the sociologist Jessica Peixotto made her own occupational group of academics the focus of her research. As a community study of a professional group, Peixotto's work on her fellow Berkeley professors separated studies of their actual family budgets from the standard of living they hoped to achieve. Although she did chart the former, she found that salaries in the field were not a good indication of the growing expectation for academics to share the quality of life of a more general professional culture. Peixotto believed that academics were culturally valued in American society, writing that "[n]ot only does the public want the class; it wants the members of the profession to look like other people; to behave like other people; to take their place on even terms with other professionals."[18]

In short, academics were expected to share markers of class status with other professional, or middle-class groups, but their earnings were almost always outpaced by other fields. As among the lowest paid of the salaried professionals, academics proved to be the perfect test case for explaining class distinctions based on organization of daily life, rather than income.[19]

If income and occupational grouping, traditional markers of economic distinction, were not enough to designate class, what needed to be added to the mix? Peixotto showed that her peers' middle-class status stemmed from cultural rather than financial capital. The budgetary, social, and literary studies of the early twentieth century suggest that class is formed from the sharing of cultural attributes, as much as it is informed by the differentiation of economic, social, and political position. While culture can be as slippery a term as class itself, I (and the authors upon whom I draw) refer to the myriad productions – material

---

[17] Lynd and Lynd, 101-02.

[18] Peixotto, 21.

[19] Ibid., viii-ix; Mary Hinman Abel discusses teachers, clerks, and ministers in this same category; Abel, "Community and Personal Standards," in *American Standards and Planes of Living: Readings in the Social Economics of Consumption*, ed. Thomas Eliot (Boston: Ginn & Co., 1931) 185; see also Ellis Lore Kirkpatrick, *The Farmer's Standard of Living* (New York: Century Co., 1929) 202-203.

life, domestic organisation, foodways, print, technology, art, religion, legal codes, to name some important examples – that a group creates to express itself and its beliefs. The creation, consumption, prioritising, and ordering of these cultural productions provide means of expressing affinities among groups of people, and thus, ways of establishing communities that are identified as classes. The cultural markers of daily life are ways to "look like" or "behave like" other people and therefore identify oneself as a member of a particular class. Thus, the relationships of production, on which class distinction can rest, encompass cultural production. The middling sort did not always have control over others' labor; they were not always political leaders; nor were they the wealthiest echelon of any given community. Increasingly, however, the middling sort claimed access to cultural productions that were also important, if perhaps less obvious, as avenues to power.

If class is recast as a socioeconomic group defined by the cultural productions its members share, then identification with a particular class status becomes more accessible than it might otherwise be. This model of class consolidation is based on the connective tissue that binds a group together rather than the circumstances that set it apart from other groups. Thinking about class in terms of cohesion rather than distinction (though perhaps somewhat counterintuitive) helps to explain how such a large swath of the American population claims a place in the middle. Clearly, Americans have chosen to prioritise the bonds they do share rather than the admitted internal disparities that such a large group would of necessity display. The emergence of this sense of cohesion, of a widely shared American pattern of daily life and access to the cultural markers that defined class status, was born, ironically, out of an era of discord stretching from the Civil War into the early twentieth century. The Gilded Age and Progressive era witnessed a variety of conflicts, often along the fault lines of class, race, ethnicity, and gender, which at their core focussed on issues of access to and achievement of a shared quality of life. Whoever the agents of these struggles, whether large-scale labor uprisings or conflicts over Jim Crow laws, the varied sides shared a conviction that an American standard of living did exist.

In the early twentieth century, many cultural critics commented on this increasingly shared ideal of the expectations of daily life, which encompassed not only material goods but also access to education, leisure activities, the ability to save, and numerous other facets of social and economic standing. This ideal was not perceived as the pinnacle of attainment but as a middle-class standard.[20] In trying to explain the level or degree of this status, social scientists categorised different strata of daily life in the United States; while different authors used slightly different rhetoric, a common scheme enumerated four planes of daily life: subsistence, convenience, comfort, and luxury. Essayist F. Spencer

---

[20] I have discussed this emergence of the standard of living in much greater depth in Marina Moskovitz, *Standard of Living: The Measure of the Middle Class in Modern America* (Baltimore: Johns Hopkins University Press, 2004).

Baldwin defined these terms as early as 1899: "A necessary is something indispensable to physical health; a convenience is something that relieves from slight pain or annoyance [...] a comfort [...] is a common and inexpensive means of enjoyment; a luxury [...] is an unusual and expensive means of enjoyment." [21] Middle-class life was said to correspond to the level of comfort. Jessica Peixotto referred to the "comfort standard" as the "new single standard" in the United States.[22] The economist Simon Patten concurred, considering the middle class as "sufficiently representative of 'normal' standards."[23] Thus, the comfort attained by the American middle class was widely represented as a national way of life.

Still, in referring to the "comfort standard" as a national ideal, Baldwin, Peixotto, Patten and their peers were certainly not saying that the majority of Americans lived in the same degree of comfort. The ideal of a comfortable quality of life was widely shared, even if the attainment of that ideal was not; these shared expectations were enough to provide cohesion to a broad group of people. All of these authors pointed, whether directly or indirectly, to aspiration as the key to consolidating the American middle class. While of course a small percentage of the population lived well above the comfort standard, and another larger percentage lived at a plane so far below it as to not have sensed its existence, this notion of aspiration made middle-class ideals available to many. As economist Ira Wile explained, "It is but natural that aspiration, imitation, and emulation should serve as incentives to raise the lower standards to the higher levels." [24] Wile's contemporary Frank Streightoff agreed, noting the "inborn spirit of emulation" that Americans possessed.[25] Even if they exhibited a wide variety in material, financial, and social attainment, Americans would be drawn together in agreement on what they were hoping to attain. Over the twentieth century, representations of middle-class life were broadcast through a variety of media, starting, as mentioned above, with print culture and extending to other communications media, such as radio, film, and television, in both programming and advertising. Whatever their level of consumer spending, ratio of work to leisure time, or domestic organisation, many Americans had some access to these representations, and thus were able to share in the broad understanding of what it meant to be middle class. The economist Hazel Kyrk noted that the

---

[21] F. Spencer Baldwin, "Some Aspects of Luxury," *The North American Review* 168: 507, February, 1899, 155. For strikingly similar categorizations of the planes of living, see Hazel Kyrk, *Economic Problems of the Family* (New York: Harper & Bros., 1929) 372, 387; Frank Hatch Streightoff, *The Standard of Living Among the Industrial People of America* (Boston: Houghton Mifflin Co., 1911) 2; Thomas Francis Moran, "Ethics of Wealth," *American Journal of Sociology*, 6:6, May, 1901, 824; S. Agnes Donham, "Conscious Standards," in *American Standards and Planes of Living*, 477-78
[22] Peixotto, viii-ix.
[23] Thomas Eliot, Introduction to "The Standardization of Family Life," by Simon Patten, in *American Standards and Planes of Living*, 194-95.
[24] Ira S. Wile, "Standards of Living," *Journal of Home Economics*, 5, December, 1913, 410; Eliot, 194; Patten, 194-95; Kyrk, 381.
[25] Streightoff, 2.

spectrum of Americans' spending habits was in quantity rather than type, showing that many had the same vision of what items should be included in the household budget, even if their purchasing power varied. As she wrote in *Economic Problems of the Family*,

> Another marked characteristic of American consumption habits is their similarity from class to class. Variations are not in kind, merely in degree. This is the result of a democratisation process that is the product not only of the social and political structure but of an educational system which was to some extent deliberately planned for this purpose.[26]

While Kyrk pointed to American education as the mechanism for inculcating a middle-class standard of living, many of her peers looked to a more tangible mechanism: the widespread acceptance and availability of credit. If the economist Wile pointed to "aspiration, imitation, and emulation" as one means of identifying with the middle class, he also recognised the influence of credit arrangements. As he explained to a national conference on home economics in 1913, "the instalment business has made possible the acquisition of well-furnished homes that would otherwise be impossible."[27] The Lynds also commented on the trend toward paying by instalment, "which turns wishes into horses overnight."[28] While networks of credit had existed in local contexts for generations, these systems gradually became codified business practices rather than individual, face-to-face arrangements between buyers and sellers. [29] The twin cultural and financial mechanisms of emulation and credit explain how aspiration enables a broad swath of the population, with potentially limited financial resources, to consider themselves members of the middle class.

But what about the "upper" end of the broad middle? Why does aspiration explain a desire to claim middle-class status, but not a desire to achieve an elite status? I believe there are two answers to this question. The first stems from the planes of living described above. Building on a longstanding scepticism of luxury, many Americans seem uncomfortable admitting to the "unusual and expensive means of enjoyment" that Baldwin outlined. The concern with the increased social and economic stratification in the United States that found such a receptive audience in the Progressive Era has not abated, nor has that stratification. Claiming membership in the middle class and a cohesive relationship with a broad sector of the American population prioritises a shared cultural influence over a disparity in economic and political power. At the same time, a claim to middle-class status is justified because the shared ideal of the standard of living

---

[26] Kyrk, 381.
[27] Wile, 417; Kyrk, 424-25; Peixotto, viii-ix.
[28] Lynd and Lynd, 81-82 (see especially n. 18); quotation from p. 82.
[29] For a more thorough discussion of consumer credit see Lendol Calder, *Financing the American Dream* (Princeton: Princeton University Press, 1999) and Martha Olney, *Buy Now, Pay Later: Advertising, Credit, and Consumer Durables in the 1920s* (Chapel Hill: University of North Carolina Press, 1991).

is dynamic, and usually pitched just ahead of broad attainment. As Wile wrote, "[s]tandards level upwards. The luxuries of yesterday are the necessities of today [...] There is no absolute standard of living save as an ideal; and when the highest standards of today are realized, they will fall short of the standards that will then be used."[30] Thus, the upper reaches of the middle class may always stretch the boundaries of their community and retain their place within it. For these reasons, again, what binds the group together is as important as what sets it apart from others, and helps explain the overwhelming self-identification of the middle class.

The broad self-identification of middle-class status that blossomed in the twentieth century had one additional precondition: the ability for Americans to understand their place in a national context. For many Americans, the multiple small settings of daily life did not (and do not) provide exposure to the socioeconomic diversity of the nation. In their attempt to characterise "typical" Americans in *Middletown*, the Lynds in fact struggled with how the middle class was defined. As noted above, the Lynds used a binary class division, between the business and working classes, as the central distinction in Muncie's population. The Lynds avoided the tripartite designations of lower, middle, and upper class as not truly representing the experience of daily life in Muncie. Their rejection of the tripartite class divisions, despite encouragement from their advisors to use them, stemmed primarily from their belief that in a town the size and stature of Muncie, there was no true upper class, as might have existed in a metropolitan area.[31] In order to perceive of themselves as residing in the middle of a larger socioeconomic and cultural spectrum, the citizens of Muncie would also need to take a broader, perhaps national, view of the community they inhabited. From the turn of the twentieth century onward, Americans have turned to the myriad examples of national culture that they do encounter daily in order to establish their sense of being "in the middle."

Cultural markers of American life, such as dress, domestic organisation, working patterns, leisure activities, or even local legal codes, began to transcend regional variation due to national media outlets, transportation technology, and internal migration. This increasingly national culture allowed Americans to see themselves in a broader context than previous generations had. In particular, the distinctions between urban and rural societies were eroding. Home economist Christine Frederick discussed this fluidity in terms of consumer behaviour, writing in 1924, "the farm woman once wore little else but gingham and alpaca. She buys copies of Fifth Avenue models today, and her daughter, whose face was innocent of aught but freckles, now possesses the standard female laboratory of toilet articles."[32] As before, these cultural changes were charted not only in aca-

---

[30] Wile, 410-11; see also, Baldwin, 155; Kyrk 376; Streightoff 2; Abel, 183.

[31] Lynd and Lynd, 22-23 (see especially n. 3); Galen Fisher, "Notes on Small City Manuscript," 6 May 1927 and S. Went, "General Comments," 5 May 1927, both in Container 7, File: Comments on Manuscript, LP.

[32] Christine Frederick, "New Wealth, New Standards of Living and Changed Family Budgets," *An-

demic texts but also in popular fiction. The popular writer Edna Ferber conveyed the exact same sentiment as Frederick's in her depiction of the fictional town of Winnebago, a "little Mid-Western town." Ferber described the residents: "The Winnebagoans seem to know what is being served and worn, from salad to veilings, surprisingly soon after New York has informed itself of those subjects."[33] In a variety of media Americans were being told that they were increasingly alike from coast to coast. These shared patterns of daily life were particularly important in providing a sense of middle-class identity in the towns and small cities in which the majority of Americans lived, where the gradations of socioeconomic status may have been less apparent. Widespread self-identification as members of the middle class arose from association and comparison on a national level.

The broad self-identification of middle-class status that has characterised American society in the twentieth century also may betray a pride in how that status compares to other nations. Again, Americans have tended to choose not the pinnacle but the average of American life to hold up as an example. As early as 1907, essayist Joseph Jacobs envisioned how such national comparisons of quality of life could be made. Writing in the *American Magazine*, Jacobs imagined "The Middle American," whose typicality derived from the median of every measurable facet of life, from personal statistics such as height and weight, to residential location within the United States, to income. Jacobs explained his purpose in carrying out such an exercise: "The value of such a figure, if we could obtain it, is great, especially for comparative purposes [....] To compare the bulk of one nation with another, our only method seems to be to compare the Middle Man of each nation with that of the other."[34]

Jacobs' essay showed one more appeal of middle-class identity: the opportunity to represent the nation. In a very recent representation of American life, the television series *The West Wing*, the fictional politicians debate whether or not the term "average American" will be perceived as "pejorative." One character insists,

> This may come as a shock to you but eighty per cent of the people in this country would use the word "average" to describe themselves. They do not find the term deprecating. Indeed being considered an average American is something they find to be positive and comforting.[35]

Whether or not the screenwriter Aaron Sorkin based these lines on actual polls, they do ring true in a nation in which such a large majority identify with the middle class. Fifty years earlier, Robert Lynd pointed to this satisfaction with a

nals of the American Academy of Political and Social Science, 115, September, 1924, 79; see also Kirkpatrick, 6-8 and passim.

[33] Edna Ferber, *Fanny Herself* (New York: Frederick A. Stokes Co., 1917) 52-53.

[34] Joseph Jacobs, "The Middle American," *American Magazine*, 63, March 1907, 526.

[35] *The West Wing*, Season 1, Episode 21, "Lies, Damn Lies, and Statistics," written by Aaron Sorkin, directed by Don Scardino.

middling lot in life as an American characteristic. He wrote of the middle class, "...we Americans have never been wont to regard it as a term of reproach, our feeling being: 'Aren't we all?'" [36] The vast majority of Americans clearly agree.

Selected Bibliography

Bederman, Gail. *Manliness & Civilization: A Cultural History of Gender and Race in the United States, 1880-1917.* Chicago: University of Chicago Press, 1995.

Bingham, Alfred. *Insurgent America: Revolt of the Middle Classes.* New York: Harper and Brothers, 1935.

Bulmer, Martin, Kevin Bales, and Kathryn Kish Sklar, eds. *The Social Survey in Historical Perspective, 1880-1940.* Cambridge: Cambridge University Press, 1991.

Calder, Lendol. *Financing the American Dream.* Princeton: Princeton University Press, 1999.

Campbell, Helen. *Prisoners of Poverty: Women Wage Workers, Their Trades and Their Lives.* Westport, CT: Greenwood Press, 1970. Reprint 1887.

Carnes, Mark C. and Clyde Griffen. *Meanings for Manhood: Constructions of Masculinity in Victorian America.* Chicago: University of Chicago Press, 1990.

Chapin, Robert. *The Standard of Living of Workingmen's Families in New York.* New York: Charities Publication Committee, 1909.

Diner, Steven J. *A Very Different Age: Americans of the Progressive Era.* New York: Hill and Wang, 1998.

Eliot, Thomas, ed. *American Standards and Planes of Living: Readings in the Social Economics of Consumption.* Boston: Ginn & Co., 1931.

Gilkeson, John S. Jr. *Middle-Class Providence, 1820-1940.* Princeton: Princeton University Press, 1986.

Greenwald, Maurine and Margo Anderson, eds. *Pittsburgh Surveyed: Social Science and Social Reform in the Early Twentieth Century.* Pittsburgh: University of Pittsburgh Press, 1996.

Hanna, Archibald. *Mirror for the Nation: An Annotated Bibliography of American Social Fiction, 1901-1950.* New York: Garland, 1985.

Henderson, Yandell and Maurice Davie, eds. *Incomes and Living Costs of a University Faculty.* New Haven: Yale University Press, 1928.

Hofstadter, Richard. *The Age of Reform.* New York: Vintage, 1955.

Hornstein, Jeffrey. *A Nation of Realtors: A Cultural History of the Twentieth-Century American Middle Class.* Durham: Duke University Press, 2005.

Horowitz, Daniel. *The Morality of Spending: Attitudes Toward the Consumer Society in America, 1875-1940.* Baltimore: Johns Hopkins University Press, 1985.

---

[36] Robert Lynd, Lecture Notes, 3.

Igo, Sarah. "America Surveyed: The Making of a Social Scientific Public, 1920-1960." Ph.D. Diss. Princeton University, 2001.

Jacobson, Matthew Frye. *Whiteness of a Different Color: European Immigration and the Alchemy of Race*. Cambridge: Harvard University Press, 1998.

Kirkpatrick, Ellis Lore. *The Farmer's Standard of Living*. New York: Century Co., 1929.

Kyrk, Hazel. *Economic Problems of the Family*. New York: Harper & Bros., 1929.

Lukas, J. Anthony. *Big Trouble: A Murder in a Small Western Town Sets Off a Struggle for the Soul of America*. New York: Simon and Schuster, 1997.

Lynd, Robert S. and Helen Merrell Lynd. *Middletown: A Study in Modern American Culture*. New York: Harcourt, Brace and Co., 1929.

McNeely, John H. *Salaries in Land-grant Universities and Colleges*. Washington DC: Government Printing Office, 1932.

Minter, David. *A Cultural History of the American Novel*. New York: Cambridge University Press, 1994.

Modlin, Charles E. Ed. *Sherwood Anderson's Love Letters to Eleanor Copenhaver*. Athens: University of Georgia Press, 1989.

Moskowitz, Marina. *Standard of Living: The Measure of the Middle Class in Modern America*. Baltimore: Johns Hopkins University Press, 2004.

Olney, Martha. *Buy Now, Pay Later: Advertising, Credit, and Consumer Durables in the 1920s*. Chapel Hill: University of North Carolina Press, 1991.

Omi, Michael and Howard Winant. *Racial Formation in the United States: From the 1960s to the 1990s*. New York: Routledge, 1994.

Painter, Nell Irvin. *Standing at Armageddon: The United States, 1877-1919*. New York: W.W. Norton, 1987.

Peixotto, Jessica B. *Getting and Spending at the Professional Standard of Living: A Study of the Costs of Living an Academic Life*. New York: Macmillan, 1927.

Reilly, Kevin. "Corporate Stories: *Fortune* Magazine and the Making of a Modern Managerial Culture." Ph.D. Diss. University of Massachusetts-Amherst, 2004.

Riley, Denise. *"Am I That Name?": Feminism and the Category of "Women" in History*. Minneapolis: University of Minnesota Press, 1988.

Ross, Dorothy. *The Origins of American Social Science*. Cambridge: Cambridge University Press, 1991.

Rubin, Joan Shelley. *The Making of Middlebrow Culture*. Chapel Hill: University of North Carolina Press, 1992.

Scott, Joan Wallach. *Gender and the Politics of History*. New York: Columbia University Press, 1988.

Streightoff, Frank Hatch. *The Standard of Living Among the Industrial People of America*. Boston: Houghton Mifflin Co., 1911.

public resources, it is essential to reanimate the labor movement. Such a movement seeks the creation of a strong progressive government and the establishment of an economic democracy in the United States.

In support of such a movement, I offer in this paper a normative critique of U.S. power, which I regard as imperial and unjust and I argue that it has grown, in part, because of the systemic alienation of organized labor from mainstream American politics. I then provide a critical analysis of the 1895 case *In re Debs* – a paradigmatic event in U.S. labor history – and in light of this case I argue for the progressive rethinking of labor in the U.S. by highlighting the importance of equity and social justice in labor relationships.

The United States as Empire

As argued by Susan Owen and Peter Ehrenhaus, contemporary America can be characterized as an empire.[6] This empire can be understood in at least two senses. The first is the traditional notion of empire as conquest. In American law, conquest became a constitutionally sanctioned method for bestowing property rights on settlers when the U.S. Supreme Court formally extinguished the property claims of Native Americans after they had been dispossessed of their land through European colonization (and in many cases exterminated). As explained by the Court, "Conquest gives a title which the Courts of the conqueror cannot deny [...] The title by conquest is acquired and maintained by force. The conqueror prescribes its limits."[7] By reifying as law what had been done in practice, the Court gave legal sanction to further transgressions against the remaining Native American communities. Implicit in this ruling is also a policy of judicial non-interference with further expansion of the territorial United States.

Such expansion accelerated in the years following the Civil War, in which the U.S. began to grow as a world power. In recent years, this power has been increased and extended to dominate almost every nation on Earth.[8] So pervasive is this power that even staunch supporters of U.S. global influence are beginning to recognize this influence as "imperial."[9] The classic expression of U.S. imperial power was articulated in 1898 by Senator Albert J. Beveridge. In his "The March of the Flag" address, Beveridge, an ardent supporter of the annexation of the Philippines, argued that God made the United States "the master organizers of the world to establish system where chaos reigns [...] He has made us adept in government that we may administer government among savages and

---

[6] Susan Owen and Peter Ehrenhaus "Animating a Critical Rhetoric: On The Feeding Habits of American Empire" *Western Journal of Communication*, 57, 1993, 170.

[7] *Johnson v. M'Intosh*, 21 U.S. 543 (1823), 589.

[8] Michael Parenti, *Against Empire* (San Francisco: City Lights Books, 1995).

[9] Dimitri K. Simes, "America's Imperial Dilemma," *Foreign Affairs* 82, Nov-Dec 2003, 91-103.

senile peoples."[10] Beveridge's sentiment is alarming. More than one hundred years later, the U.S. government behaves as if this was *still* foreign policy, as in President George W. Bush's ill-pursued "War on Terrorism" and its conquest of Afghanistan, Iraq, and perhaps other nations in the near future. Such practices – the projection and manipulations of American power overseas – should be anathema to nations such as the U.S., which claim justice and equality as definitive ideals. All the great empires of history – Greek, Roman, Spanish, British, French, Japanese, German, and the like – were established on the principle that one race, culture, or economic class has the right to conquer and to subject as many other nations as possible.

Although the United States and other historic empires have (or had) the ability to invade and to occupy other nations, each mistook its power for a mandate that was often couched in religious or eugenic language.[11] The use of power in this way is contemptible, and critical citizens must become pedagogical so that others may learn to rue and reject the imperial ambitions of our government. Fundamental to this task is a recognition of the part of ourselves that is compliant with imperial ambitions, the part of us that benefits from the calculus of oppression so central to the practice of U.S. politics. Until the latter part of the twentieth century, empire was established and maintained through military force and accepted by the colonizer's legal system. The Athenians, Romans, Spanish, Italians, Danish, Portuguese, French, British, and Germans were all at one time expansionist societies, conquering, expropriating, and enslaving much of the world. Each had their day in the sun and all failed, eventually, divested of honor and shamed as a people. Currently, however, the world has evolved such that traditional military conquest is difficult to maintain; thus, the world has entered a second phase of empire. Owen and Ehrenhaus refer to this new phase as involving "the intricate orchestration of American cultural, political and economic institutions, and [...] their attendant social practices."[12] This empire, they argue, is organic – it is a living, growing, self-conscious force concerned with consumption and expansion. This U.S. empire "has voracious appetites; it thrives by feeding upon those less well positioned in the world, and its perpetuation requires domination over those both within its boundaries and without."[13] Thus, the practice of empire has become – in many instances – less overtly violent; involving, instead, the financial manipulations of economies and the colonization of minds through mass-mediated propaganda and the promotion of consumer escapism – what Michael Carbone calls "our anti-critical

---

[10] Cited in John H. Sloan, "American Imperialism" in *America in Controversy: History of American Public Address*, ed. DeWitte Holland, 131 (Dubuque, IA: Wm. C. Brown Company Publishers, 1973).

[11] Marouf A. Hasian, *The Rhetoric of Eugenics in Anglo-American Thought* (Athens: University of Georgia Press, 1996).

[12] Owen and Ehrenhaus, 130.

[13] Ibid.

mass culture with its managed information."[14] At least internally, "American empire accomplishes its hegemony largely through the creation of diversions – distractions of desire that integrate the individual into the broader constellation of institutional relations: consumer, voter, spectator, patriot, fan, etc. Empire thrives precisely because of the given consent, complicity, and absorption of those upon whom it feeds."[15]

A similar critique has been articulated by Michael Hardt and Antonio Negri who view the United States as, on the one hand, embodying progressive ideals – such as a commitment to the protection of civil liberties – while, on the other, failing to enact a democratic society in which rich and poor have equal and substantive access to education and legal protection.[16] Instead, America has become a flourishing global empire. Fundamental to this empire is communication, which "not only expresses but also organizes the movement of globalization"[17] and cultural norms. Symptomatic of this communication is the fragmentation of identity among communities, both domestically and internationally. Such fragmentation is often mistakenly characterized as a symptom of a new vision of the world, captured by the term "postmodernism." Like others, I am suspicious of this term and recognize that the post-modern world is little more than a hyper-modern world, a world of "turbo-capitalism."[18] In the words of Ben Agger, "There is absolutely nothing 'post' about the current modernity, which is fundamentally continuous with capitalism from the mid-19th century in the sense that capitalism is characterized by private property, sexism, racism, and the domination of nature."[19] The so-called post-modern world has reified the worst aspects of capitalism, which no longer faces the restraints of a concerted working-class challenge. Missing from our contemporary world is the ability of individuals to identify with others for progressive transformation. Because critical transformation is grounded in a communal identification with others, the loss of this identification makes the practice of a working-class praxis more difficult. The fact that the critical theory of the Frankfurt school was situated in the context of a communication paradigm (loosely speaking) is not surprising, as the critical persona, communication, and community are all interrelated phenomenon.[20] Hardt and Negri are optimistic, however, when they note

---

[14] "Empowering the Liberal Arts: Analysis and Paradigms From Critical Theory," *Quarterly Journal of Ideology*, 12, 1988, 8. Also see Alex Carey, *Taking The Risk Out of Democracy* (Urbana: University of Illinois Press, 1997).

[15] Owen and Ehrenhaus, 171.

[16] Michael Hardt and Antonio Negri. *Empire* (Cambridge, MA: Harvard University Press, 2001).

[17] Ibid., 32.

[18] Edward N. Luttwak, "Power Relations in the New Economy," *Survival*, 44, 2002, 13-16.

[19] Ben Agger, *The Decline of Discourse: Reading, Writing and Resistance in Postmodern Capitalism* (New York: Falmer, 1990) 6.

[20] See Rolf Wiggershaus, *The Frankfurt School: Its History, Theories, and Political Significance* (Cambridge, MA: MIT Press, 1995)

that, "the passage to Empire and its processes of globalization offer new possibilities to the forces of liberation."[21]

The political left long has dreamed of a pronounced internationalism in which people transcend religious, ethnic, and national boundaries and unite for the cause of the greater human good, like the World Social Forum. Throughout the twentieth century, however, groups of people or nations developed a progressive consciousness *independent* of other groups or nations, with little coordination between them; thus, most efforts to empower the working-classes across nations have failed.[22] Now, with the globalization of empire, a profound homogenization is emerging among nations and people. Thus, if class-consciousness (i.e., a critical class self-identification, however conceptualized) ever re-emerges as an important historical force, the emergence of this consciousness will likely be perceived much more uniformly around the world.[23] Working-class solidarity will then no longer be subsumed by nationalist identification, as was the case with the Second International during the First World War.[24] In short, with globalization comes the potential for world-wide working-class solidarity and a transcendence above the provincialism of nationality and the territoriality such nationality fosters.

Empowering Labor: Lessons Learned from In Re Debs

As suggested above, the United States often exemplifies the type of power that is antithetical to the construction of humane, inclusive, and equitable community life and must be countered domestically and internationally. An important reason why the United States has attained this type of deleterious power stems from the fact that the emergence of U.S. power has not been successfully humanized and tempered by organized labor within its borders. This condition can be challenged, encouraging the U.S. to join with the other industrialized nations in allowing the working-class to help determine the conditions of work for the benefit of the entire society. For this reason, developing a stronger labor consciousness in the United States is an essential precondition for the transformation of U.S. society, which is an important prerequisite for progressive change internationally. While this development does not preclude other possible routes to a progressive future, the history of the twentieth century, and the dire world-wide conditions at the start of the twenty-first century – the collapse of socialism and social democracy as credible politics, the growth of the World Bank, International Monetary Fund, and the World Trade Organization, and the in-

---

[21] *Empire*, xv.
[22] Max Elbaum, "What Legacy From the Radical Internationalism of 1968?," *Radical History Review*, 82, 2002, 39.
[23] Greg Smithsimon, "Transnational Labor Organizing: Opportunities and Obstacles for Unions Challenging Multinational Corporations," *Socialist Review*, 27, 1999, 65-93.
[24] Ronald Aronson, "Hope After Hope," *Social Research*, 66, 1999, 474.

creasingly consequential U.S. "war on terrorism," make it difficult to imagine progressive social change without such working-class consciousness and unifying discourse.

The marginalization of organized labor, which continues to be a condition of contemporary life, involves the failure of U.S. society to develop a viable labor party. Related to this point is the idea that the concerns of labor are unimportant in normative political deliberation. Throughout the industrialized world, the acceptance of organized labor in national economic and social planning has led to substantial and positive effect on the lives of millions of workers and has contributed to a more humane society in nations where labor is treated with dignity. Measured in benefits, security, and the length of the work week, the conditions of labor throughout much of Western Europe are better than that of the majority of U.S. workers.[25]

The alienation of U.S. labor stems in large part from the post-Civil War drive for industrialization. Leading this drive were important industrialists of the nineteenth and early twentieth centuries, such as Andrew Carnegie, Jim Fisk, Henry Ford, John Paul Getty, Jay Gould, John P. Morgan, John D. Rockefeller, Leland Stanford, and Cornelius Vanderbilt, who asserted themselves as a powerful class in national politics.[26] Collectively, this group of people and others comprised the unofficial but powerful aristocracy of the U.S. Through their manipulations – which Lee Artz and Bren Ortega Murphy describe as "bribery, deceit, and terror" these men achieved a heightened degree of power, privilege and luxury.[27] Decisions made by these industrialists helped forge an antagonistic relationship between industry and labor that worked to the detriment of labor and to the suffering of millions of workers and their families. One dimension of their power was their ability to harness the armed force of the state and the legal system to suppress collective action by the working-class as a method for advancing labor's inclusion in the national community. As Dianne Avery observes, "Economic harm became blurred with physical harm; peaceful economic coercion became synonymous with coercion through violence. The talk of violence both masked and revealed the judges' real fears: fears of great union strength and autonomy, of class warfare, of anarchy, of loss of control, of change."[28] In destroying the capacity of labor to engage in collective action, the government confiscated the only effective tool that labor had to achieve con-

---

[25] This, however, has started to change as European leaders succumb to the anti-labor pressures of globalization. See Asbjorn Wahl, "European Labor: the Ideological Legacy of the Social Pact," *Monthly Review*, 55, 2004, 37-50.

[26] Michel Beaud, *A History of Capitalism: 1500-1980* (New York: Monthly Review Press, 1983), 96.

[27] Lee Artz and Bren Ortega Murphy, *Cultural Hegemony in the United States* (Thousand Oaks, CA: Sage, 2000) 240.

[28] Dianne Avery,"Images of Violence in Labor Jurisprudence: The Regulation of Picketing and Boycotts, 1894-1921," *Buffalo Law Review*, 37, 1988, 12.

crete results. As discussed below, the 1895 case of *In re Debs* exemplifies this phenomenon.[29]

In 1893, a particularly strong recession swept the nation and business at the Pullman factory plummeted. Pullman compensated by firing 4,000 of his 6,000 workers, who immediately lost their living quarters;[30] the remaining workers had their wages cut by 30%.[31] In the face of these pay cuts, there was no equivalent cut in rent for company housing or utilities. Attempts by the workers to arbitrate the issue with Pullman were met with stern refusal: "There is nothing to arbitrate," Pullman declared arrogantly.[32]

Representatives from the Pullman workers went to the annual meeting of the American Railway Union (ARU) to enlist its support. Eugene Debs, founder and leader of the ARU, had recently achieved a victory in a strike against the Great Northern Railroad, and so the Pullman workers approached Debs with anticipation and hope. After some debate and emotional argument, the Pullman workers succeeded in receiving support from the ARU. Initially, the ARU was careful to boycott only trains carrying Pullman cars. This was a strategic and well-calculated plan, as Debs clearly comprehended that big industry – in particular, the railroads – enjoyed the political and military support of the federal government and that political counter-pressure was the only effective way to initiate change. This approach also reflected Debs' philosophical commitment to electoral politics, since he "disagreed strenuously" with labor organizations which repudiated "political activity" and engaged in violence and industrial sabotage.[33] Pullman, however, understood Debs' strategy and ordered his cars attached to a variety of different trains – particularly to those carrying the U.S. mail – to frustrate Deb's plan, forcing the ARU to either give up the strike or to intensify the strike's effect. The ARU reluctantly chose the latter, causing two-thirds of the U.S. railroads to become mired in the strike. By causing the strike to expand (and the mail to halt), Pullman successfully federalized the strike, creating a pretext for the U.S. government to intervene, which it did – violently. The government marshalled 14,000 state and federal soldiers against the strikers, killing 35 workers.[34] The U.S. Supreme Court sanctioned such violence:

---

[29] *In re Debs*, 158 U.S. 564 (1895). In United States law, the name of a case is followed by the law book in which it appears. In this case, the U.S. refers to the *United States Reports*, the official outlet for decisions issued by the United States Supreme Court. The first number "158" is the volume number of that title. The number "564" is the page number where the decision can be found.

[30] Liston Edgington Leyendecker, *Palace Car Prince: A Biography of George Mortimer Pullman* (Niwot, CO: University Press of Colorado, 1994) 229.

[31] Howard Zinn, *A People's History of the United States* (New York: Harper Perennial, 1980), 274.

[32] Quoted in Melvyn Dubofksy and Foster Rhea Dulles, *Labor in America: A History* 6th ed. (Wheeling, IL: Harlan Davidson, Inc., 1999) 160.

[33] David M. Rabban, "The IWW Free Speech Fights and Popular Conceptions of Free Expression Before World War I," *Virginia Law Review*, 80, 1994, 1065.

[34] Zinn, *A People's History of the United States*, 275.

> The entire strength of the nation may be used to enforce in any part of the land the full and free exercise of all national powers and the security of all rights entrusted by the constitution to its care. The strong arm of the national government may be put forth to brush away all obstructions to the freedom of interstate commerce or the transportation of the mails. If the emergency arises, the army of the nation, and all of its militia, are at the service of the nation, to compel obedience to its laws.[35]

The irony here is patent. Debs, in coordinating the ARU, worked hard to avoid violence (as well as violent rhetoric), and to be conscientious of federal interests. Furthermore, Debs "consistently counselled moderation and restraint" and warned the strikers to respect railroad property.[36] Debs' rhetoric and method of effectuating social change was, in the short term, to withhold labor and, in the long term, to build a popular labor political party (he helped form the Socialist Party of America in 1901).

From the point of view of the progressive community committed to social justice, the government's violence in suppressing the strike was unnecessary, as the strike was essentially peaceful before the federal government interfered. Furthermore, Governor John Peter Altgeld of Illinois, who had constitutional authority to resolve the conflict, opposed federal interference. In a letter Altgeld sent to President Grover Cleveland, he explained,

> At present some of our railroads are paralyzed, not by reasons of obstruction, but because they cannot get men to operate their trains... As Governor of the State of Illinois, I ask the immediate withdrawal of Federal troops from active duty in this State.[37]

Along with the mayors of 50 U.S. cities, Altgeld urged Pullman to address the concerns raised by the workers.[38] Aside from the military suppression of the strike, the federal government also unleashed a series of legal assaults against the ARU. As many as 400 union members were arrested, including Debs.[39] The federal government charged Debs and other leaders of the union with conspiracy – in this case, conspiracy to violate the Sherman Anti-Trust Act. Although the Sherman Act was created to break up business monopolies, most Americans do not realize that the Act was enforced against labor unions years before it was enforced against business trusts.[40] The Bill of Indictment positioned the defendants as follows:

> In the month of May, 1894, there arose a difference or dispute between the Pullman Palace Car Company and its employees, as the result of which a con-

---

[35] *In Re Debs*, 582.
[36] Dubofksy and Dulles, 162.
[37] Ibid.
[38] Leyendecker, 226.
[39] Dubofksy and Dulles, 164.
[40] Avery, 53-54.

siderable portion of the latter left the service of the car company; that thereafter the four officers of the railway union combined together, and with others, to compel an adjustment of such dispute, by creating a boycott against the cars of the car company; that, to make such boycott effective, the railroads running out of Chicago [were prevented] from operating their trains, and were coming to extend such boycott against Pullman sleeping cars by causing strikes among employees of all railroads attempting to haul the same.[41]

To suppress such conspiracy, the judiciary issued an injunction precluding Debs from discussing or coordinating the strike. Debs violated this legal command and was jailed on contempt charges. The Supreme Court affirmed the conviction and gave constitutional sanction to labor injunctions as a potent weapon of class warfare. From "then on," notes Lawrence M. Friedman, "the injunction, in the hands of a strong-minded judge, was a mighty adversary that organized labor had to reckon with. The injunction was swift, and it could be murderously inclusive – broad enough in its contours to cover a total situation, outlawing every aspect of a strike and effectively crushing it."[42] The severity of the federal reaction to this and to other strikes, including contemporary strikes, begs an inquiry into the federal interest at stake in these issues. In the following subsections, I identify and engage three such interests – protection of the mail, protection of commerce, and resistance to social reform and political dissent.

Protection of the Mail. The first federal interest discerned in the Pullman Strike is the responsibility of the government to run and to regulate the postal service. This interest is articulated by the Constitution, as noted by the Court: "Among the powers expressly given to the national government [in Article 1, section 8 of the Federal Constitution] are the control of interstate commerce and the creation and management of a post-office system for the nation."[43] Ostensibly, President Cleveland took this mandate so seriously that, in ordering the military suppression of the strike, he declared: "If it takes every dollar in the Treasury and every soldier in the United States to deliver a postal card in Chicago, that postal card should be delivered."[44]

Such interest, however, does not provide a morally satisfactory justification for violently repressing the Pullman strike. Mail is an expression of community, communication, and social bonding. Only when mail fulfils these roles does the mail system attain its utility. By itself, mail – or, indeed, government – is undeserving of respect, as both gain importance only in the context of community. What matters is the health of that community and the actions of individuals to cultivate and to support that health. To respect the expressions of community (such as its civic, political, and industrial institutions) while ignor-

---

[41] *In Re Debs*, 567.
[42] *A History of American Law* 2nd ed. (New York: Simon & Schuster, 1985) 557.
[43] *In re Debs*, 579.
[44] Quoted in Dubofsky and Dulles, 163.

ing the substance of human life within that community, is to ignore the most essential value that underlies democratic society – substantive equality in which
all individuals are valued and protected as human beings with human physio-
logical and psychological needs.

Furthermore, in the context of this and other labor disputes, the community
itself has broken down. The proper government response to such a situation is
to reconstruct the health of the community. Consider the following analogy. If
weak foundations cause a structure to collapse, the strengthening of that foundation is needed before a new structure can be erected. As in this analogy, security
for a community is derived from the internal strength of the community consti-
tuting the structure, and not from the superficial reinforcement of an untenable
social reality. This logic applies more generally to the social construction of
property and crime. As Howard Zinn notes:

> [The] huge proportion of poor people in jail for crimes against property suggests
> that prisons are inevitable counterparts of banks. And so long as we have a sys-
> tem that breeds fierce and unequal competition for scarce resources ... some
> steel bars will be needed to protect money, and others to confine human be-
> ings.[45]

The government's responsibility is to reduce class antagonism by encouraging
mediation and compromise between industry and labor, and between the
wealthy and the poor, which it clearly does not do. As I argue below, the construction of community involves an inclusive political vision of a society that is
both just and fair, compassionate and inclusive. By elevating a communication
form (in this case, the mail) over people (or to elevate individual wealth over a
community's needs), the federal government misread the source of a nation's
strength: A nation is only as strong as the communities of which it is composed.
A society that privileges material wealth over community strength will cease to
function as a society and will decay into plutocracy, oligarchy, or worse. In this
sense, George W. Bush is a portent of horrors to come.

Protection of Commerce. The second government interest at stake concerned the government's fear that a disruption in the rail service would ad-
versely affect the health of commerce. Similar to the Constitutional authority in
Article I, Section 8, for the government's regulation of the mail, Congress has
express authorization from the Constitution to exclusively regulate interstate
commerce. Given that Chicago was the choke point of the national railroad system in which 24 railroads converged, a major strike in that city threatened the
national distribution of goods.[46] Such a strike, therefore, would constitute an un-

---

[45] Howard Zinn, *The Zinn Reader: Writings on Disobedience and Democracy* (New York: Seven Stories Press, 1997) 446.
[46] David Ray Papke, "Eugene Debs as Legal Heretic: The Law-Related Conversion, Catechism, and
Evangelism of an American Socialist," *University of Cincinnati Law Review*, 63, 1994, 343.

lawful usurping of powers vested in Congress, to the detriment of the entire nation. As argued by the government prosecutor:

> By reason of said unlawful combination and conspiracy and the acts and doings aforesaid thereunder, the supply of coal and fuel for consumption throughout the different states of the Union, and of grain, breadstuffs, vegetables, fruits, meats, and other necessaries of life, has been cut off, interrupted, and interfered with, and the market therefore made largely unavailable, and dealers in all of said various products and the consumers thereof have been greatly injured, and trade and commerce therein among the states has been restrained, obstructed, and largely destroyed.[47]

This government interest is suspicious, I argue, for a number of reasons. In the most general sense, the purpose of any strike is to highlight the value of labor, raise wages, and improve working conditions. The more that society recognizes that, at its core, there exists a fundamental dependence among all its members, the more likely the intrinsic value of labor will be recognized by that society. This is a fundamental market principle: Labor is paid according to market worth. Strikes, in effect, are a way of determining the market worth of an industry. If a strike by railroad employees cripples the nation, that is a *prima facie* indication that these workers are undervalued. Recognizing the value of workers removes the disruption and ensures the future wellbeing of the system.

More specifically, the asserted interest of the federal government is disingenuous. The strike, in this instance, was focused solely on Pullman's luxury sleeping cars and did not target the federal mail, nor did the strike target produce transports or any other perishable goods. The record clearly indicates that Debs and his union did not intend to paralyze the country, destroy the economy, or overthrow the government. The strike, nevertheless, was positioned by the mass media as subversive. With hyperbole characteristic of the yellow press of the day, the *New York World* declared that the strike was "a war against the government and against society."[48]

In short, there is a strong sense in which the response of the federal government was disproportionate to its interest. Although the federal government has a clear role to play in assuring social order and tranquillity, this same government has an even more pressing responsibility to act on behalf of the common good of all of its citizens, not merely for the privileged few who control influential industries. Why, for instance, was Pullman, who attached his luxury cars to regular freight cars (including the mail cars), without blame from the perspective of the federal government? Why was Pullman not punished or otherwise rebuked for refusing to negotiate with his employees or for exacerbating employee discontent to prolong the strike? Finally, why, in light of the fact that the U.S. Attorney General who coordinated the military suppression of the

---

[47] *In re Debs*, 570.
[48] Quoted in Dubofksy and Dulles, 160.

strike was himself a former corporate attorney for the railroad industry and a personal friend of many railroad owners, were Pullman and his agents not culpable for their undemocratic influence that militarized the conflict and, thereby, ensured an outbreak of violence? Clearly, the systemic inequality that existed between Pullman and the ARU was not reflected in the law's determination of culpability in which the stronger party was exonerated and the weaker party punished for the strike and its consequences.

Resistance to Social Reform and Political Dissent. The third government interest is more revealing of the government's motivation for crushing the striking workers and for imprisoning its leaders and hundreds of the rank-and-file members. The federal government has a longstanding interest in preventing popular democratic activism – activism not controlled or contained by either of the two political parties in this country. When such activism (such as the street democracy prevalent in the 1960s) falls outside the control of elite power, this expression of politics is declared contrary to "ordered liberty" and Constitutionalism. This interest explains why social movements such as the civil rights and labor movements that attempt to expand the notion of community and political enfranchisement in the United States, no matter how patriotic or just, usually meet with substantial resistance from the establishment. In upholding the power of the federal government to imprison Debs and other union members, the Supreme Court preached a "lesson" to the defendants and to the larger working community. With these remarks, the Court crystallized the establishment's fear of grassroots political change:

> It is a lesson which cannot be learned too soon or too thoroughly that under this government of and by the people the means of redress of all wrongs are through the courts and at the ballot box, and that no wrong, real or fancied, carries with it legal warrant to invite as a means of redress the co-operation of a mob, with its accompanying acts of violence.[49]

Under this rationale, the civil rights movement, as well as most other progressive social movements in the United States, would be rendered illegitimate, as their mere existence would have been considered a "mob" threatening "democratic" processes.

By rendering the "mob" undemocratic, the Court is alienating the expression of "we, the people" (the vast bulk of the U.S. population that has never been part of the governing economic elite, and in whose interest such government seldom acts). For example, the North Carolina Agricultural & Technical State University students who demonstrated on February 1, 1960, for integration at a Woolworth's in Greensboro, N.C. – sparking similar protests around the country – would have laughed at the Court for asserting that the redressing of social wrongs must be accomplished at the ballot box or before the judiciary.

---

[49] *In re Debs*, 599.

These students knew better. If struggling people in the United States are to depend on judges and voting alone to improve the conditions of their lives, this society would be vastly more impoverished. This has been the experience of labor. For decades before labor grew militant, workers petitioned both the judiciary and the legislature for relief and received little if any redress to their concerns. Therefore, there is little reason to assume that, absent the threat of mass civil disobedience, the government and the judiciary will act on behalf of labor and the poor in the future.

In addition to a profound resistance to popular political organization outside of systemic Constitutional channels, the government, until relatively recently, expressed a consistent interest in punishing speech that rejected government policy or encouraged others to examine critically government motives.[50] This resistance can be traced to the Alien and Sedition Acts of 1801, and to the fear by the Federalist Party of domestic support for the French Revolution. Although the Alien and Sedition Acts only existed for a few years, such laws mushroomed in the United States from the Civil War period onward (for example, the Federal Espionage Act of 1917). Of course, prior to the Civil War, there was no First Amendment protection for slaves or anyone who spoke out against slavery. Southern legislatures frequently passed death sentences on Northern abolitionists and made possession of abolitionist literature a capital offence.

Many of the laws against criminal syndicalism identified "anarchism" as the ideology to be outlawed; in practice, however, the statutes were intended to suppress most dissent; as other labor groups supplanted anarchism in the late nineteenth century, these laws were applied to them. Throughout this period, large newspaper chains experienced little government harassment because they often parroted the views of the economic and ruling elite. On the other hand, when average citizens sought to express alternative views that violated the state's sense of security or threatened established interests, they were routinely silenced.[51]

What we learn from this brief analysis of *In re Debs* is that the government and laws of the United States privilege the interest of an elite minority in this country at the expense of most members of the national and international working class community. In the past, this had led to much strife and even warfare. In an effort to combat this crass classism, I discuss, in the section below, a new model of labor relations, emphasizing the importance of equity and social justice in how business and government treats its workers and citizens.

---

[50] *Brandenburg v. Ohio*, 395 U.S. 444 (1969). Since the attacks on the U.S. of 2001, I question our society's continuing commitment to the tolerance articulated in *Brandenburg* which establishes a high bar for government prosecution of seditious speech.

[51] Patricia Cayo Sexton, *The War on Labor and the Left* (Boulder, CO: Westview Press, 1991), 135-136.

The Importance of Equity and Social Justice in Labor relations

In principle, democratic culture demands equity among citizens and does not privilege private property above all other values. As Martin Luther King, Jr., observed, "Property is intended to serve life, and no matter how much we surround it with rights and respect, it has no personal being. It is part of the earth man walks on; it is not man."[52] Equity, however, does not mean a forced equality that ignores individual strengths and weaknesses, as all citizens are not similarly situated in terms of motivation, intelligence, moral character, or physical stamina. Equity must not be equated with a crude social levelling. The goal of a progressive society is not to make everyone poor; rather, the goal of a progressive society is to provide for the basic material and cultural needs of all that society's citizens and allow them the intellectual freedom to explore, reorganize, critique, and debate.[53] At the most fundamental level, equity involves a profound social commitment to the human community. A person's lack of wealth is as irrelevant to that person's status as a human being as is that person's sexuality or ethnic identifications. The individual human should be respected and his or her human needs guaranteed.

All people are fundamentally the same, as all other species of animals are fundamentally the same among members of their classification, and should be treated as such. I reject all metaphysical assumptions of the inherent importance of any exclusive community and work (and encourage others to work) toward creating a society grounded in pragmatic assumptions of solidarity, cooperation, kindness, and reciprocity. In other words, for sustained progressive change to occur in the United States, a practical sense of hope must be forged. Social and economic justice is not inevitable. Moral evolution is seldom driven by top-down initiative. When such evolution occurs, the driving force of change is usually the result of community vision and mass struggle. By definition, such vision is grounded in hope. With hope, vision achieves its strength in the ability of individuals to imagine a better life; this imagination, subsequently, becomes the blueprint for progressive change.

My unqualified commitment to – and respect for – the individual human acknowledges that among all classes of people there is a fundamental interdependence. This interdependence is an essential nutrient for the health of collective life and represents an important normative value in progressive politics. Out of respect for the fundamental co-dependence of all humans, the different social classes must strive to provide each other the necessities for a life of dignity. No single class of people can survive independent of all other classes. Human potential is dependent upon cultural diversity for its realization; human

---

[52] Martin Luther King, Jr., *The Trumpet of Conscience* (New York: HarperCollins, 1987) 56.
[53] Ariel Dorfman, "Ideology, Exile, Language: An Interview With Ariel Dorfman," *Salmagundi*, 82-83, 1989, 146.

beings blossom only in the context of other humans. Thus framed, class cooperation is the *topos* of the economic vision I am advocating.

Under this new model of political economy, industry can continue to organize for the production of social goods, and important incentives remain for motivated people to amass a comfortable level of *useful* wealth (as opposed to *superfluous* wealth). This distinction between types of wealth is pragmatic, not metaphysical. Wealth should be used to reduce human suffering in the world; indeed, I cannot imagine any other justification for it. When squandered on decadence, wealth doubly harms the under-resourced. Usable wealth is wealth that people utilize to secure necessary items such as food, shelter, health care, clothing, as well as some modest material comforts. Superfluous wealth, on the other hand, is wealth wasted on "conspicuous consumption" – such as multi-million dollar celebrity weddings, multi-million dollar bonuses for corporate officers, or houses valued at tens of millions of dollars – all of which insult the dignity of the working-class and highlight the moral poverty of the non-working-class elite.[54]

While our current system allows people to make these types of consumptive and wasteful choices, there is no necessary reason to do so. Part of the current malaise in U.S. society is that Americans are more offended by restricting the opportunities of the affluent in how they spend their money than they are offended by the condition and suffering of the poor (for example, the repeal of the Estate Tax and tax breaks for the super-wealthy). In contrast, the economic model that I support provides for an equitable distribution of society's wealth and opportunities. When this economic change occurs, the class tensions that plague the current economic arena will be recast into what I term *relationships of mutuality*. Such relationships recognize and honor the fundamental consubstantiality of all human beings.[55] Such relationships can help mediate the effects of the arbitrary – yet inevitable – symbolism that divides human communities. In mediating such effects, relationships of mutuality deny U.S. elites a rationalization for structural inequality. Within relationships of mutuality, the working class will continue to produce good and services, as this is their important contribution to society. However, management and owners – rather than hoarding that wealth for themselves – will invest that wealth back into the well-being of the workers, their families, and their communities. This act constitutes industry's essential contribution to society. As articulated by John J. Maresca:

> [T]oday a business can no longer be seen as a creator of wealth solely for its owners. The role of business as a creator of wealth is broader than that. Business is the principal engine for generating wealth for society as a whole – for the entrepreneur and the owners, but also for the employees who must receive fair salaries, for the community which receives tax revenues to fund schools

---

[54] Thorstein B. Veblen, *The Theory of the Leisure Class* (Amherst, NY: Prometheus Books, 1998).

[55] Kenneth Burke, *A Rhetoric of Motives* (Berkeley: University of California Press, 1969).

and other public institutions, and for suppliers and sales organization and their employees up and down the business stream.[56]

Under the working-class industrial model I have proposed, the concerns of labor are essential for management, as the health of the industrial enterprise would be correlated to worker satisfaction. If the producers themselves are not satisfied, the production process becomes a sham and the objects produced cease to be a societal benefit. No product, no matter how necessary, can be considered a benefit if the method of production offers no quality of life to the producer – the historical nexus of sugar and slavery is a paradigmatic example.[57] Labor that does not affirm humans and, instead, reduces them to objects for manipulation, is a form of oppression. Humans labor to live and to construct community; they do not live to labor for the sole gain of another.

Under a system of equity in which mutuality of relationships is established, industry would still be encouraged to generate "profit," but the profit generated would be socially focused. Because society supports the conditions for industrial wealth, the profit from such enterprise properly belongs to society. Managers and owners are merely stewards of this wealth. While such classes are entitled to compensation for this responsibility, their fundamental duty is to channel their power toward ends supportive of society that makes their enterprise possible. The end result of this system is a more just society, marked by increased citizen satisfaction and overall productivity. Historically, labor unions have worked (however imperfectly) toward such a vision. As Richard Rorty notes, at "their best, labour unions are America at its best. Like the civil rights movement, the union movement is a model of Americans getting together on their own and changing society from the bottom up – forcing society to become more decent, more democratic and more humane."[58]

Under the equity model of labor relations, the greatest countries would not be those that create concentrated wealth, but the societies in which the most low-level workers are guaranteed that their economic and social needs are firmly met. This move is not intended to turn paupers into princes, but to construct a world in which neither extreme is acceptable. Without such guarantees of economic equality, without economic justice, the protections of political equality that U.S. citizens respect are not secure; in fact, much of this political equality has been steadily eroding as the public realm becomes increasingly subjected to unrestrained market forces and the concurrent growth of economic disparity in which large amounts of U.S. political autonomy have been turned over to non-elected, global, financial institutions.[59] The loss of such autonomy

---

[56] "A New Concept of Business," *The Washington Quarterly*, Spring, 2000, 161.

[57] Richard S. Dunn and Gary B. Nash. *Sugar and Slaves: The Rise of the Planter Class in the English West Indies, 1624-1713* (Chapel Hill, NC: University of North Carolina Press, 2000).

[58] *Philosophy and Social Hope* (New York: Penguin, 1999) 256.

[59] M. Lane Bruner, "Global Constitutionalism and the Arguments Over Free Trade," *Communication Studies*, 53, 2002, 30.

threatens the rights and privileges that the U.S. government – or, indeed, *any* government – is supposed to secure for its citizens.

Critics of the equity model might argue that being rich is inherently virtuous, and that free markets can help the entrepreneur become wealthy; the entrepreneur, in turn, spreads the wealth (hence the idiom, "The rising tide raises all boats"). Yet, while tremendous wealth has been generated by free markets this wealth – with few exceptions – creates social problems like immorality, gluttony, depletion of vital resources, social isolation, and cultural callousness. Moreover, the wealth generated by world markets has not been rationally or fairly distributed. Simply, markets make few rich and most poor. As of 2002, for example, the developing nations had a total debt of approximately $2.5 trillion.[60] A few people in the developing world have become billionaires, but their wealth does little to uplift the conditions of their impoverished co-patriots. Thus, the market's focus on the material wealth of a select group misses a fundamental point about humans and their needs. Meaningful wealth comes not from BMWs, diamond rings, or nuclear arsenals but from healthy bodies and healthy spirits and from communities that are uplifting and dignifying – meeting human needs for love, inclusion, self-fulfilment, and joy. Karl Marx may have been wrong about many things, but he was correct in warning that people should not mistake money for life.

Conclusion

Fundamental to my notion of labor articulated in this chapter is equity and economic justice. The U.S. system of property works best when everyone has some property, and the system works least effectively when a handful of people control most of the property while the rest of us remain tenants and servants. The underlying theory behind private property is that people will do their best work with pride and feel integrated into the community when they have the right of sole possession over some resource that cannot be taken from them. However, the flip side of this assumption is that when people have no property, when the available wealth is monopolized, they have no investment in their community or in their occupation and thus have no reason to do their best work or to invest emotional capital into their surroundings. Under the current system, people without property are alienated, and when millions of such people exist, societies become destabilized, the rich fearful, and governments more punitive in an effort to further entrench the privileges of the aristocracy against the claim of the poor for an equitable share of society's wealth. This is the world to which we are heading rapidly.

---

[60] Sohan Sharma and Surinder Kumar, "Debt Relief – Indentured Servitude for the Third World," *Race & Class*, 2002, 45.

While individuals clearly have agency, politics occurs mainly at the level of the collective. Each individual is too weak and is often distracted by self-serving pressures to work for the common good. Moreover, powerful industrialists continue to attain political and economic power because of institutionalized norms and policies (i.e., the socio-legal foundations of *laissez-faire* capitalism and neo-liberalism). These policies allow the rich to sacrifice humanistic values – such as those allowing for the dignity, healthy, and security of the laboring classes – to their own greed. Because of this, I do not recognize the current neo-liberal model as appropriate for producing wealth. Simply, the United States needs to enact a different morality and different economic values; fundamental to this task is repudiating – not excusing – the harmful practices of the past and the rebuilding of a strong, forward-looking, and progressive labor party. Americans need to recognize that wealth should not be treated as an end in itself. How wealth is created and used is more important than its mere existence. If this were not true, there would be less ground upon which to repudiate slavery. Eugene Debs and others in the U.S. labor movement organized and agitated so that future generations of workers would not forget this vital point, which we, as a society, are becoming in danger of losing.[61]

Selected Bibliography

Agger, Ben. *The Decline of Discourse: Reading, Writing and Resistance in Postmodern Capitalism*. New York: Falmer, 1990.

Aronson, Ronald. "Hope After Hope." *Social Research* 66 (1999): 471-494.

Artz, Lee and Bren Ortega Murphy. *Cultural Hegemony in the United States*. Thousand Oaks, CA: Sage, 2000.

Avery, Dianne. "Images of Violence in Labor Jurisprudence: The Regulation of Picketing and Boycotts, 1894-1921." *Buffalo Law Review* 37 (1988): 1-117.

Beaud, Michel. *A History of Capitalism: 1500-1980*. New York: Monthly Review Press, 1983.

Brandenburg v. Ohio, 395 U.S. 444 (1969).

Bruner, M. Lane. "Global Constitutionalism and the Arguments Over Free Trade." *Communication Studies* 53 (2002): 25-39.

Burke, Kenneth. *A Rhetoric of Motives*. Berkeley: University of California Press, 1969.

---

[61] An earlier version of this paper appeared in the on-line journal *Reconstruction: Studies in Contemporary Culture*. See http://www.reconstruction.ws/042/swartz.htm. Readers interested in my larger defence of working class political and cultural unity and the role of critical intellectuals and scholars in fighting for economic justice and social democracy should see my *In Defence of Partisan Criticism* (New York: Peter Lang, 2005).

Carbone, Michael. "Empowering the Liberal Arts: Analysis and Paradigms From Critical Theory." *Quarterly Journal of Ideology* 12 (1988): 1-14.

Carey, Alex. *Taking The Risk Out of Democracy*. Urbana: University of Illinois Press, 1997.

Chomsky, Noam. *Profit Over People: Neoliberalism & Global Order*. New York: Seven Stories Press, 1998.

Dorfman, Ariel. "Ideology, Exile, Language: An Interview With Ariel Dorfman." *Salmagundi* 82-83 (1989): 142-163.

Dubofksy, Melvyn and Foster Rhea Dulles. *Labor in America: A History*. 6th ed. Wheeling, IL: Harlan Davidson, Inc., 1999.

Dunn, Richard S. and Gary B. Nash. *Sugar and Slaves: The Rise of the Planter Class in the English West Indies, 1624-1713*. Chapel Hill, NC: University of North Carolina Press, 2000.

Ehrenreich, Barbara. *Bait and Switch: The (Futile) Pursuit of the American Dream*. New York: Metropolitan Books, 2005.

____. *Nickel and Dimed: On (Not) Getting By in America*. New York: Metropolitan, 2001.

Elbaum, Max. "What Legacy From the Radical Internationalism of 1968?" *Radical History Review* 82 (2002): 37-64.

Friedman, Lawrence M. *A History of American Law*. 2nd ed. New York: Simon & Schuster, 1985.

Hardt, Michael and Antonio Negri *Empire*. Cambridge, MA: Harvard University Press, 2001.

Hasian, Marouf A. *The Rhetoric of Eugenics in Anglo-American Thought*. Athens: University of Georgia Press, 1996.

Johnson v. M'Intosh, 21 U.S. 543 (1823), 589.

King, Jr., Martin Luther. *The Trumpet of Conscience*. New York: Harper-Collins, 1987.

Luttwak, Edward N. "Power Relations in the New Economy." *Survival* 44 (2002): 13-16.

Leyendecker, Liston Edgington. *Palace Car Prince: A Biography of George Mortimer Pullman*. Niwot, CO: University Press of Colorado, 1994.

Maresca, John J. "A New Concept of Business." *The Washington Quarterly* (Spring, 2000): 155-163.

Moberg, David. "Union Busting, Past and Present: Charting an Old American Tradition." *Dissent* (Winter, 1992): 73-80.

Owen, Susan and Peter Ehrenhaus. "Animating a Critical Rhetoric: On The Feeding Habits of American Empire." *Western Journal of Communication* 57 (1993): 169-177.

Papke, David Ray. "Eugene Debs as Legal Heretic: The Law-Related Conversion, Catechism, and Evangelism of an American Socialist." *University of Cincinnati Law Review* 63 (1994): 339-375.

Parenti, Michael. *Against Empire*. San Francisco: City Lights Books, 1995.

Phillips, Kevin. *Wealth and Democracy: A Political History of the American Rich*. New York: Broadway Books, 2002.

Postman, Neil. *Amusing Ourselves to Death*. New York: Penguin, 1985.

Rabban, David M. "The IWW Free Speech Fights and Popular Conceptions of Free Expression Before World War I." *Virginia Law Review* 80 (1994): 1055-1158.

Rorty, Richard. *Philosophy and Social Hope*. New York: Penguin, 1999.

Sexton, Patricia Cayo. *The War on Labor and the Left*. Boulder, CO: Westview Press, 1991.

Sharma, Sohan and Surinder Kumar. "Debt Relief – Indentured Servitude for the Third World." *Race & Class* 43:4 (2002): 45-56.

Shipler, David K. *The Working Poor: Invisible in America*. New York: Vintage, 2005.

Simes, Dimitri K. "America's Imperial Dilemma." *Foreign Affairs* 82 (Nov-Dec 2003): 91-103.

Sloan, John H. "American Imperialism." *America in Controversy: History of American Public Address*. Ed. DeWitte Holland. Dubuque, IA: Wm. C. Brown Company Publishers, 1973. 123-134.

Smithsimon, Greg. "Transnational Labor Organizing: Opportunities and Obstacles for Unions Challenging Multinational Corporations." *Socialist Review* 27 (1999): 65-93.

Swartz, Omar. *In Defense of Partisan Criticism*. New York: Peter Lang, 2005.

Theriault, Reg. *The Unmaking of the American Working Class*. New York: New Press, 2003.

Veblen, Thorstein B. *The Theory of the Leisure Class*. Amherst, NY: Prometheus Books, 1998.

Wahl, Asbjorn. "European Labor: the Ideological Legacy of the Social Pact." *Monthly Review* 55 (2004): 37-50.

Wiggershaus, Rolf. *The Frankfurt School: Its History, Theories, and Political Significance*. Cambridge, MA: MIT Press, 1995.

Zinn, Howard. *The Zinn Reader: Writings on Disobedience and Democracy*. New York: Seven Stories Press, 1997.

___. "Economic Justice: The American Class System." *Declarations of Independence: Cross-Examining American Ideology*. New York: Harper Perennial, 1990, 147-181.

___. *A People's History of the United States*. New York: Harper Perennial, 1980.

(Re)Examining Class: Transnational Workers and Nationalist Struggles in the late 19th Century United States

Malini Cadambi & Evan Matthew Daniel (New School for Social Research)

This essay introduces Cuban cigar makers and Indian agricultural workers as transnational subjects involved in concerted class struggle in the United States while simultaneously engaging in counter-hegemonic struggles with their imperial oppressors abroad. Drawing on the theories of E.P. Thompson, Herbert Gutman, Donna Gabaccia, and William Sewell, we argue that both groups constructed collective identities based on their class positions as well as their notions of nationality as colonial subjects. The Cuban and Indian workers engaged in similar forms of collective action in the U.S. despite the differing economic and social situations in their respective homelands, with which there was a significant and continuous interaction.

In trying to relate the lives of the cigar makers to those of the agricultural workers, our own understanding of class had to be broadened to encompass these workers' cultural backgrounds, social milieu, political experiences, and religious identities, among other things. Many of these workers travelled back to their countries of origins and, as with the case of some of the Indian workers who belonged to a revolutionary party known as Ghadar, travelled to other locales including Germany, Japan, and Southeast Asia in an effort to further their political aims. These back and forth movements of bodies, literature, information, money, etc. complicate them as historical subjects. It is for this reason we find using a transnational historical approach valuable.

Theoretical Framework

Class in America is a puzzle. It is not as clear-cut as in European nations that have experienced feudalism and monarchies as well as revolutions opposed to those forms of social, economic and political organization. In Europe, class position and differentiation appear more clearly delineated and class action has been defined as consisting of certain prescribed actions, e.g., union organization or general strikes.

Yet such a seemingly united working-class has never existed in the United States. Class in the U.S. has always been much more complicated by race, ethnicity, and religion. This has led some scholars to conclude that there is either (a) no class consciousness in the United States (e.g., Sombart's question of "Why Is There No Socialism in the United States?"[1]) or (b) that class is not a useful category of analysis in the U.S. (i.e., "We're all middle-class."). This bi-

---

[1] Werner Sombart, *Why Is There No Socialism in the United States?* Edited and translated by Patricia M. Hocking and C.T. Husbands (White Plains, NY: International Arts and Sciences Press, 1976).

furcation in labor scholarship "misses the rich and complex worlds of working-class political consciousness and associations that most often fall somewhere between those two poles."[2]

While class – as a social grouping in America – is difficult to delineate, class as a category of analysis is even fuzzier. At one time, class was tethered to a strictly materialist definition, prefiguring all other relationships. This primacy of class, however, is now generally understood as producing, at best, limited understandings of various groups, and, at worst, completely erroneous assumptions as to the motivations of those groups.

Following in the footsteps of Thompson, Gutman sought to analyze the "cultural baggage" working people – and in particular immigrants – brought with them from the old world to the new and from a rural way of life to an industrial era. Rather than focus on the structural changes in capitalism that transformed generations of working people, Gutman instead examined "the ways in which the behavior of working people affected the development of the larger culture and society in which they lived."[3] William Sewell's recent work calling for interdisciplinary approaches to labor history emphasizes the "arbitrary nature" of dichotomizing the "ideal" and the "material."[4] Instead, Sewell stresses that

> [W]e must imagine a world in which every social relationship is simultaneously constituted by meaning, scarcity, and power... [and] the discursive features of the social relationships are themselves always constitutively shaped by power relations and conditions under scarcity.[5]

While sceptical of Sewell's calls for post-materialist rhetoric, Michael Hanagan agrees that "labor history is laden with an unproblematized reliance on dialectics, totalism and teleology."[6] In short, we should neither privilege the physical or the ideational since both constitute the "stuff" of human experience. In this regard, our research on Cuban cigar makers and Indian land workers attempts to understand both groups' ideological underpinnings through their lived experiences as laborers.

The development of trade unions and formation of class were conceptualized by Thompson as national processes. Unfortunately, there has been limited development and revision of Thompson's analysis. As Ira Katznelson laments, "[o]ne aspect of the new social history is that Thompson's

---

[2] Eric Arnesen, Julie Greene, and Bruce Laurie, *Labor Histories: Class, Politics and the Working-Class Experience* (Chicago: University of Illinois Press, 1998) 6-7.

[3] Herbert G. Gutman, *Work, Culture, and Society in Industrializing America: Essays in American Working-Class and Social History* (New York: Alfred A. Knopf, 1976) xii.

[4] William Sewell, "*Toward a Post-Materialist Rhetoric for Labor History*" in Lenard B. Berlanstein, ed. *Rethinking Labor History* (Urbana: University of Chicago Press, 1993) 15-38.

[5] Sewell, "Toward a Post-materialist Rhetoric for Labor History," 33.

[6] Berlanstein, ed. *Rethinking Labor History*, 190.

genius and the scope of his achievement have prompted attempts at imitation [....]"[7] The work of Katznelson and fellow political scientist Aristide Zolberg is one noteworthy exception to this trend but labor historians continue to apply Thompson's concept of the "making" of a working class – be it American or Mexican or Chilean – almost as if these developments are strictly circumscribed within specific nation-state borders. This is partly understandable as the specific national institutions, political culture, and so on shape a nation's distinctive history of union formation. However, this emphasis on the centrality of the nation-state has meant less attention paid to sub-national processes, such as the formation of regional identities and transnational influences including ideologies and work cultures, as well as to subaltern groups – those not commonly studied or regarded as legitimate workers.[8] Close to fifteen years after its initial publication, David Brody addressed these deficiencies when he acknowledged that, "we cannot expect to develop a new synthesis of American labor history on the lines of *The Making of the English Working Class.*"[9]

The "linguistic turn" further complicated the concept of class by moving from a strictly materialist definition (typically, but not exclusively, emphasizing relations to the means of production) towards non-materialist conceptions that privilege language and/or culture. For some scholars this paradigm has bifurcated the academic landscape, for others it has just made scholarship richer. Immigration historians Donna Gabaccia, Franca Iacovetta, and Fraser Ottanelli saw no tension between material feminist analysis and post-modern feminist analysis in doing their decade-long project on Italian migration and labor but, rather, found a middle ground providing for more complex analysis:

> For us, a sensitivity to women's multiple identities emerged from our fairly tra-
> ditional bottom-up approach to women's lives and from an understanding of a
> feminist labor scholarship that...had already begun in the 1970s and 1980s to
> deconstruct class and to demonstrate the complicating influence of language,
> rhetoric, and ideology on social practice, class consciousness, hierarchies of
> power, and contested meanings and identities.[10]

Benedict Anderson posits that nations are "imagined communities."[11] If this is indeed the case, the "imagining" has far too often been identified as being pre-

---

[7] Ira Katznelson and Aristide Zolberg, *Working Class Formation: Nineteenth-Century Patterns in Western Europe and the United States* (Princeton: Princeton University Press, 1986) 11.

[8] Subaltern workers can be See Marcel Van der Linden's discussion of sub-altern working class studies

[9] David Brody. "The Old Labor History and the New: In Search of An American Working Class," *Labor History*, 20:1, 1979, 122.

[10] Donna Gabaccia, Franca Iacovetta, and Fraser Ottanelli, "Laboring Across National Boarders" and Michael Hanagan and Marcel Van der Linden, "New Approaches to Global Labor History" in *International Labor and Working Class History*, 66, Fall, 2004, 71.

[11] Benedict Anderson, *Imagined Communities: Reflections on the Origins and Spread of Nationalism* (London: Verso, 1983).

scribed by elites. That is, nation building has been typically viewed as the do-main of the privileged few. Operating in a similar vein, the traditional historiog-raphy of Latin American and South Asian labor has focused on the role of the elites in state formation, implicitly or explicitly denying that the popular classes – workers, peasants, etc. – had an impact in this sphere. More recent scholarship proposes a different view by presuming that popular-class mobilization is an es-sential element in shaping states and concepts of national identity.[12] Further-more, transnational studies are discovering that these processes also occur *be-yond* national boundaries.[13] As the research of Gabaccia, Iacovetta and Ottanelli clearly shows, nation building among Italy's peasants and workers began out-side Italy.[14]

Furthermore, these studies have also revealed that class formation and the development of national identity were occurring concurrently. Scholars are only recently analyzing migration as an ongoing interactive process in which mi-grants fashioned new identities based on their concurrent participation in the politics of both "old" and "new" countries.[15] A transnational approach illumi-nates these phenomena and acknowledges that capitalism, labor markets, labor regimes and workers' movements have never been phenomena enclosed solely national territories.[16]

An increasing interest in transnational history followed in the wake of the gains and debates of the linguistic turn.[17] On the most general level, transnational history is described by historian Hartmut Kaelble as the history of transfers and exchanges of people and ideas between different cultures.[18] Marcel Van der Linden argues for widening the focus of analysis in historical works addressing working class develop-ment and formation. There will be an increased urgency to understand national movements within the global milieu as historians expand their knowledge about the working classes in greater numbers of countries.

---

[12] See for example Ruth Berins Collier and David Collier, *Shaping the Political Arena: Critical Junc-tures, the Labor Movement and Regime Dynamics in Latin America* (Princeton: Princeton University Press, 1991) and Florencia E. Mallon, "Indian Communities: Political Cultures, and the State in Latin America, 1780-1990," *Journal of Latin American Studies*, 24, supplement, 1992, 35-53.

[13] See Gabaccia, Iacovetta, Ottanelli. "Laboring Across National Boarders," 1-11 and 57-77.

[14] Donna R. Gabaccia and Fraser M. Ottanelli eds. *Italian Workers of the World: Labor Migration and the Formation of Ethnic States* (Urbana and Chicago: University of Illinois Press) 200; Gabaccia, Iacovetta, and Ottanelli, "Laboring Across National Boarders," 61.

[15] Hanagan and Van der Linden, "New Approaches to Global Labor History," 7.

[16] Gabaccia et al. "Laboring Across National Boarders," 57.

[17] Of particular interest to labor historians are the impact of language and nonmaterial motivations for collective action and solidarity. See William H. Sewell, *Work and Revolution in France: The Lan-guage of Labor from the Old Regime to 1848* (Cambridge: Cambridge University Press, 1980) and "Toward a Post-materialist Rhetoric for Labor History."

[18] Hartmut Kaelble "Social History In Europe: Introducing The Issues," *Journal of Social History*, Fall, 2003.

Van der Linden cites two reasons for this shift. First, aspects of specificity and generality can only be discerned by examining what is occurring within and across national borders. Secondly, and more pertinent to our research on Cuban cigar makers and Indian agricultural workers, is that working-class formation and restructuring are "not neatly contained within particular national borders; it is a process in which voluntary and forced immigration and emigration have a great influence."[19]

The studies of Cuban cigar makers and Indian land workers are merely introduced in this essay to highlight the relevance of using transnational, multidisciplinary approaches toward working-class history. Both groups of workers have extraordinary histories of which we have only begun to fully explicate, especially in regards to their radical ideological development vis à vis their working lives.

Cuban Cigar Makers: Class, Identity and Ideology[20]

Mass Cuban immigration to the United States during the mid-to late-nineteenth century was influenced by two factors. The first and most frequently cited reason by historians is political, the Ten Years War occurring from 1868 to 1878. A second is economic, specifically the international trade in tobacco between Cuba and the United States in the years preceding the Ten Years War. These factors facilitated the emergence of the cigar industry in the United States. Cuban tobacco capitalists such as Martínez Ybor spearheaded extensions of the island's cigar industry first in Key West, Florida and later Tampa and New York City, providing the locus for working-class emigrations that would continue into the twentieth century.

In 1857, the United States responded to Spanish trade restrictions by passing its own retaliatory measure, the 1857 McKinley Tariff. The tariff limited the number of Cuban cigars entering the market by raising the duty on finished cigars but not raw Cuban tobacco. The American tobacco interests were partly responsible for the tariff since it protected them from Cuban competition. In Cuba, the tariff had a disastrous effect. Cigar workers were unemployed, panic ensued, and many manufacturers went bankrupt. Unemployed laborers became a political and social problem for the Spanish government.

The outbreak of the Ten Years War forced many Havana cigar factories to close and, as a result, unemployed workers emigrated to Key West in search of work. The armed struggle between separatists and supporters of the crown set into motion the first of a series of population dislocations. Separatists and sym-

---

[19] Marcel van der Linden, *Transnational Labour History: Explorations* (Ashgate, Burlington, 2003) 3.

[20] Due to space considerations we can only briefly summarize our research into the transnational world of Cuban cigar makers. For a fuller explication see Evan Daniel, "A Single Universe: Cuban Cigar Makers in Havana and South Florida, 1853-1899," in *Florida's Labor and Working-Class Past: Three Centuries of Work in the Sunshine State*, Forthcoming from University Press of Florida, 2006.

pathizers seeking to escape the anticipated wrath of Spanish colonial authorities scattered throughout Europe, Latin America, and the U.S. In general, the wealthiest patricians settled in Europe while the middle-class and most professionals immigrated to the Northeastern cities of the U.S. – New York, Philadelphia, and Boston. The majority of cigar makers emigrated to Florida (first in Key West and later Tampa) and New York City.

The Panic of 1857 and increasing duties on Cuban finished tobacco due to the United States Civil War resulted in a major reorganization of the Cuban cigar industry. Several of the more resourceful manufacturers, seeking to penetrate the high tariff wall, relocated their operations to the U.S. While most relocated to Key West, and later, Tampa, tobacco capitalists also moved operations to New York City. The first cigar factories were established in New York City in the 1860s. By the end of 1868 – the first year of the Ten Years War – some 100,000 Cubans sought refuge abroad. With the end of the War in February 1878, many working-class Cubans who had fled to the U.S. returned home. But, in the five-year period after 1885, the level of immigration from Cuba more than tripled.

Cuban *torcedores* (cigar makers) were a distinctive work group in many respects. They had a collective identity and anarchist ideology that was fostered by their unique work culture, shared by Cuban cigar makers both on the island and in the U.S. As skilled workers, Cuban cigar makers had a relatively high level of workplace autonomy. Through their fashionable attire, their consciousness of their own "manliness," and long-standing shop floor customs that allowed them to regulate their own hours of labor or to take home free cigars ("smokers") at the end of a workday, cigar makers were able to secure a measure of autonomy uncommon among other workers. Cooperative work practices and craft pride fostering a mutualist ethos also helped them control their working conditions and resist managerial authority.[21] This work culture was transplanted from Cuba to the émigré communities in South Florida and New York City.

The cigar makers were politically educated on the job through the shop-floor readers, or *lectors*. But the Lectors were far more than simple propagandists, they facilitated the development of a collective working class identity and a common Cuban identity.[22] The political material read by the lectors was highly influenced by what was being read to cigar makers in Cuba at the time with anarchist tracts in the majority. A typical workday would begin with current events read from Cuban newspapers followed by a section from a popular novel, such as Emile Zola's Germinal, and, after lunch, the day would conclude with readings from Cuban anarchist and working-class periodicals including *La*

---

[21] Patricia Cooper, *Once a Cigar Maker: Men, Women, and Work Culture in American Cigar Factories, 1900-1919* (Urbana: University of Illinois Press, 1987) 16.

[22] Louis A. Pérez, Jr., *Essays on Cuban History: Historiography and Research* (Gainesville: University Press of Florida, 1995) 25.

Aurora, El Productor, and *El Despertar* in addition to Paris' *les Temps nou-veaux* and *Barcelona's El Productor*.

In the formative years of cigar making, the worker-owner relationship was quite simple. Economic historian L. Glenn Westfall states,

> Farmers growing tobacco usually sold a few cigars to supplement their income, a small group of enterprising businessmen calling themselves 'brokers' collected cigars from farmers. Their brand name was placed on the cigars which were sold to Havana merchants for distribution.[23]

Small tobacco shops, called *chinchales* (bedbugs), were set up to meet the growing demands for cigars. Brokers later hired full-time workers to produce cigars and the increased market demands resulted in the construction of factories.

Although in many respects an artisanal craft, by 1855 the factory system was an integral part of the industry. Cuba was on the verge of a small but significant industrial revolution. In less than fifty years, a total transformation of the tobacco trade had taken place. While cigar making was only a supplement to farm income in 1800, by 1850 it became a highly valued industrial skill while global market demands for Cuban tobacco continued to increase.

In Cuba, collective identity was fostered by the close spaces of the *factoria*. Whether engaging in labor or listening to the *lecturas*, this proximity meant that free and unfree workers were in constant contact with each other. Mutual benefit associations, the *lectura*, labor periodicals, and eventually strikes facilitated solidarity between workers of different ethnicities and races

The large measure of autonomy in artisanal cigar making combined with the tendency of cigar makers to populate the same neighborhoods led to greater class cohesion as craft solidarity was expanded from the workshop to the bar or café. Proletarians, by contrast, were much more geographically dispersed and did not live in clearly delineated neighborhoods. Although both proletarians and artisans operated within factory walls, artisans were able to take their own breaks, roll their own cigars and come and go as they pleased. The relative quiet in cigar factories allowed for levels of socializing unheard of in industrial factories where noisy machinery made thinking – much less conversation – a chore and where a minute lack of attentiveness on the part of the worker could result in a missing finger, leg or death.

The higher salaries of skilled artisans meant that they had more money to spend on union dues in comparison to their proletarian brothers and sisters. Higher incomes also meant that artisans had an advantage over proletarians in strike situations because they had more savings to fall back on. Yet skilled cigar

---

[23] L. Glenn Westfall, *Don Vicente Martínez Ybor, the Man and his Empire. Development of the Clear Havana Industry in Cuba and Florida in the Nineteenth Century* (New York: Garland Publishing, Inc., 1987) 10.

makers managed to win the support of semiskilled workers in strikes as many had relatives among the semiskilled and unskilled and joint-strikes were organized. Some union leaders also supported joint-strikes as they viewed the assaults by employers on the organizations of the unskilled as the first step in cracking down on their own organizations.

Joan Casanovas argues that since free and unfree labor worked together in tobacco manufacturing, non-whites and probably even self-hired slaves participated in the strikes. Furthermore, slaves, indentured Chinese laborers and free blacks became part of the audience during the readings in the factories.[24] People of differing races and ethnicities participated in strikes together and in this climate of class confrontation socialist and anarchist propagandists first emerged publicly in Cuba, attracting a growing number of workers to their respective causes. During this period, their propaganda reached a broad sector of the urban popular classes in Cuba. Casanovas contends that the anarchists' approach fostered class ties among people of diverse race, political sympathy, and origin (peninsular and creole). [25] In an openly white-supremacist society, anarchists constantly called for an alliance of all workers regardless of race in their propaganda organs.

The Cuban anarchists attempted to create bonds of solidarity between workers across racial and national lines through intellectual and material support, while the Spanish government and employers increasingly appealed to ethnic and racial divisions on the Island. During a strike by revolutionary cigar makers in Key West in 1893, the Spanish government distributed posters in Cuba advertising available jobs in Key West. This created division in the unions between Spaniards, who were viewed as strike breakers, and Cuban Creoles.[26] Jean Stubbs remarks that during the anti-colonial struggle, "despite their good intentions as to treating all workers equally, regardless of color, race and nationality – and possibly because of this – it was easy to point to many Spanish anarchists who were against the national independence movement of being anti-Cuba."[27]

Cuban workers also appealed to nationalism to stop European immigration to Cuba and called for strikes to demand preferential treatment for Cuban workers. Ultimately, as Alejandro de la Fuente notes, "race operated along national and ethnic lines, considerably weakening workers' bargaining capacity"

---

[24] Joan Casanovas, "Slavery, the Labour Movement and Spanish Colonialism in Cuba (1850-1890)," *International Review of Social History* (Amsterdam), 40:3, 1995, 376. See also Joan Casanovas, *Bread, or Bullets!: Urban Labor and Spanish Colonialism in Cuba, 1850-1898* (Pittsburgh: University of Pittsburgh Press, 1998).

[25] Aline Helg, *Our Rightful Share: The Afro-Cuban Struggle for Equality 1886-1912* (Chapel Hill: University of North Carolina Press, 1995) 26, 38.

[26] John C. Appel. "The Unionization of Florida Cigar makers and the Coming War with Spain," *The Hispanic American Historical Review*, 36:1, February, 1956, 44.

[27] Jean Stubbs, *Tobacco on the Periphery: A Case Study in Cuban Labour History, 1860-1958.* (Cambridge: Cambridge University Press, 1985) 106.

as employers sought to divide the working class.[28] However, working-class organizations tended to recognize these divisive tactics as the work of employers and the state. Consequently, unions and other working-class organizations labored to bridge the potential racial and ethnic divisions, incorporating whites, blacks, and Spaniards into their leadership ranks. De la Fuente correctly notes that the articulation of "a notion of non-racialized class identity" helped to bring "class" into the forefront of Cuban politics after independence.[29] This greatly contributed to the appeal of a Cuban "racial democracy" and galvanized support for independence among the Cuban working classes in the émigré communities of Key West, Tampa and New York City.[30]

Louis Pérez argues that by the 1890s the movement for *Cuba Libre* moved to the fore and working class action to the rear; "Class was subordinated to nationalism."[31] This is largely, though not completely, due to the influence of José Martí on labor militants in the émigré communities. Martí made the first of a series of visits to Key West and Tampa in early 1892. By the end of the year, during a visit to Tampa, Martí announced the creation of the Cuban Revolutionary Party (PRC), dedicated to Cuban independence.

The first revolutionary club of Cuban émigrés, the Patriotic Association of Key West, had been set up as early as 1869, the year in which cigar manufacturer Martínez Ybor transferred his factory and workers to the region. Over the next twenty-five years, 46 small organizations of this type sprung up in Florida wherever there were émigré communities. Cuban women were instrumental to the development and proliferation of these centers. Recreational centers, schools, and revolutionary clubs for Cubans were formed as far north as Philadelphia and New York. By 1896 Tampa's Cubans had formed forty-one patriotic clubs.[32] While living in exile in New York, Martí travelled to meet with anarchist unionists in Florida.

For Martí, *Cuba Libre* signified not only a nation free of Spanish rule but also a country free from racism, exploitation, and oppression. Martí's populism was an attempt to link labor and management in the common cause of independence. Many leading cigar manufacturers including Vicente Martínez Ybor, Domingo Villamil, Teodoro Perez, and Ceceilion Henriquez, publicly identified with Cuban independence. Eduardo Hidalgo Gato, the Key West cigar magnate

---

[28] Alejandro de la Fuente, "Two Dangers, One Solution: Immigration, Race and Labor in Cuba, 1900-1930," *International Labor and Working-Class History*, 51, 1997, 30-49.

[29] Alejandro de la Fuente, "Myths of Racial Democracy: Cuba 1900-1912," *Latin American Research Review*, 34:3, 1999, 39-73.

[30] Kirwin Shafer. "Cuba para todos: Anarchist Internationalism and the Cultural Politics of Cuban Independence," *Cuban Studies*, 31, 2000, 49-50.

[31] Louis A. Pérez, Jr. *Essays on Cuban History: Historiography and Research* (Gainesville: University of Florida Press, 1995) 25.

[32] Gary R. Mormino and George E. Pozzetta. *The Immigrant World of Ybor City: Italians and Their Latin Neighbors, 1885-1985* (Chicago: University of Illinois Press, 1990) 79.

and Martí's close personal friend, donated tens of thousands of dollars to the separatist cause.

PRC leadership took this cross-class alliance as necessary not only in Cuba but in the expatriate communities in Key West and Ybor City as well. Martínez Ybor was one of the first tobacco capitalists who outsourced production in Key West in order to avoid the 1857 McKinley Tariff on finished cigars. After a succession of work disruptions and a major fire, Martínez Ybor founded his namesake company town on the outskirts of Tampa in 1885. These expatriate communities were a vital source of funds for the separatists. The wives of Cuban workers regularly saved one day of their husband's earnings in support of Cuba Libre.[33] *"El dia de la Patria"* (one day's work for the homeland) became the theme song of Ybor City's Cubans in the 1890s.[34] A threatened strike in February 1896 prompted Tomás Estrada Palma, the chief of the New York delegation, to visit Ybor City to urge workers to return to the factories on behalf of *Cuba Libre*. The PRC recognized the support provided to the cause of independence by Martínez Ybor. Furthermore, Benjamin Guerra, the secretary-treasurer of the PRC, owned a cigar factory in Tampa.[35]

So when war again erupted in 1895, Cuban anarchists in the émigré communities and on the island engaged in the armed struggle. In this war, the goal for the cigar makers was greater than independence: it was global social revolution. What differentiated the struggle in 1895 from all the previous wars against Spain was the acknowledgement that inequality was the effect of the Cuban social system, not merely a by-product of Spanish colonial rule. Therefore, the only remedy was a transformation of the entire class and racial structures of Cuban society.

Cuban cigar makers in Cuba, South Florida and New York City existed in a transnational milieu. They were members of the same organizations, read the same newspapers, and participated in the same strikes. However, the autonomy of the cigar making craft led to real and perceived divisions between cigar makers and other workers. And life in Cuba was certainly not identical to life in the United States.

The autonomy of Cuban cigar makers facilitated the development of a cluster of work patterns, attitudes, and traditions that tended to pull cigar makers away from collective action among the broader working-class. Many highly skilled cigar makers – especially those who controlled apprentices – considered themselves a "class apart" and resisted changes that threatened their status. Moreover, the cigar industry in the U.S. manifested its own brand of upward mobility. Unlike many other manufacturing industries, the cigar trade required no outlay or investment in expensive machinery or specialized buildings and en-

---

[33] Nancy A. Hewitt, *Southern Discomfort: Women's Activism in Tampa, Florida, 1880s-1920s* (Chicago: University of Chicago Press, 2001).
[34] Mormino and Pozzetta, 80.
[35] Pérez, 30.

terprising cigar makers often aspired to open their own shops. In this economic environment frugal and market-savvy cigar makers become bosses and owners in their own right. While not large, these one – or two – man chinchales were always plentiful, supplying graphic evidence of the process at work.

The economic opportunity of the chinchal also reinforced Anglo republican notions of free labor.[36] As opposed to socialist conceptions of a proletarian working-class, republicans posited the ideal of a small-scale producer whether independent farmer or craftsman.[37]

The divergent messages of class conflict enunciated by radicals, on the one hand, and capitalist enterprise exemplified by the chinchal, on the other, coexisted in an uncomfortable balance. During times of labor strife radicals frequently played roles in shaping union destinies. Socialists, syndicalists, and anarchists joined with their fellow cigar workers, often in leadership positions, and struggled against the forces of management. Their appeals to class-consciousness and worker solidarity were effective in organizing workers and promoting strike efforts. During periods of tranquillity the influence of these individuals waned. In these circumstances cigar makers may have listened with intent to discussions of the class war, but apparently were making plans to become factory owners themselves.[38]

The world that cigar makers inhabited was in dramatic flux, in an era that constantly demanded fluidity with which to address the changes in work, society, and nation. They were constantly renegotiating their relationship to work and to the state as transnational subjects who actively maintained a multitude of connections even after "settling for good" elsewhere.

Indian Land Workers: Class, Identity and Ideology

During the same time period that cigar makers were forced to relocate due to global economic and political factors, workers from Northern India were also emigrating for similar reasons. Beginning in the late nineteenth century, laborers from Northern India arrived in the Pacific Northwest to work in the timber and agricultural industries. Many of these workers were involved in an expatriate movement in the U.S and Canada, called *Ghadar* (mutiny), which sought to violently overthrow the British from India. Some Indian workers were also involved in radical labor organizations including the Industrial Workers of the World (I.W.W.), as well as anarchist and communist movements. The various economic, social and political struggles these immigrants were involved in did not constitute mutually exclusive domains; contact with other workers in the la-

---

[36] David R. Roediger, *The Wages of Whiteness: Race and the Making of the American Working Class* (New York: Verso Press, 1991) 44.

[37] See Eric Foner, *Free Soil, Free Labor, Free Men: The Ideology of the Republican Party Before the Civil War* (New York: Oxford University Press, 1970) 11-39.

[38] Mormino and Pozzetta, 113-114.

bor movement and anti-colonialist movements encouraged an overlap between struggles and cross-pollenization of revolutionary activity.

These workers (Indians) were comprised of farm laborers and former farm owners, primarily from the Punjab province. Beginning in the mid-nineteenth century, significant changes transformed Punjabi agrarian society including improved irrigation, regressive land laws and taxation, increased money-lending and new relationships between landholders and tenants.[39]

These changes to rural society along with other factors contributed to an exodus of Punjabi male laborers leaving to British colonies such as Hong Kong, Singapore, and Canada in the late nineteenth century. Other factors that encouraged emigration included recurrent famines in India, along with high rates of poverty[40], British impressments of laborers to build Canadian railways, and aggressive promotion of jobs and high wages in North America by steamship companies.

The early wave of immigrants to North America, nearly all male, originally went to Canada, primarily to British Columbia, for employment in the timber and agricultural industries. As mentioned earlier, the bulk of the early immigrants were from the Punjab province and nearly ninety percent of the immigrants to North America were Sikhs.[41] Increasingly restrictive immigration laws in Canada[42], a rapidly growing agriculture industry and stories of higher

---

[39] See Himadri Banerjee, "Changes in Agrarian Society in the Late Nineteenth Century," in *Five Punjabi Centuries: Polity, Economy, Society and Culture, c. 1500-1900*, ed Indu Banga (New Delhi: Manohar, 1997) 333-340.

[40] According to LaBrack and Leonard, during the mid-nineteenth century in India, improved irrigation methods contributed to decreased mortality rates. Landowning families, with more children vying for limited shares of property, encouraged the movement of their young, able-bodied sons overseas for employment. See LaBrack and Leonard, "Conflict and Compatibility in Punjabi Immigrant Families in Rural California, 1915-1965," *Journal of Marriage and Family*, August, 1984, 46:3, 527.

[41] Within India, Sikhs have a distinct identity and history apart from the broader culture, too complex to explicate for the purposes of this essay. However, it is worth mentioning the immediate political/religious identification that was taking place among Sikhs in India, since this was undoubtedly influential in the political action that these workers were engaged in within the U.S. Michael Angelo demarcates three major periods of Sikh history prior to 1947, the year of India's independence from Britain. The Age of the Gurus from 1469 to 1708 saw the development of Sikhism vis-à-vis its succession of gurus. A "heroic age" from 1708 to 1849, a period of intense struggle for Sikhs to individuate themselves as a community as well as an era marked by Sikh sovereignty over the Punjab province. The next period, from 1840-1947, is the era of British control throughout the region. The second and third periods show, very broadly, the political development of Sikhs in India. The transition from a period of cultural and political distinction from Hindu and Muslims in India is followed by a period of subjugation by the British. This political history was very likely carried by at least some members of the Indian immigrants who came to Canada and subsequently to the U.S. As Angelo notes, "[t]his experience forced a critical reappraisal by the Sikhs of their institutional identity, both as subjects of a colonial foreign power and as a minority whose political and religious existence were challenged by larger Muslim and Hindu constituencies." See Michael Angelo, *The Sikh Diaspora: Tradition and Change in an Immigrant Community* (Garland Publishing, Inc: New York, 1997) 4.

[42] In 1908, Canada enacted a law barring immigrants from entering the country unless they came from their country of citizenship via a continuous journey. At the time, it was impossible for Indians to

wages eventually brought these workers into the United States and down along the Pacific Coast. Some settled in the timber regions of Washington and Oregon while others continued further south into Northern and Central California. By 1907, there were nearly 5,000 Indians in the U.S.

Unlike the cigar makers who tended to settle and practice their craft in an area, Indian laborers were by and large migrant workers who moved seasonally to wherever they could find work along the coast. Beginning at the end of the nineteenth century, California underwent such monumental shifts in farm production as improved irrigation systems, the completion of the transcontinental railroad, and the introduction of new cash crops, such as sugar beets and citrus plant. These all transformed agricultural society into its modern, industrialized form. "Factories in the field" was how Carey McWilliams termed this new breed of large, industrial farms that subsisted on large quantities of cheap, expendable labor willing to do monotonous, backbreaking work.[43]

Indian agricultural workers were often met with hostility which led to exclusionary practices, discriminatory legislation[44], and violence. Irrespective of the numbers of Indian immigrants and the overstated economic threat they posed to other laborers, their arrival into the U.S. was often characterized as the "Hindoo scare"[45] or "the turban invasion," after the headdress that many Sikh men wore[46]. The Dillingham Commission, in its 1911 report on U.S. immigration, characterized the position of Indians on the Pacific Coast as "almost uni-

make an unbroken journey from India to Canada. In 1914, an Indian-Canadian businessman, Gurdit Singh, attempted to challenge this law by leasing a ship, the Komagata Maru, in Asia and encouraging Indian passengers to undertake the historical voyage. Upon arriving in British Columbia, however, the ship was not allowed to dock. The passengers were forced to remain aboard without additional food or water. The ship was ultimately forced to return to India where British authorities met the passengers with gunfire, killing a number of them. The incident encapsulated the racism Canadian Indians had been experiencing and began a period of mobilization among the immigrants. Violence erupted after the departure of the Komagata Maru. The Canadian authorities attempted to suppress Ghadar activity. A Canadian policeman, William Hopkinson, was identified as being integral in this suppression and was murdered by Mewa Singh during the trial of an agent provocateur, Bela Singh. Mewa Singh was convicted and hanged by the Canadian government in 1915. Mewa Singh was seen as a martyr to the cause of oppressed Canadian Indians. See Khushwant Singh, *A History of the Sikhs (Volume 2): 1839-1964* (Princeton: Princeton University Press, 1966).

[43] Carey McWilliams, *Factories in the Field: The Story of Migratory Farm Labor in California.* (Berkeley and Los Angeles: University of California Press, 2000).

[44] The Asian Exclusion Act of 1882-1924, the Asian Land Law of 1913, which barred Asians from owning land, and the Barred Zone Immigration Act of 1917, undoubtedly influenced the lives of these immigrants, engendering a feeling of marginalization and spurring (revolutionary) political action. Indian immigrants felt they were a people with no land.

[45] While the Indian immigrants were comprised of others besides Hindus, they were collectively referred to as Hindus. Even the Dillingham Commission notes this error in making another error in the characterization of Hindu as one caste: "The East Indians in the Pacific coast States include Sikhs, Mohammedans, and Afghans (who are also the Mohammedan faith). They are all known as "Hindus," though, strictly speaking, they are not all of the Hindu caste." U.S. Senate, Immigration Commission. *Reports of the Immigration Commission*, 1911, 325.

[46] See Roger Daniels, *History of Indian Immigration to the United States: An Interpretive Essay* (Cincinnati: University of Cincinnati Press, 1989).

versally regarded as the least desirable race of immigrants thus far admitted to the United States."[47]

While some Sikh men discontinued wearing a turban, others continued to use it. The Dillingham Commission noted the Sikhs' long hair and turbans as a hindrance to obtaining employment, "their strange appearance is a handicap to them."[48] The report continues, "The native article of dress, the turban, which is also allowed to become very dirty, has created prejudice. Some of the East Indians in California have cut their long hair because of the heat, but even these men continue to wear their native headdress."[49] The continued use of the turban in the U.S. is significant since it was a visual marker of distinction but also demonstrated the Sikhs' desire to maintain their religious and cultural identity, even in the face of discrimination and the pressure to assimilate. This is contrasted with some Muslim small businessmen who sold tamales in San Francisco: "They are all Mohammedans and consequently wear their hair short without turbans. As a result of these changes in their appearance they are not generally known to be East Indians."[50]

The Dillingham Commission also notes that many Indians had to contend with a language barrier. While the Japanese and Chinese farm workers generally organized into work "gangs," Indian workers were noted as being more "individualistic" but were forced to search for work in gangs due to their limited English. The leader of the Indian work groups was usually the one with the best English and received a nominal stipend for translating on behalf of the group, again unlike the Japanese and Chinese work groups who had gang bosses that received a commission of their workers' wages.[51]

In 1912, Sikhs started the *Khalsa Diwan* in Holt, California. This organization offered accommodation and aid to indigent and transient workers and students as well as a place where revolutionary ideas and activities were promoted.[52] Also that same year, Sikhs built their first *gurdwara* (temple) in the U.S. in Stockton, California. The gurdwara became the focal point for the community, drawing Sikhs from all parts of the Pacific Northwest. While these migrant workers travelled together and would meet along the Pacific Coast searching for work, these sites provided physical spaces where men, living transitory lives, could rest and interact with other Indians away from the broader society. These were places where men of different religions and backgrounds interacted. Even though the gurdwara was a Sikh temple, Muslims and Hindus took refuge in the temple, especially when they were new arrivals to the area.

---

[47] U.S. Senate, Immigration Commission. *Reports of the Immigration Commission*, 1911, 349.
[48] Ibid, 337.
[49] Ibid, 342.
[50] Ibid, 344.
[51] Ibid, 336.
[52] Sucheng Chan, *Asian Americans: An Interpretive History* (Boston: Twayne Publishers, 1991) 74-75.

Students who came to study would meet migrant workers, something that was probably unlikely in India. Information and ideas about life in India and life in the U.S. were exchanged.

These meetings provided the incipient start to the Ghadar party. Ghadar party meetings began loosely from 1907 and continued into the 1930s, with the party's most influential years lasting from 1913 to 1917. Headquartered in San Francisco, Ghadar was started as an explicitly anti-colonial movement. The party openly advocated the use of violence in removing British authority from India. Ghadar literature called for an international uprising of Indians to bear arms and organize themselves along working-class lines. The party positioned itself against non-violent anti-colonial forces in India as well as, what they regarded derogatorily as conciliatory political parties, such as the Indian National Congress, that attempted to work within the system.

The Ghadar party also took a hard line against collaborationist trade unions and socialist organizations both in India and the U.S. What they advocated was revolution along class lines: "[T]hose who are honestly fighting for national independence, must realize that it can be only own through a victorious revolutionary struggle of the masses united in their class organizations."[53] There was a profound faith found in the workers in India, echoed in a Ghadar pamphlet:

> The militant mass actions of the Indian proletariat and peasantry mark a new phase in the national revolutionary movement in India, in which the struggle of the mass of workers and peasants, whose class interests can never be reconciled with imperialist domination will become the principal driving force in the struggle of the Indian people for complete freedom. Therein lies the strength of the growing revolutionary movement of India and the guarantee of its final victory over British Imperialism.[54]

News articles from the period show that Indian workers were also actively involved in organized labor activities. Some Indian farm workers were involved in what became known as the Wheatland Hopfield Riots in Northern California in 1913. In August 1913, migrant hops pickers in Yuba County, California protested the abominable working conditions at the Durst Hop Ranch. A strike was authorized for August 3. Indian workers were originally brought in as scab replacements for striking farm workers. However, they were convinced instead to not cross the picket line and join the striking workers.

The Wheatland incident was an I.W.W. led action that was the largest and most ethnically diverse agricultural action in California at the time with workers speaking some twenty-seven different languages. The action resulted in the death of a District Attorney, convictions of I.W.W. organizers, and a clamp down on agricultural organization in California. In the San Francisco Bay area,

---

[53] "Resolutions of the League against Imperialism for India" (San Francisco: The Hindustan Gadar Party. Date unknown) 8. See bibliography for complete information.
[54] Ibid, 6.

Ghadar members, including leader Har Dayal, had been in contact with various anti-colonial activities and revolutionaries. Ghadar members were invited to I.W.W. meetings, associated with expatriate Irish, and had been in contact with socialists and anarchists including Emma Goldman and Alexander Berkman.

Ghadar activists also maintained ties with German officials, both parties hoping to use their mutual desire to undermine the British to their advantage. Ghadarites thought Britain would be distracted by the activities of World War I and decided to make attempts at fomenting revolution from outside India's borders. Capitalizing on this opportunity, the German government provided considerable assistance to the Ghadar party. In a two-pronged effort to both destabilize Britain as well as to garner support of anti-imperialist groups, such as Irish-Americans, Germany provided advice and arms to the party. In October 1914, Germany authorized the purchase of ten to twenty thousand rifles and their shipment to India on the *Maverick* via the Pacific. The plan was thwarted at various points due in part to the gross overstatement of Ghadar sympathizers in India by Ghadar leader, Ram Chandra, and also to terrible incompetence of German organizers who were unable to secure working ships and maintain a schedule. A second shipment of arms was attempted June 15, 1915 this time through New York aboard the *Djember*. However, the *Djember* and its revolutionary cargo never went far due to the early discovery of the plan by British agents at New York.

Beginning in 1916, the Ghadar party experienced internecine fighting stemming from accusations of misappropriation of funds as well as religious differences. The Ghadar party splintered into factions, suffering a similar fate to many other radical groups throughout history. In April 1917, U.S. federal agents began arresting various Ghadar members for treason. The trial, U.S. versus Franz Bopp, et al., began November 1917 and ended April 1918 with all the accused pleading not guilty. The trial exposed the infighting within the party and ended with one member, Ram Singh, shooting to death Ram Chandra in the courthouse. Ram Singh was immediately shot by the court's marshal. All of the accused but one American were adjudged guilty were given sentences ranging from thirty days to two years with some also receiving fines.

Conclusion

From the late nineteenth to early twentieth century, Cuban *torcedores* (cigar makers) exemplified the highly autonomous work culture of skilled artisans and their newspapers and workplace orators, or, *lectors*, articulated an explicitly internationalist anarchist ideology.[55] For Cuban cigar makers, anarchist ideology

---

[55] Anarchism is a complex and multi-faceted ideology with individualist, mutualist, collectivist, syndicalist and communist tendencies. In the case of Cuban cigar makers, anarchism may be most broadly defined as the forms and ideas of libertarian socialism that emerged from the First International with an emphasis on direct action, workers self-management and anti-parliamentarianism. The

was mobilized against domestic capitalists and imperial Spain. Cuban anarchists did not frame the war against Spain as a strictly nationalist struggle. Instead they promoted the war as a legitimate struggle against imperialism that would pave the way for a broader social revolution.

Many of the Indian land workers who started coming to the U.S. in the late nineteenth century brought their economic and political frustrations as colonial subjects with them. Their experiences in the U.S. – at times financially beneficial yet tempered with racism and discrimination – compounded with the subjugated political life they lived in India. These agricultural workers' political participation in the U.S. ranged from organized labor activity – including involvement with the Industrial Workers of the World – to forming the Hindu Association of the Pacific Coast, more commonly known as the Ghadar Party, an organization that advocated and instigated armed rebellion against the British in India. These immigrant Indian agricultural workers were minority subjects of different states, had potentially conflicting class interests yet coalesced to engage in various revolutionary struggles transnationally.

Anarchist ideology and working-class identity were nurtured by the work culture of Cuban cigar makers. For example, notions of international proletarian solidarity across boundaries of race or color were fostered by the close working conditions and diverse work force of the cigar factories. Their work culture, in turn, was influenced by anarchist ideology as evidenced by their advocacy of self-management and participation in direct action. The identity of Cuban cigar makers was also constructed through workplace relations and community ties. The unique anarchist ideology, class identity and work culture of Cuban cigar makers was international as the working conditions and ethnic composition within Cuban cigar factories varied little whether located in Havana, South Florida, or New York City. Likewise, a shared ideology could also be found on both sides of the Florida straits and up the Atlantic coast.[56]

Demographic data points to the need for a reexamination of the importance of New York as a perennial center for Cuban immigrants and as an arena for important events in Cuban history. The need – and opportunities – for research into the origins and development of this community of Cubans are tremendous.

Transnational historical research is in its formative stages. A fluid or multiple-identities approach is one attempt to migrate from previous arguments

---

two tendencies with the most relevance are those of the mutualists – associated with Pierre Joséph Proudhon – and the collectivists – associated with Mikhail Aleksandrovich Bakunin – as these two tendencies had the greatest influence in the development of working-class ideology on the island. For general surveys of anarchist ideology see Paul Avrich, *Anarchist Portraits* (Princeton: Princeton University Press, 1988); Daniel Guérin, *Anarchism: From Theory to Practice* (New York: Monthly Review Press, 1970); George Woodcock, *Anarchism: A History of Libertarian Ideas and Movements* (New York: New American Library, 1974).

[56] Hewitt, 11.

regarding whether to prioritize gender, race, and class in labor studies, to reconstructing how gender identity, race identity, and class identify shape each other.[57] This often leads, as in this paper, to an acknowledgement that different class and political identities in combination produce multi-faceted individuals and groups. However, keeping transnational working classes in mind, it is also necessary to recognize that people with multifaceted identities have multiple interests and can therefore create collectivities in various ways.

Indeed, as much as Martí – and later, the symbol of Martí – served to unify the Cuban émigré community, he also meant different things to different people. Martí's successors in the PRC and the editors of *Patria* focused on the political question, while others considered Martí's social doctrines as primary, with Cuban workers and labor leaders emphasizing socio-economic issues.[58]

Diversity was the movement's principal source of strength. It sustained Cuban resolve in so far as Cubans generally agreed on the necessity to separate from Spain. However, class and political diversity was also the movement's principal weakness. The diverse class origins and political ideologies of Cuban separatism gave rise to fractious political conflicts. Ambiguity of purpose produced ambiguity in policy. Leadership fragmented. In the end, the institutional agencies around which the forces of Cuba Libre had organized were more competitive than complementary, and the only real unifying bond was the will to wage war against Spain.[59]

The Indian land workers who came to North America and, eventually, Northern California, came primarily from the Punjab province with the majority being Sikhs. Despite the predominance of this one religious and regional group, their activities in Northern California – ranging from a temple in Stockton and social activities to the labor activity to the Ghadar Party – consciously down-played religious and (Indian) regional differences. Instead, their common cause of overthrowing the British from India helped forge a common Indian revolutionary identity. This is not unlike other anti-colonial movements that construct a common identity in the face of a common enemy.

But the Ghadarites openly opposed existing anti-colonial groups in India, including Gandhi, Nehru and part of the Indian National Congress that chose the non-violent route. To some degree, they portended Subhash Chandra Bose' military and political agitation from forces outside India and Bose' theory that Britain's preoccupation with the war – World War II – would be ripe for Indian revolution. The Ghadarites attempted a movement intertwined with class revolution and was influenced by both communist and anarchist ideologies, unlike

---

[57] van der Linden, *Transnational Labour History*, 149.
[58] See Gerald Poyo, "*With All for the Good of All*": *The Emergence of Popular Nationalism in the Cuban Communities of the United States, 1848-1898* (Durham and London: Duke University Press, 1989).
[59] Louis A. Pérez Jr., *José Martí in the United States: The Florida Experience* (Tempe: Center for Latin American Studies, Arizona State University, 1995) xvii.

Bose, who was convinced that India would be served well with authoritarian socialism. The Ghadarites unique history of being a marginalized, stateless people whether in the U.S., Canada or India, produced unique political subjects. Their ability to re-imagine their imagined communities made them more than passive actors.

Transnational historical research is in its formative stages. A fluid or multiple-identities approach is one attempt to migrate from previous arguments regarding whether to prioritize gender, race, and class in labor studies, to reconstructing how gender identity, race identity, and class identity shape each other.[60] This often leads, as in this paper, to an acknowledgement that different class and political identities in combination produce multifaceted individuals and groups. However, keeping transnational working classes in mind, it is also necessary to recognize that people with multifaceted identities have multiple interests and can therefore create collectivities in myriad ways.

Selected Bibliography

Anderson, Benedict. *Imagined Communities: Reflections on the Origins and Spread of Nationalism*. London: Verso, 1983.

Arnesen, Eric, Julie Greene and Bruce Laurie. *Labor Histories: Class, Politics and the Working-Class Experience*. Chicago: University of Illinois Press, 1998.

Appel, John C. "The Unionization of Florida Cigar makers and the Coming War with Spain." *The Hispanic American Historical Review*, 36:1 (1956): 38-49.

Avrich, Paul. *Anarchist Portraits*, Princeton: Princeton University Press, 1988.

Bakunin, Mikhail Aleksandrovich. *The Political Philosophy of Bakunin: Scientific Anarchism*. Compiled and Ed G. P. Maximoff, Glencoe: Free Press 1953.

Banerjee, Himadri. "Changes in Agrarian Society in the Late Nineteenth Century" *Five Punjabi Centuries: Polity, Economy, Society and Culture,* c. *1500-1900*. Ed. Indu Banga. New Delhi: Manohar, 1997. 333-340.

Brody, David. "The Old Labor History and the New: In Search of An American Working Class," *Labor History* 20:1 (1979): 111-26.

Casanovas, Joan. "Slavery, the Labour Movement and Spanish Colonialism in Cuba (1850-1890)," *International Review of Social History* 40:3 (1995): 367-382.

_____. *Bread, or Bullets!: Urban Labor and Spanish Colonialism in Cuba, 1850-1898*. Pittsburgh: University of Pittsburgh Press, 1998.

Chadney, James G. *The Sikhs of Vancouver*. New York: AMS Press, 1984.

---

[60] Van der Linden, *Transnational Labour History*, 149.

Chan, Sucheng. *Asian Americans: An Interpretive History*. Boston: Twayne Publishers, 1991.

_____. "Chinese Livelihood in Rural California: The Impact of Economic Change, 1860-1880." *Working People of California*. Ed. Daniel Cornford. Berkeley and Los Angeles, California: University of California Press, 1995. 57-81.

_____. *This Bittersweet Soil: The Chinese in California Agriculture, 1860-1910*. Berkeley and Los Angeles: University of California Press, 1986.

Chandrasekhar, S., ed. *From India to America: A Brief History of Immigration: Problems of Discrimination, Admission and Assimilation*. La Jolla, California: Population Review Publications, 1982.

Collier, Ruth Berins and David. *Shaping the Political Arena: Critical Junctures, the Labor Movement and Regime Dynamics in Latin America*. Princeton: Princeton University Press, 1991.

Cooper, Patricia. *Once a Cigar Maker: Men, Women, and Work Culture in American Cigar Factories, 1900-1919*. Urbana: University of Illinois Press, 1987.

Daniel, Evan M. "A Single Universe: Cuban Cigar Makers in Havana and South Florida, 1853-1899." *Florida's Labor and Working-Class Past: Three Centuries of Work in the Sunshine State*. Gainesville: University Press of Florida, 2006.

Daniels, Roger. *History of Indian Immigration to the United States: An Interpretive Essay*. Cincinnati: University of Cincinnati Press, 1989.

de la Fuente, Alejandro. "Two Dangers, One Solution: Immigration, Race and Labor in Cuba, 1900-1930." *International Labor and Working-Class History* 51 (1997): 30-49.

_____. "Myths of Racial Democracy: Cuba 1900-1912." *Latin American Research Review* 34:3 (1999): 39-73.

Deol, Gurdev Singh. *The Role of the Ghadar Party in the National Movement*. Delhi: Sterling Publishers, 1969.

Dolgoff, Sam ed. and trans. *Bakunin on Anarchism*. Montréal: Black Rose Books, 1980.

Dreyfus, Michel. *Liberté, Égalité, Mutualité: Mutualisme et Syndicalisme, 1852-1967*. Paris: Atelier, 2001.

Dubofsky, Melvyn. *We Shall Be All: A History of the Industrial Workers of the World*. New York: Quadrangle Books, 1969.

Edwards, Stewart ed. *Selected Writings of Pierre-Joseph Proudhon*. Trans. Elizabeth Fraser. Garden City: Anchor Books, 1969.

Essenwein, George. *Anarchist Ideology and the Working Class Movement in Spain, 1868-1898*. Berkeley: University of California Press, 1989.

Foner, Eric. *Free Soil, Free Labor, Free Men: The Ideology of the Republican Party Before the Civil War*. New York: Oxford University Press, 1970.

Fraser, Thomas G. "Germany and Indian Revolution, 1914-1918." *Journal of Contemporary History*, 12 (1977): 255-272.

Gabaccia, Donna R. and Fraser M. Ottanelli, eds. *Italian Workers of the World: Labor Migration and the Formation of Ethnic States*. Urbana and Chicago: University of Illinois Press, 2001.

Gabaccia, Donna, Franca Iacovetta, and Fraser Ottanelli. "Laboring Across National Borders: Class, Gender, and Militancy in the Proletarian Mass Migrations." *International Labor and Working-Class History* 66 (2004): 57-77.

Guérin, Daniel. *Anarchism: From Theory to Practice*. New York: Monthly Review Press, 1970.

Gueslin, André. *L'invention de l'économie sociale: idées, pratiques et imaginaires coopératifs et mutualistes dans la France du XIXe siècle*. Paris: Economica, 1998.

Gutman, Herbert G. *Work, Culture, and Society in Industrializing America: Essays in American Working-Class and Social History*. New York: Alfred A. Knopf, 1976.

Hall, Greg. *Harvest Wobblies: The Industrial Workers of the World and Agricultural Laborers in the American West, 1905-1930*. Corvallis, Oregon: Oregon State University Press, 2001.

Hanagan, Michael. *The Logic of Solidarity: Artisans and Industrial Workers in Three French Towns, 1871-1914*. Champaign: University of Illinois Press, 1980.

Hanagan, Michael and Marcel Van der Linden. "New Approaches to Global Labor History." *International Labor and Working Class History*, 66 (2004): 1-11.

Helg, Aline. *Our Rightful Share: The Afro-Cuban Struggle for Equality 1886-1912*. Chapel Hill: University of North Carolina Press, 1995.

Hewitt, Nancy A. *Southern Discomfort, Women's Activism in Tampa, Florida: 1880s-1920s*. Chicago: University of Chicago Press, 2001.

Hobsbawm, Eric J. *Primitive Rebels: Studies in Archaic Forms of Social Movement in 19th and 20th Centuries*. Manchester: Manchester University Press, 1959.

Juergensmeyer, Mark. "The Ghadar Syndrome: Nationalism in an Immigrant Community." http://www.lib.ucdavis.edu/punjab/ghadarsyndrome2.html (Consulted March 27, 2007.)

Kaelble, Hartmut. "Social History in Europe: Introducing the Issues." *Journal of Social History* (Fall 2003): 29-35.

Katznelson, Ira and Aristide Zolberg. *Working Class Formation: Nineteenth-Century Patterns in Western Europe and the United States*. Princeton: Princeton University Press, 1986.

LaBrack, Bruce and Karen Leonard. "Conflict and Compatibility in Punjabi-Mexican Immigrant Families in Rural California, 1915-1965." *Journal of Marriage and the Family* 3 (1984): 527-537.

Leonard, Karen. "Ethnicity Confounded: Punjabi Pioneers in California." *Sikh History and Religion in the Twentieth Century.* Ed. Joseph T. O'Connell, et al. Toronto: University of Toronto, 1988. 314-333.

Mallon, Florencia E. "Indian Communities: Political Cultures, and the State in Latin America, 1780-1990." *Journal of Latin American Studies* 24, supplement (1992): 35-53.

Mathur, L.P. *Indian Revolutionary Movement in the United States of America.* New Delhi: S. Chand and Company, 1970.

McWilliams, Carey. *Factories in the Field: The Story of Migratory Farm Labor in California.* Berkeley and Los Angeles, Ca. Univer   sity of California Press, 2000 [1935].

Melendy, Brett. *Asians in America: Filipinos, Koreans, and East Indians.* Boston: Twayne, 1977.

Mormino, Gary R. and George E. Pozzetta. T*he Immigrant World of Ybor City: Italians and Their Latin Neighbors, 1885-1985.* Chicago: University of Illinois Press, 1990.

Pérez, Louis A. Jr. *Essays on Cuban History: Historiography and Research.* Gainesville: University of Florida Press, 1995.

_____. *Martí in the United States: The Florida Experience.* Tempe: Center for Latin American Studies, Arizona State University, 1995.

Poyo, Gerald. *"With all for the Good of All": The Emergence of Popular Nationalism in the Cuban Communities of the United States, 1848-1898.* Durham: Duke University Press, 1989

Proudhon, Pierre Joseph. *General Idea of the Revolution in the Nineteenth Century,* London: Freedom Press, 1923.

Puri, Harish K. "The Ghadar Movement: A New Consciousness." *Five Punjabi Centuries: Polity, Economy, Society and Culture, c. 1500-1900.* Ed. Indu Banga. New Delhi: Manohar, 1997. 157-179.

"Resolutions of the League against Imperialism for India." San Francisco: The Hindustan Gadar Party. Date unknown. Gadar Collection. Bancroft Library. University of California, Berkeley.

Roediger, David R. *The Wages of Whiteness: Race and the Making of the American Working Class.* New York: Verso Press, 1991.

Sewell, William H. *Work and Revolution in France: The Language of Labor from the Old Regime to 1848.* Cambridge: Cambridge University Press, 1980.

_____. "Toward a Post-Materialist Rhetoric for Labor History." *Rethinking Labor History.* Ed. Lenard B. Berlanstein. Urbana: University of Chicago Press, 1993. 15-38.

Shaffer, Kirwin. "Cuba Para Todos: Anarchist Internationalism and the Cultural Politics of Cuban Independence." *Cuban Studies* 31 (2000).

Singh, Khushwant. *A History of the Sikhs, Volume 2: 1839-1964*. Princeton: Princeton University Press, 1966.

Sombart, Werner. *Why Is There No Socialism in the United States?* Ed. and trans. Patricia M. Hocking and C.T. Husbands. White Plains, NY: International Arts and Sciences Press, 1976.

Stubbs, Jean. *Tobacco on the Periphery: A Case Study in Cuban Labour History, 1860-1958*. Cambridge: Cambridge University Press, 1985.

Thompson, E.P. *The Making of the English Working Class*. New York: Vintage Books, 1966.

U.S. Senate, Immigration Commission. *Reports of the Immigration Commission: Immigrants in Industries, Part 25: Japanese and Other Immigrant Races in the Pacific Coast and the Rocky Mountain States*. Washington, D.C.: Government Printing Office, 1911.

van der Linden, Marcel. *Transnational Labour History: Explorations*: Burlington, 2003.

Westfall, L. Glenn. *Don Vicente Martínez Ybor, the Man and his Empire. Development of the Clear Havana Industry in Cuba and Florida in the Nineteenth Century*. New York: Garland Publishing, Inc., 1987.

Woodcock, George. *Anarchism: A History of Libertarian Ideas and Movements*, New York: New American Library, 1974.

PART II

THE DISCOURSE OF CLASS

Defining Working-Class Realities in Chicago and Rocksburg, PA: 'Partial Descriptions'

Rosalie Murphy Baum (University of South Florida)

In a world in which all verbal texts are increasingly considered "fictions" – that is, subjective verbal constructions – the genres of the short story and novel have become more and more respected as social constructions of reality. Theorists in the 1970s and 1980s, like Dominick LaCapra and Lloyd S. Kramer, have argued that all linguistic texts – e.g., history, biography, ethnographic narrative, short story, novel – are subjective and should not assume to establish "*the* account of the world as it actually existed," but instead presuppose that any text's "partial descriptions always exclude a great many other kinds of important informa- tion."[1] There is, as Hayden White states in 1978, "no such thing as a *single* cor- rect view of any object under study but […] *many* correct views, each requiring its own style of representation."[2]

In the late 1950s the traditional literary canon with its tendency to espouse "a *single* correct view" and an aesthetic hierarchy was being seriously ques- tioned by thinkers like Richard Hoggart and Raymond Williams. Their rejection of the standard "the best that has been thought and said" (advocated by critics like F. R. Leavis and T. S. Eliot in the tradition of Samuel Taylor Coleridge, Thomas Carlyle, and Matthew Arnold) gradually made it "fashionable to talk about race or gender," while class remained an "uncool subject."[3] Many "cor- rect views" reflecting race and gender led to the discovery and appreciation of a seemingly unlimited range of styles of literary representation; but in a society increasingly segregated by class, even "a landscape of economic apartheid," the subject of class and the study of working-class literature continued to be ne- glected.[4] bell hooks has even suggested that "[r]ace and gender can be used as screens to deflect attention away from the harsh realities class politics ex- poses."[5]

Although the teaching of working-class literature – often with an emphasis upon literature written by men and women from working-class backgrounds – began in the early 1980s, Working-Class Studies did not become an acknowl- edged field until the mid-1900s, and it still has a tense relationship with "the

---

[1] Lloyd S. Kramer, "Literature, Criticism, and Historical Imagination," *The New Cultural History*, ed. Lynn Hunt (Berkeley: University of California Press) 118.
[2] Hayden White, *Tropics of Discourse: Essays in Cultural Criticism* (Baltimore: Johns Hopkins Uni- versity Press, 1978) 46.
[3] bell hooks, *Where We Stand: Class Matters* (New York: Routledge Press, 2000) vii.
[4] Janet Zandy, Preface to *What We Hold in Common: An Introduction to Working-Class Studies* (New York: Feminist Press, 2001) x.
[5] hooks, 7.

bullying voice of theory."[6] Generally, however, practitioners of Working-Class Studies argue that working-class cultural studies emphasizes "a collective sensibility," "relies heavily on autobiography as a genre," and "rarely [offers] isolated or romanticized individualism."[7] The literature focuses upon work as its primary subject, portraying "a pace of activity controlled by machinery, supervisors, or a time clock," while attempting "to reproduce the boredom of sameness, of mindless repetition."[8] It displays "a distrust of authority and an aversion to paternalism;" often focuses upon crisis, perhaps "loss of persons through death, loss of job or means of survival, loss of values through a quest for upward mobility" or a loss of religion or hope; and presents "the realistic speech patterns of people who do not speak standard English nor conduct conversations along intellectually analytic lines."[9] In addition, Nicholas Coles points out how differently working-class literature can affect readers: to some offering "revelations of social worlds they had never imagined" as "they respond like readers of documentary realism, with shock, concern, sometimes political questioning;" to others, relating "the inside stories of their own heritage, the history of families like theirs."[10]

Frank Norris's "A Deal in Wheat" (1902), a short story of Chicago, and the pseudonymous K. C. Constantine's *Grievance* (2000), a novel of Rocksburg, Pennsylvania, are excellent examples of two working-class texts that present very different views (not a "*single* correct view") of economic collapse and the personal endurance of workers. Using very different narrative strategies and styles of representation, they suggest that class is more learned than inherent, learned both from "the significant others" in charge of the individual's early socialization and in confrontation with groups that define the characters dissociatively until the characters learn to make such dissociative designations themselves.[11] "A Deal in Wheat" recounts the Lewiston family's loss of their farm in Kansas when stock market speculators force the price of grain so low that many wheat growers are destroyed. It is the story of a family's move from the country to the city, with all of the trials suffered by the unemployed in the city, including the failure of a small factory because of foreign competition. *Grievance* is an account of industrial failure, insurance loopholes, and fraud that destroy steelworkers and foremen in a small town and contribute – along with international events like the Vietnam War and personal conflict and loss – to a culture in decline. Both works focus upon the results of socio-

---

[6] Zandy, Introduction to *What We Hold in* Common, xv.

[7] Ibid., xiv.

[8] Renny Christopher and Carolyn Whitson, "Toward a Theory of Working Class Literature," *Thought and Action: The NEA Higher Education Journal*, 71, 1999, 73.

[9] Ibid., 74, 76, 73.

[10] Nicholas Coles, "Democratizing Literature: Issues in Teaching Working-Class Literature," *College English*, 48, 1986, 677.

[11] Peter L. Berger and Thomas Luckmann, *The Social Construction of Reality: A Treatise in the Sociology of Knowledge* (New York: Anchor Books, 1967) 131.

economic change, emphasizing the huge gap between the have-nots and the haves, describing oppressed workers and oblivious capitalists.

Norris's work was written at a time when authors believed they could describe "every-day life" objectively; they could "report" the "simple, the natural, the honest."[12] The goal of the realists, and later of naturalists like Norris, was truth – to be "true to the motives, the impulses, the principles that shape the life of actual men and women."[13] Thus, Norris's story was written from what today would be described as a hegemonic perspective, with a monologic narrating voice relating scenes (almost pantomimic in character) that lead to an allegorical conclusion of victimization. Norris presents an impressionistic reality screaming for social reform with the detachment of an outsider/observer, always an artist. The "real" voice of the working class is not heard. Constantine, a contemporary writer, searches for what Kramer calls "lost voices." In Constantine's case these are the ethnic and working-class voices "that [usually] pass unnoticed through the historiography of social elites, politics and culture."[14] His novel is polyphonic, with significant dialogic encounters and an open-ended conclusion.

Some practitioners of Working-Class Studies today would be comfortable with Constantine's literary representation, much less comfortable with Norris's.[15] They would insist that working class literature must be written by members of the working class only, even if there is no clearly articulated class consciousness; and Norris (after his father's brief rags-to-riches period) clearly enjoyed a privileged childhood. Thus, such critics would believe Norris lacked "class knowledge," whether learned from within – that is, from "the significant others" of a person's socialization – or from without, in conflict with other socio-economic subcultures. As Zandy argues, "Class knowledge comes from experience and story, history and memory, and from the urgency of witnessing. Class solidarity is born from perception of common struggles and common enemies."[16] Some readers would also feel that Norris, an outsider, is portraying the "ideology of 'the deserving poor'" and that his canonical aesthetic representation is condescending since it romanticizes workmen.[17]

Constantine, on the other hand, the son of a house painter, describes in an interview that he "happened to have been born at the height of the Great De-

---

[12] William Dean Howells, "Selections from *Criticism and Fiction*," in *American Realism: A Shape for Fiction*, ed. Jane Benardete (New York: G. P. Putnam's Sons, 1972) 71-73.

[13] Ibid., 95. Norris considered naturalism to be a blend of romanticism and realism. See "A Plea for Romantic Fiction" in *The Responsibilities of the Novelist and Other Literary Essays* (1903)

[14] Kramer, 124-25

[15] For example, Renny Christopher, Carolyn Whitson, Nicholas Coles, Ingrid von Rosenberg, and Carole Snee.

[16] Janet Zandy, Introduction to *Calling Home: Working Class Women's Writing – An Anthology* (New Brunswick: Rutgers University Press, 1990) 8.

[17] Laura Hapke, "A Wealth of Possibilities: Workers, Texts, and the English Department," in *What We Hold in Common: An Introduction to Working-Class Studies*, ed. Janet Zandy (New York: Feminist Press, 2001) 139.

pression in an industrial town that nearly dried up and blew away as a result of it and I'll never shake that experience."[18] Constantine is an insider: he has lived the life that would give him "class knowledge." In addition, his literary representation is far less self-consciously aesthetic.

Paul Lauter and most practitioners, however, argue that working-class literature is that written about the working classes, whether or not the author has attained "class knowledge" through personal experience. Lauter embraces "high," "popular," and "mass" culture in working-class literature, thus defining a place for Norris, who worked with now-codified literary strategies some consider elitist, and for Constantine, who reflects the dominant literary culture but works with multiple ethnic and working-class voices. Supporting Lauter's view, Richard Hoggart cautions that working-class writers have "temptations to error" in the portrayal of the working class: for example, they may experience nostalgia for old ways rather than welcome the new, be "unwarrantedly sharp" toward features of working-class life they disapprove of, or overvalue features that meet their approval.[19]

Many practitioners of Working-Class Studies would agree, however, that both Norris and Constantine portray the working class in its most recent definition. Few today consider "working class" to be simply an economic designation. Most argue that education, kind of work, "[s]tyle and taste and awareness are as important as money."[20] Many believe the most important factor is power and authority: working-class people "have relatively little control over the pace or content of their work, and aren't anybody's boss. They produce the wealth of nations, but receive from that wealth only what they can buy with the wages their employers pay them."[21] Increasingly practitioners also insist that "working class" is not a fixed designation: the older categorizations no longer work. Each individual's life is a process, beginning with the influence of "significant others" and continuing through years of supportive and oppositional forces and subcultures. As John Frow argues, class must be thought of as a process. People go through "processes of class formation [...] played out through particular institutional forms and balances of power [...] through desires, and fears, and fantasies."[22] Both Norris and Constantine emphasize class as process in their works: both represent content members of the working class eventually trapped

---

[18] "Grievance," in *Crime Time* (May 28, 2005): www.crimetime.co.uk/features/kcconstantine.-php/. Born in Modesto, California, Constantine prefers that his real name not be used. He feels strongly that publishers "turn writers into commodities" and that every manuscript should be "submitted anonymously."

[19] Richard Hoggart, *The Uses of Literacy*, 2nd ed. (New Brunswick: Transaction Publishers, 2000) 4-5.

[20] Paul Fussell, *Class: A Guide Through the American Status System* (New York: Summit Books, 1983) 27.

[21] Michael Zweig, *The Working Class Majority: America's Best Kept Secret* (Ithaca: Cornell University Press, 2000) 3.

[22] John Frow, *Cultural Studies and Cultural Value* (Oxford: Clarendon Press, 1995) 59.

by "institutional forms and balances of power" that impoverish them. The focus of their fiction is "the power some people have over the lives of others, and the powerlessness most people experience as a result."[23] Whether it is 1902 (Norris) or 2000 (Constantine), the story is still that of Jacob Riis in 1890: "Long ago it was said that 'one half of the world does not know how the other half lives.' That was true then. It did not know because it did not care."[24]

Norris's short story, "A Deal in What," is divided into five sections, with the divisions dramatizing the separation between the exploited and the exploiters: laborers and capitalists never appear in the same section. The laboring Lewistons, the couple who once worked the soil and produced wheat on their Kansas farm, open and close the story in Sections I and V. The speculators, the bull Hornung and the bear Truslow, appear in the middle three sections, in Hornung's office and the pit (the Chicago Board of Trade).[25] Norris's narrative strategies are primarily those of the romance, as defined by William Gilmore Simms and Nathaniel Hawthorne in the first half of the nineteenth century and clarified by Richard Chase in his 1957 study of the American novel. The characters remain two-dimensional throughout. They are abstractions: typifying the capitalist-speculator and the workman, with the simple working couple in Section I impoverished and helpless and the bull and bear speculators of the middle three sections vital and exuberant as they challenge each other and exult in a world of power, privilege, and wealth.

The story offers almost the economy of drama, with Sections I through IV relying upon dialogue and using minimal description, explanation, and summary. Section V, the concluding section, however, is strikingly different. The narrator – who has remained in the background, revealing his characters through minimal gesture, action, and speech, not individualizing them with insight into their thinking and beliefs – exchanges his modulated voice for a sometimes poignant, sometimes passionate, but an always anguished voice and turns to summary and image to create an allegory of victimization. He is clearly the distanced narrator who romanticizes the fate of the working class, incapable of creating "the voice of self-representation of the class."[26]

In this section, Sam Lewiston is waiting in a bread line in Chicago on a rainy night after one crisis after another: the loss of his ranch in Kansas and then the loss of a job in his brother's hat factory that could not compete with "cheap Belgian and French products." (His wife is staying with her sister in Topeka.) Norris's water imagery suggests the slow and steady deterioration of Lewiston:

---

[23] Zweig, *Working Class Majority*, 11.

[24] Jacob A. Riis, *How the Other Half Lives* (1890), ed. David Leviatin (New York: Bedford Books, 1996) 59.

[25] Investors who buy stock with the anticipation that prices will rise or try by speculation to effect a rise are bullish; those who believe prices will fall or try by selling stock to effect a fall are bearish.

[26] Ingrid von Rosenberg, "Militancy, Anger, Resignation: Alternative Moods in the Working-Class Novel of the 1950s and Early 1960s," in *The Socialist Novel in Britain: Towards the Recovery of a Tradition*, ed. H. Gustav Klaus (New York: St. Martin's Press, 1982) 146.

the "sodden, stupefied" and exhausted man is "always sinking, sinking" into the "ooze of the lowest bottom;" the "great ebb" sweeps over him, engulfs him, shuts him up in darkness." There is no dialogue in Section V. There are no individuals, but hundreds of silent people, a "shapeless throng," in front of a bakery at one a.m. The method of representation is impressionistic, mythic, even archetypal:

> There was something ominous and gravely impressive in this interminable line of dark figures, close-pressed, soundless; a crowd, yet absolutely still; a close-packed, silent file, waiting, waiting in the vast deserted night-ridden street; waiting without a word, without a movement, there under the night and under the slow-moving mists of rain. ("A Deal in Wheat")

These are "workmen, long since out of work, forced into idleness by long-continued 'hard times,' by ill luck, by sickness." bell hooks would describe their social condition as "a form of class warfare that increasingly goes unnoticed."[27]

The "wheel of [Lewiston's] fortunes" does, however, change at the very end of the short story. Lewiston finds a job – prophetically, given the world of today, in a service industry – and eventually his wife joins him as they make a new start. But the narrator stresses that "Lewiston never forgot." He lets Lewiston's thoughts – "dimly" beginning to understand the nature of competitive capitalism – conclude the short story. Lewiston has seen "the cogs and wheels of a great and terrible engine" that had caught him and so many others, and he knows he may be one of the only survivors. In the "battle between Bear and Bull," covered in the Chicago press, he has recognized his own insignificance: "The farmer – he who raised the wheat – was ruined upon one hand; the working man – he who consumed it – was ruined upon the other." The bear and the bull, however, those "who never saw the wheat they traded in," lived a very different life. They were free to gamble "in the nourishment of entire nations," to practice, even enjoy, "their tricks, their chicanery and oblique shifty 'deals'" as they went "their appointed way, jovial, contented, enthroned, and unassailable."

In a country in which many authors have romanticized agricultural life and emphasized the dangers and corruption of urban life, [28] Norris presents the farmer *and* the urban worker as morally superior to urban capitalists. He clearly agrees with Joseph Hollingworth, who in 1830 wrote that, "Manufacturing breeds lords and Aristocrats, Poor men and slaves." But he does not agree, with Hollingworth and others, that only the farmer can be "independent [...] industrious, Healthy and Happy."[29] Lewiston may once have thought of himself as

---

[27] hooks, 46.
[28] See, for example, Henry Nash Smith, *Virgin Land* (1950); Leo Marx, *The Machine in the Garden* (1964); and Annette Kolodny, *The Lay of the Land* (1975).
[29] Joseph Hollingworth. Letter Nov. 8, 1830. "The Hollingworth Family."

self-sufficient, industrious, reliable, decent, moral – attributes encouraged by "the significant others" of his primary socialization in rural Kansas – but his secondary socialization, "the acquisition of role-specific knowledge, the roles being directly or indirectly rooted in the division of labor,"[30] have taught him in Chicago that he is one of the powerless ones in the "institutionalized practice of dominance and subordination on which the social order is founded."[31] He is simply one in the "monolithic collections of socially identical people"[32] who, in Norris, acquiesce to "institution-based 'subworlds.'"[33]

With its emphasis upon the different kinds of reactions working-class people have to events and forces beyond their control, *Grievance* offers multiple realities and "lost voices" not found in Norris's "A Deal in Wheat," in which the exploited farmers and laborers lack voices and respond – individually and collectively – with bewilderment and numbness. In Constantine the issue of will power and the individual's control over his life is central among workers – blue-collar laborers, factory foremen, and state and local police officers – who define their lives in terms of purpose, reliability, and endurance. The novel's characters are very individual, sometimes idiosyncratic; and the narrator, relying upon dialogue and scene rather than summary, allows readers to see events and beliefs from different points of view. The structure of the novel revolves around the polyphony that often characterizes working-class literature. *Grievance* opens with violence in Detective Ruggiero "Rugs" Carlucci's professional life, the murder of James Deford Lyon, CEO of an international company, and in his personal life, a physical attack on him by his mentally unstable mother. Dialogue and recurring flashbacks to the 1970s and 1980s by various characters then offer multiple accounts of the causes of the violence and reveal three dialogic texts: exchanges between Rugs and his mother, a therapist-lover and Rugs, and a murderer and Rugs. Each text unfolds an authentic reading of deeply traumatic experiences. The emotional center of the novel is the "'deep shit'" that characterizes the lives of the two main characters.[34] "Rugs" Carlucci, age

---

http://www.osv.org/learning. See also William Conlogue, *Working the Garden: American Writers and the Industrialization of Agriculture* (Chapel Hill: University of North Carolina Press, 2001).

[30] Berger and Luckmann, 138.

[31] Coles, 672.

[32] Michael Zweig, ed., Introduction to *What's Class Got to Do With It? American Society in the Twenty-First Century* (Ithaca: Cornell University Press, 2004) 8.

[33] Berger and Luckmann, 138. Berger and Luckmann argue that an individual's primary socialization is followed by secondary socializations, in which "partial" but "more or less cohesive realities" - with "normative," "affective," and "cognitive components" - become an individual's "sub-worlds." For example, secondary socialization defines "roles," "role-specific vocabularies," rituals, and symbols "directly or indirectly rooted in the division of labor" (138-40).

[34] K. C. Constantine, *Grievance* (New York: Mysterious Press, 2000), 192. All further references to the novel are in made in parentheses. This discussion of *Grievance* focuses narrowly upon the portrayal of the working class in the novel, but does not represent the accomplishment of the novel: its sensitivity to the mentally ill, a complex son-mother relationship, a perceptive psychiatric social

46, Vietnam veteran, bachelor, caretaker of his mentally ill mother, and lover of (therapist) Franny is a detective sergeant in the small town of Rocksburg. John Joseph Czarowicz, age 66, son of an alcoholic father, Korean veteran, father of two sons (the older killed in Vietnam), former foreman at Conemaugh Steel, pensionless retiree with three part-time jobs, and caretaker of a wife who has slowly died of cancer is a murderer.

The setting of the novel is not simply one of a culture in decline, but also of a small, "third-class city" of depressed and angry blue collar and managerial citizens (both defined as working-class by the privileged), suffering a sense of injustice and treachery (41). In many ways the people of Rocksburg are a repre-sentative cross-section of small-town America. There are Korean and Vietnam vets, dysfunctional and loving families, and alienated and caring children. There is the usual competition and ambition found in the world of business, law en-forcement, and politics and an ethnic tension revealed by names with and with-out hyphens as well as slurs like "dago," "polack," "hunkie," and "nigger." But Rocksburg is also a Rust Belt town. Conemaugh Steel, the main employer, had started cutting back on employees in the late fifties, eventually merging and moving to Brazil in 1985 under the "visionary" leadership of James Deford Lyon. Rocksburg has become, in the words of attorney Panagios Valcanas, "'Empty rusty buildings, a whole lotta people on welfare, and a whole lotta real estate generating no taxes for the city or the schools.'" (62) Detective Carlucci recalls that "'Last census, the city tax collector found out there were more than four hundred houses empty in town.'" (80)

The struggle that Norris portrayed in 1902 between capitalist-speculators on one side and farmers and urban workers on the other becomes, in Constantine's twenty-first century world, a complex system with capitalists, government, charitable foundations, politicians, and law enforcement on one side and workers on the other. The deep malaise of Rocksburg stems from the fact that many in the working class – laborers and foremen at Conemaugh Steel – have witnessed, over a period of some thirty years, a socio-economic-political system that has robbed them of their livelihoods and pensions, but, most pain-fully, of their dignity. Once respected members of the working class, "John Q. Citizen[s]" – solid citizens with skills who have done their jobs well and been "reliable" and "dependable" – have watched helplessly for decades as their class status changed (201). They have become the poor: "'worthless,'" unemployed, purposeless, a burden on society (207).

In Constantine, the socio-economic changes are more complex than in Norris: the institutional structure of the town and nation is far more complex. The day of the Carnegie-type steel industry with "'integrated companies [...] from ore to coal to coke to finished product and all the transportation necessary

---

worker who becomes Rugs' romantic interest, or even Rugs' ethical decisions much less the gentle and bold ironies of the work.

between fields and plants [...] was history.'" (62) However, CEO Lyon's "visionary" ten-year plan leads to immense profits for stockholders as he moves Conemaugh Steel through Chapter 11 reorganization in 1982, merges the company with Knox Iron and Steel, moves the new company to Brazil in 1985, and cancels all pensions, including those of the so-called managerial class. By the late 1990s, when the novel begins, the steelworkers "'might be hangin' around the union hall, but they sure as shit ain't punchin' no clocks or cashin' no checks, 'cept welfare, the ones let 'em lien their house.'" (160)

When the hated Lyon and then Frankie Krull, head of the local steelworkers union, are shot in 1985, Chief Nowicki declares very simply that, "'every guy [Lyon] put on the street's a suspect.'" (45) The smouldering anger in the town is obvious as the investigators focus upon the eight surviving foremen in the area who were among the 23 who years before had filed class actions against Conemaugh Steel Corporation and the United Steelworkers of America. Luke J. Stefanko declares, "'Hell, if I had any guts I'da done it myself, goddam right. Oh I ain't sorry that prick [Lyon's] dead [...] Bastard got rich on his stocks while we got poor. Jesus, hundreds of guys missed all that work all those years? Some of 'em still ain't working.'" (102) And John Czarowicz, the murderer, bluffs, "'Why the hell would it bother me [that he died that way]? You wanna know when I got bothered, you should've talked to me when they laid me off,'" "'Boom, bam, thank you ma'am, fuck you, you're history.'" (104, 197) "'Or when I found out I didn't have no pension or when my wife got cancer and many of the bills were turned over to a collection agency,'" "'and those bastards, [those collectors] called ya all kinda names – .'" (104, 157)

But the definition of the working class in Rocksburg extends beyond the simple relationship between blue collar and managerial workers of Conemaugh Steel and the company's financial officers. In what he calls a "'reality check,'" (221) District Attorney Howard Failan reminds Rugs of the many "institution-based 'subworlds'" in Rocksburg and the nation.[35] The tax-exempt foundations – where Lyon has shielded most of his money – "'pay for exactly what they want to pay for, and [...] don't pay for anything else;'" the wealthy get "'exactly the kind of government they want because it's exactly the kind they've paid for.'" (220) In short, "'the world is running now exactly the way that Lyon and his pals in all the Duquesne Clubs all over the world want it run.'" (221) True, DA Failan continues, the "John Q. Citizen[s]"/workmen of the world are necessary to the members of the Duquesne Clubs of the world. They are the people who work in the factories until the factories become unprofitable; who fight in Korea or Vietnam when "'the fellas down at the Duquesne Club [want] the commies stopped;'" (221) who police the grounds of the Lyons' home when the angry workers riot; who arrest, try, and execute the Czarowiczes of the world when they dare to break out of their assigned roles and, in this case, kill

---

[35] Berger and Luckmann, 238.

one of the privileged and powerful. But it is Mrs. Jessica Hale Bernhardt Lyon, "'of the Philadephia Hale Bernhardts, and that's with no hyphen and don't you forget it,'" who can call Detective Rugs Carlucci "'you little nematode,'" "'You arrogant dog dropping,'" and "'You insufferable pile of excrement.'"(10, 21, 25) It is the Lyons of the world who "'pay for the campaigns to put people they want – like me [Failan]'" and Chief Detective George Sporcik – into office (220). And it is Rugs' role as Detective Sergeant of Rocksburg, DA Failan reminds him, to be "'the exemplary public servant [...] and I emphasize the word *servant*, understand?'" (222) Clearly Rugs, the blue collar workers, and the foremen have their roles defined for them by groups that define them dissociatively: "relative power on the economic side of things translates, not perfectly but to a considerable extent, into cultural and political power."[36]

Much of the polyphony of *Grievance* examines dissociative designations, with a person's need to be respected or even acknowledged as he struggles with assigned roles, "appropriate norms," and powerlessness.[37] Trooper Milliron sees Czarowicz as a nobody, a calculating murderer, simply a man headed for death row. DA Failan and Chief Sporcik, living on the fringes of the privileged, are driven to make an immediate arrest because of the calls they are receiving from "'the national media [...] but also from people in government, elected and nonelected, everybody from the FBI to the SEC.'" (50) Fearing issues that may arise at trial and embarrass them or politically powerful people, they arrange for the unimportant Czarowicz to be murdered and quickly announce his death as a suicide. During earlier questioning, however, Czarowicz insists upon his significance: "'There's some people think I ain't worth the space I take up. Or the time. Least that's how they treated me. Or how they thought they could treat me. But I'm a man.'" (195)

Rugs is the main spokesman for those who, like attorney Valcanas and retired Chief Mario Balzic, believe they understand Czarowicz. Despising "the institutional forms and balances of power" that have trapped Czarowicz,[38] Rugs tries to explain that Czarowicz thinks "'what he did was justice,'" not murder; that is why there is "'not a flicker of remorse in that man's tone or expression or body language,'" (163) Rugs believes there are men who

> "will endure anything. They will put up with anybody's shit in this world, man, they will ask no questions, they don't care how you fuck with them, all they ask is half a chance, that's all. Just keep it even, that's all they want [...] But you back one of these guys up and take away their half a chance? When they see one of their buddies go down, and people are still tryin' to fuck with 'em, man, it's war." (162)

Rugs says he knew men like Czarowicz in Nam:

---

[36] Zweig, *Working Class Majority*, 4.
[37] Berger and Luckmann, 139.
[38] Zweig, *Working Class Majority*, 11.

"None of 'em knew what Nam was about any more than [Czarowicz] knew what Korea was about. But once they got there, it was them and their buddies against everybody else, that's all it was [...] it was cover your buddy's ass and he'll cover yours, that's all, whatever it took." (161-2)

And when Czarowicz married, his wife became his "buddy." Thus, when he saw "'his buddy" [wife] go down'" – with his unemployment, their lack of a pension, and finally her cancer – "'in his mind there were people responsible for puttin' his buddy down, and he took them out.'" (163) Further, Rugs believes Czarowicz was not seeking the ordinary "'eye-for-eye, tooth-for-tooth justice'" when he shot Lyon. He was seeking "'indignity for indignity. Years and years of it.'" (207) Czarowicz did not intend to kill Lyon: he wanted to cripple him, paralyze him, by a shot to his spine, so that Lyon could experience the helplessness, dependence, and indignity of the many Czarowiczes he had created.

Constantine's novel, although written by an author with a working-class background, does not have many of the characteristics often identified with working-class literature. Constantine has created a world in which there are a number of working-class voices rather than "a collective sensibility;" in fact, the working-class voices of Rugs and Czarowicz are more consistent with those of the attorney Valcanas and former Chief Mario Balzic – definitely middle class – than with those of other members of the working class. Work is a significant focus and clearly basic to an individual's identity, but even more important are ethical decisions and the quality of human interaction and compassion. Certainly there is "a distrust of authority," and the precipitating cause of the murders is one crisis after another. Still, the crises are really over before the murders occur; it is the death of Czarowicz's wife that frees him from crisis so he can attempt to paralyze Lyon in order to introduce the insensitive man to helplessness and hopelessness. In addition, the novel's portrayal of the "subjective consciousness" of two working men, a long-suffering man who becomes a murderer and a detective incapacitated by his anguish for both his mentally ill mother and a murderer, recalls the canonical "humanitarian narrative," described by Thomas W. Laqueur as beginning in the 18th century.[39]

An important issue, then, arises from this examination of the very different works of Norris and Constantine: labeling literature as "working-class" may discourage a broad range of representation, canonical and non-canonical, from writers without and with working-class backgrounds. In addition, using the category "working-class literature" denies the complexity of social structure and

---

[39] Thomas W. Laqueur, "Bodies, Details, and the Humanitarian Narrative," in *The New Cultural History*, ed. Lynn Hunt (Berkeley: University of California Press, 1989) 178. Laqueur notes "a new cluster of narratives" beginning in the 18th century that describes the suffering and deaths of ordinary people "in extraordinarily detailed fashion," focusing upon the body as "locus of pain," "common bond" between those who suffer and those who help, and "object of scientific discourse."

may obscure the accomplishment of literary texts that do not display many of the characteristics associated with "working-class literature."

It is generally acknowledged that there are "many working classes, each to be investigated whilst avoiding the unitary anthropological gaze."[40] Practitioners of Working-Class Studies attempt a balance between "the great number of differences, the subtle shades, the class distinctions, within the working-classes themselves" and a designation of "the majority who take their lives much as they find them, and in that way are not different from the majority in other classes."[41] A few look to social reform to further the effect of those qualities in their individual and collective lives.

But with increasing emphasis upon class as process and upon "sites of class experience," "situated knowledges,"[42] rather than upon the deification of fixed categories of class, practitioners of Working-Class Studies may conclude that establishing working-class cultural studies as an alternate hegemony will actually undermine an understanding of the complex and variegated working class. The dangers for Working-Class Studies are similar to those for subaltern studies. As Robert Young has pointed out, Gayatri Spivak is always "vigilant [...] to the hidden ways in which nominally radical, or oppositional historians can often unknowingly, or even knowingly, perpetuate the structures and presuppositions of the very systems which they oppose."[43] For example, an emphasis upon a class subject may very well obscure "the diversity of subject positions which each individual is obliged to take up or refuse" during her or his lifetime.[44] Neglect of the dynamic and shifting process of class for the individual, the mutualities and negotiations across classes, and the complex texture of power and powerlessness in not only economic, but also cultural, social, and political areas may obscure the highly contextual nature of working-class culture as an integral part of the "common culture" of every human being.[45]

Working-Class Studies must not evolve in an oppositional position to the traditional or dominant culture: it must be incorporated into a "common culture." An intertextuality that juxtaposes the rich heteroglossia of traditional *and* working-class texts, both canonical and non-canonical, would contribute to defining a "common culture," rich with "dominant," "residual," and "emergent" cultures.[46] The goal should be to embrace "the full range of human practice, human energy, human intention" with the "continual making and remaking of

---

[40] Sally R. Munt, ed., *Cultural Studies and the Working Class* (New York: Cassell, 2000) 10.

[41] Hoggart, 7-8.

[42] Munt, 11.

[43] Robert Young, *White Mythologies: Writing History and the West* (New York: Routledge Press, 1990) 161-62.

[44] Ibid, 162.

[45] Raymond Williams, *Culture & Society: 1780-1950* (New York: Columbia University Press, 1958) 317..

[46] Raymond Williams, *Problems in Materialism and Culture* (New York: Verso, 1980) 39.

an effective dominant [because common] culture."[47] Labeling new approaches or emphases "alternative meanings and values," "alternative opinions and attitudes, even some alternative senses of the world," creates the danger of establishing monolithic parallel or even dominant-subordinate hegemonies, *and* perpetuates the idea of "others" rather than interesting, valuable peers.[48] A "common culture" demands an intellectual project focused upon all texts as analytic renderings of "systems of culturally-mediated social relations between classes."[49]

Selected Bibliography

Berger, Peter L., and Thomas Luckmann. *The Social Construction of Reality: A Treatise in the Sociology of Knowledge*. New York: Anchor Books, 1967.

Chase, Richard. *The American Novel and Its Tradition*. New York: Doubleday Anchor Books, 1957.

Christopher, Renny and Carolyn Whitson. "Toward a Theory of Working Class Literature." *Thought and Action: The NEA Higher Education Journal* 71 (1999): 71-81.

Coles, Nicholas. "Democratizing Literature: Issues in Teaching Working-Class Literature." *College English* 48 (1986): 664-80.

Constantine, K. C. *Grievance*. New York: Mysterious Press, 2000.

Frow, John. *Cultural Studies and Cultural Value*. Oxford: Clarendon Press, 1995.

Fussell, Paul. *Class: A Guide Through the American Status System*. New York: Summit Books, 1983.

"Grievance," *Crime Time*
http://www.crimetime.co.uk/features/kcconstantine.php/.
(Consulted May 28, 2005).

Hapke, Laura. "A Wealth of Possibilities: Workers, Texts, and the English Department." *What We Hold in Common: An Introduction to Working-Class Studies*. Ed. Janet Zandy. New York: Feminist Press, 2001. 132-141.

Hoggart, Richard. *The Uses of Literacy*. 2nd ed. New Brunswick: Transaction Publishers, 2000.

Hollingworth, Joseph. "The Hollingworth Family." Letter Nov. 8, 1830. http://www.osv.org/learning/. (Consulted March 27, 2007.)

hooks, bell. *Where We Stand: Class Matters*. New York: Routledge Press, 2000.

---

[47] Ibid, 43.
[48] Ibid., 39.
[49] Richard Johnson, "What is cultural studies anyway?" in Unpublished Occasional Paper #74. Birmingham: Center for Contemporary Cultural Studies (1983) 7.

Howells, William Dean. "Selections from *Criticism and Fiction.*" *American Realism: A Shape for Fiction.* Ed. Jane Benardete. New York: G. P. Putnam's Sons, 1972. 68-108.

Kramer, Lloyd S. "Literature, Criticism, and Historical Imagination." *The New Cultural History.* Ed. Lynn Hunt. Berkeley: University of California Press, 1989. 97-130.

LaCapra, Dominick. *History and Criticism.* Ithaca: Cornell University Press, 1985.

____. *Rethinking Intellectual History.* Ithaca: Cornell University Press, 1983.

Laqueur, Thomas W. "Bodies, Details, and the Humanitarian Narrative." *The New Cultural History.* Ed. Lynn Hunt. Berkeley: University of California Press, 1989. 176-206.

Lauter, Paul. "Working-Class Women's Literature: An Introduction to Study." *Women in Print I.* Eds. Joan E. Hartman and Ellen Masser-Davidow. New York: MLA, 1982. 109-134.

Munt, Sally R. "Introduction." *Cultural Studies and the Working Class.* Ed. Sally R. Munt. New York: Cassell, 2000. 1-16.

Norris, Frank. "A Deal in Wheat." http://www.geocities.com/short_stories_page/norrisdealinwheat.html. (Consulted March 27, 2007.)

Riis, Jacob A. *How the Other Half Lives.* Ed. David Leviatin. New York: Bedford Books, 1996.

Rosenberg, Ingrid von. "Militancy, Anger, Resignation: Alternative Moods in the Working-Class Novel of the 1950s and Early 1960s." *The Socialist Novel in Britain: Towards the Recovery of a Tradition.* Ed. H. Gustav Klaus. New York: St. Martin's Press, 1982. 145-65.

Snee, Carole. "Working-Class Literature or Proletarian Writing?" *Culture and Crisis in Britain in the '30s.* Ed. Jon Clark et al. London: Lawrence and Wishart, 1979. 165-191.

White, Hayden. *Tropics of Discourse: Essays in Cultural Criticism.* Baltimore: Johns Hopkins University Press, 1978.

Williams, Raymond. *Culture & Society: 1780-1950.* New York: Columbia University Press, 1958.

Williams, Raymond. *Problems in Materialism and Culture.* New York: Verso, 1980.

Young, Robert. *White Mythologies: Writing History and the West.* New York: Routledge Press, 1990.

Zandy, Janet. "Introduction." *Calling Home: Working-Class Women's Writing – An Anthology.* Ed. Janet Zandy. New Brunswick: Rutgers University Press, 1990. 1-16.

Zandy, Janet. "Preface." "Introduction." *What We Hold in Common: An Introduction to Working-Class Studies.* Ed. Janet Zandy. New York: Feminist Press, 2001.

Zweig, Michael. "Introduction." *What's Class Got to Do With It? American Society in the Twenty-First Century.* Ed. Michael Zweig. Ithaca: Cornell University Press, 2004. 1-17.

Zweig, Michael. *The Working Class Majority: America's Best Kept Secret.* Ithaca: ILR Press, 2000.

Class Presidents: Finding Evidence of Class Struggle in US Presidential Speechmaking

J. C. Myers and Stephen R. Routh (California State University, Stanislaus)

For generations of scholars, from the ancients to the early moderns, the dynamics of class struggle were believed to comprise the core of political life. Yet, by the end of the 20th century, a range of analysts from across the ideological and methodological spectrums had declared class struggle to be a thing of the past. In their view, new forms of political identity and new models of political mobilization had finally displaced the contest between producers and appropriators.

There are at least three reasons, however, to reopen the question of class struggle in American politics. First, many of the studies revealing class to be of diminishing political significance based their analyses on an occupational or status distinction between white-collar and blue-collar workers, rather than on the potentially more salient distinction between owners of productive resources and sellers of labor-power. Second, the vast majority of attention paid to the dynamics of class struggle has focused almost exclusively on working-class mobilization. An accurate representation of class dynamics in American politics should be able to account for the interests and actions of capital, as well as those of labor. Finally, empirically based studies have frequently examined the connections between economic circumstances and voter partisanship, but have rarely questioned the relationship between politically mobilized classes and elected officials in office. As a result, theories of the capitalist state often suffer from a lack of empirical support.

Our study attempts to make progress in these three areas by analyzing the class character of audiences to whom minor presidential speeches are delivered. While our work builds upon prior studies of presidential communications and offers insights into the nature of the modern American presidency, our findings also offer a contribution to contemporary understandings of class and class politics.

Class Struggle and the State

Class struggle may strike our ears as a distinctly modern concept, yet its early roots stretch as far back as the 5th century BCE. Whether true to the historical figure or not, Plato's characterization of Thrasymachus in *The Republic* clearly depicts him as an analyst of class politics.[1] His suggestion that different regime-types have distinct class bases is echoed by Cicero, who warns against political

---

[1] Plato, *The Republic*, trans. Raymond Larson (Arlington Heights: Harlan Davidson, 1979) 13-14.

instability arising from class conflict and advocates the uneven distribution of political rights as a solution.[2]

The early moderns were determined to probe deeper still, searching not simply for the source of a particular state's character or proclivities, but for the origin of the state itself. Without exception, they were agreed that property – and the potential for conflicts over its ownership and use – lay at the heart of specialized state institutions. For Hobbes, the likelihood of conflict over property rights was so great that all claims to such rights were essentially meaningless in the absence of a sovereign state capable of defending them against challenges.[3] Locke may have rejected Hobbes' reliance on the state for the demarcation of basic property rights, but still found the defense of property claims to be the state's central legitimate purpose.[4] It was left to Rousseau to say plainly what the others had only hinted at: that the protection of private property meant, in effect, the defence of class privilege.[5] Though his conclusions about the nature of good government differ sharply from Rousseau's, James Madison's suggestion that the greatest danger to republican government lay in the rise of factional strife between rich and poor reveals a strikingly similar understanding of class struggle and its centrality to political life.[6] Marx and Engels may now be perceived as having advanced a radically new position with their claim that the state was tied to and defined by the forces of class struggle.[7] In fact, their assessment only served to put sharper emphasis on a point that was neither new, nor particularly controversial.

By the second half of the 20th century, however, a wide gulf had emerged between those who still held that class struggle played a primary role in giving shape and purpose to the state and those who now argued that class was only one of a great number of proliferating claims on the state's attention. American political scientists, led in the 1950s and 1960s by David Truman and Robert Dahl, were the first to adopt the new paradigm.[8] Pluralism proposed that the modern industrial capitalist democracies contained a diverse range of organized and unorganized interests, none of which was capable of dominating the state. Whatever inequalities existed in such societies were non-cumulative and dispersed. G. William Domhoff, Ralph Miliband, Nicos Poulantzas, and Claus

---

[2] Marcus Tulius Cicero, *The Republic*, trans. Niall Rudd (Oxford: Oxford University Press 1998) 30-31; 58.

[3] Thomas Hobbes, *Leviathan* (Peterborough: Broadview Press, 2002).

[4] John Locke, *Two Treatises of Government and A Letter Concerning Toleration* (New Haven: Yale University Press, 2003).

[5] Jean-Jacques Rousseau, *Discourse on the Origins of Inequality* in *The Basic Political Writings*, trans. Donald A. Cress (Indianapolis: Hackett, 1987) 60; 69.

[6] James Madison, "Tenth Federalist Paper" in Alexander Hamilton, James Madison, and John Jay, *The Federalist Papers* (New York: Bantam, 1982) 44.

[7] Karl Marx and Friedrich Engels, *The Communist Manifesto* (New York: Oxford University Press, 1998) 26.

[8] David Truman, *The Governmental Process* (New York: Alfred A. Knopf, 1951); Robert Dahl, *Who Governs?* (New Haven: Yale University Press, 1961).

Offe continued to maintain that class struggle – and, in particular, the interests of a capitalist class – rose above other forces in influencing the actions of state institutions and officials, but by the late 1980s their work had largely been side-lined (even within left-political circles) by post-Marxist theorists who now appeared to find substantial common ground with the pluralists.[9] Alain Touraine and Andre Gorz announced the birth in the West of a post-industrial society lacking both a proletariat and a politics animated by class interests.[10] The new social movements of the late 20th and early 21st centuries would center themselves on the definition of non-class identities (race, ethnicity, gender, sexual preference) and the struggle for recognition and inclusion of those identities in the democratic polity.[11]

Why, then, should political scientists or social theorists continue to probe the connections between class struggle and the state? Both the pluralists' claim that all interest groups are relatively equal in their relationship to the state and the post-Marxists' claim that class struggle has been supplanted by a range of new social movements suggest the possibility for empirical verification. If, in fact, class struggle has diminished with the rise of the post-industrial society, the presence of class-based organizations in public politics should be seen to decline from the post-WWII boom years to the end of the Cold War. Similarly, if inequalities in the ownership of productive property or the accumulation of wealth do not translate into privileged connections to the state, organized representatives of business-owners and workers should be seen to receive similar levels of access to and attention from high-ranking state officials. Evidence that class-based organizations continue to loom large on the political terrain of advanced capitalist societies should lead political scientists and social theorists to re-examine the linkages between class struggle and the state.

Presidents and the Public

In the modern era of the American presidency (generally defined as beginning with Franklin D. Roosevelt's first term), presidents confront an increasingly challenging political environment. Presidential communications – the delivery of speeches and other public remarks by the Chief Executive himself – represent vital tools with which presidents attempt to advance their respective policy

---

[9] G. William Domhoff, *Who Rules America?* (Englewood Cliffs: Prentice-Hall, 1967); Ralph Miliband, *The State in Capitalist Society* (London: Winfield and Nicholson, 1969); Nicos Poulantzas, *Political Power and Social Classes* (London: New Left Books, 1974); Claus Offe, "The Capitalist State and the Problem of Policy Formation" in Leon N. Lindberg, Robert Alford, Colin Crouch, and Claus Offe, *Stress and Contradiction in Modern Capitalism* (Lexington: Lexington Books, 1975).

[10] Alain Touraine, *The Post-Industrial Society* (New York: Random House, 1971); Andre Gorz, *Farewell to the Working Class* (Boston: South End Press, 1982).

[11] Jean Cohen, "Strategy or Identity: New Theoretical Paradigms and Contemporary Social Movements," *Social Research*, Winter, 1985, 663-716; Ernesto Laclau and Chantal Mouffe, *Hegemony and Socialist Strategy* (London: Verso, 1985).

agendas. Analysts of the presidency have noted that what many regard as the central characteristic of the modern presidency is the rise of what has been termed the "rhetorical presidency." Jeffrey Tulis and Samuel Kernell both find that compared to their 19th century predecessors, presidents in the 20th century have increasingly engaged in greater amounts of presidential speechmaking and addresses to the public.[12] Presidents go forth to communicate directly with the public so as to gain support which can then be used to bring external pressure to bear on members of Congress. Such activities include, but are not limited to, televised and radio addresses, speeches to organizations, photo opportunities at various locations, and major addresses such as Inaugural and State of the Union addresses.

Modern U.S. presidents communicate directly with the public in order to overcome the inevitable gridlock spawned by the Constitution's separation of powers.[13] The American political system contains strong, inherent tendencies toward political inertia and against policy change. Over time, presidents have responded instrumentally, developing strategies with which to press their agendas. On a near hourly basis, presidents must develop and maintain coalitional support in Washington and the nation at large if there is to be any chance for the White House to win its policy battles.[14]

The choices made by presidents in addressing members of the public are far from arbitrary. Each presidential speaking appearance represents both an opportunity and an opportunity cost: an audience or group that can be appealed to directly and another that will be ignored. At one level, then, the prioritization of targeted groups will be indicative of a president's political relationships and priorities. At a broader level, as attention and access are granted to some and denied to others, a map of power relations on the political landscape is revealed.

We believe that the present study allows us to ascertain the White House's prioritization of issue areas and policy orientations by observing which groups are targeted by presidential communications. Yet, we remain mindful of some of the leading criticisms directed against the extant scholarly literature on the American presidency. In particular, concerns have arisen that the bulk of presidential scholarship is directed toward examinations of the unique psychology and idiosyncrasies of individual office-holders. As a result, normative assess-

---

[12] Jeffrey Tulis, *The Rhetorical Presidency* (Princeton: Princeton University Press, 1987); Samuel Kernell, *Going Public: New Strategies of Presidential Leadership.* 3rd ed. (Washington DC: CQ Press, 1997).
[13] Bert Rockman, *The Leadership Question: The Presidency and the American System* (New York: Praeger, 1984); Theodore Lowi, *The Personal President: Power Invested, Promise Unfulfilled* (Ithaca and London: Cornell University Press, 1985); Charles O. Jones, *The Presidency in a Separated System* (Washington: Brookings Institution Press, 2005); David Morgan, "US Presidents and the Media," *Parliamentary Affairs* 48 (1995), 503-14; Richard W. Waterman, Robert Wright and Gilbert St. Clair, *The Image-Is-Everything Presidency: Dilemmas in American Leadership* (Boulder: Westview Press, 1999).
[14] Morgan, 503.

ments are privileged, while generalizable theory building suffers.[15] Thus, prior research on presidential communications has typically focused on either content analysis of speeches (assessing patterns of rhetorical choice within speeches and the primary influences on those choices) or on the frequency and timing of speeches (discerning regularities of speechmaking and the major factors that explain those variations). Leading examples of these types of scholarly explorations include Hinckley, Tulis, Kernell, Waterman, Wright, and St. Clair, Zernicke, Ragsdale, Hart, and Stuckey.[16] By contrast, the present study pursues an empirically under-examined and theoretically under-developed area, focusing on the types of groups to whom presidents specifically direct their public remarks. We build upon Hinckley and Hart's work on specialized presidential audiences by laying out a group/remarks categorization scheme that better and more completely captures the underlying institutional and structural dynamics.[17]

Design of the Study

Our study works in two ways to test the salience of class dynamics in American presidential politics. First, we measure the levels of attention given by presidents to different types of interest groups. Second, within the range of class-based groups, we measure the levels of attention given by presidents to groups representing the interests of different classes. In both cases, the delivery of a minor speech is taken as an indicator of presidential attention.

For the purposes of this study, a minor speech is defined as remarks uttered by the president in person and addressed to a specific audience, rather than to Congress or the American people as a whole.[18] Our analysis begins with Dwight Eisenhower in 1953 and ends with the second Clinton administration in 2001. *The Public Papers of the Presidents of the United States* constitutes the sole source for the data for this study. The annual volumes of *The Public Papers* list

---

[15] George C. Edwards III, John H. Kessel, and Bery A. Rockman, *Researching the Presidency* (Pittsburgh: University of Pittsburgh Press, 1993).

[16] Barbara Hinckley, *The Symbolic Presidency: How Presidents Portray Themselves* (New York and London: Routledge, 1990); Tulis, *The Rhetorical Presidency*. See fn. 10 for reference; Kernell, *Going Public*. See fn. 10 for reference; Richard W. Waterman, Robert Wright and Gilbert St. Clair, *The Image-Is-Everything Presidency: Dilemmas in American Leadership* (Boulder: Westview Press, 1999); Paul H. Zernicke, *Pitching the Presidency: How Presidents Depict the Office* (New York: Praeger, 1994); Lyn Ragsdale, "The Politics of Presidential Speechmaking," *American Political Science Review*, 78, 1984, 971-84; Roderick Hart, *The Sound of Leadership* (Chicago: University of Chicago Press, 1987); Mary E. Stuckey, *The President as Interpreter-in-Chief* (Chatham NJ: Chatham House Publishers, 1991).

[17] Hinckley 1990; Hart 1987.

[18] Our definition of minor speeches excludes the following: major presidential addresses (Inaugural Addresses, State of the Union Addresses, any other nationally televised speech); messages associated with proclamations, executive orders, and signing legislation; nationally televised press conferences; remarks given to partisan organizations; remarks uttered during visits by visiting foreign leaders; and remarks given at airports while a president is travelling.

all presidential addresses, radio and television broadcasts, speeches to Congress, short messages related to the signing of legislation, news conferences, proclamations, executive orders, veto messages, and speeches on the road, appointment announcements, and so forth. *The Public Papers* also provides information regarding the audience receiving the President's remarks. These data have been used to classify audiences with respect to their representation of mobilized interest groups.

Table 1 shows the nine interest group categories into which we have sorted the various audiences to whom minor presidential speeches were delivered between 1953 and 2001.

Table 1. *Interest Group Designations*

DESIGNATION
Class
Education/Scientific
Ethnic
Government
Media
Religious
Service
Environmental
Other

- *Class*   This type of organization or group either represents constituents defined by their role in production or the organization/group largely concerns itself with rules governing production. Examples of this group designation include: the National Association of Manufacturers, the American Retail Federation, US Chamber of Commerce, the American Federation of Labor-Congress of Industrial Organizations (AFL-CIO), United Auto Workers, United Steelworkers of America, the National Education Association, the American Federation of Teachers, business leaders, labor leaders, The American Medical Association, the American Bar Association, the World Bank, and the International Monetary Fund. Think tanks concerned with economic policy (such as the Brookings Institution, the Heritage Foundation) are coded as *class*. Teachers' unions have been coded as *class* because of their representation of teachers as employees.
- *Education/scientific*   This type of organization or group involves itself in scientific or educational advancement issues. Examples of this group designation include: the National Academy of Sciences, the American Council on Education, and the Association of Land-Grant Colleges and Universities.
- *Ethnic*   This type of organization or group is composed of people who have come together based on shared ethnicity or shared race. Examples of this group designation include: the Polish-American Congress, the National Association for the Advancement of Colored People, Columbus Day

Celebration (Italian-Americans), German-American Day Celebration, and a Group of Hispanic Leaders. Ethnic business associations have been coded as *class*.

- *Government*   This type of organization or group consists of government employees or government officials. Examples of this group include: the National Association of Governors, the National League of Cities, the National Conference of Mayors, and the National Association of County Officials. Foreign policy organizations and institutes have been coded as *government*.

- *Media*   This type of organization or group is composed of members of the mass media. Nationally televised or broadcast press conferences do not fall into this category. Examples of this group include: the National Association of Radio and Television Broadcasters, the Association of American Editorial Cartoonists, the Inter-American Press Association, the American Society of Newspaper Editors, and the American Newspaper Publishers Association. Members of the media may represent either owners of capital or sellers of labor power. However, because of the unique interest presidents may have in communicating with the media apart from any desire to appeal to them as representatives of a class, they have been given their own category.

- *Religious*   This type of organization or group is composed of people who come together based on shared religious belief or religious tradition. Examples of this group include the National Council of Churches, Spiritual Foundations of American Democracy, World Christian Endeavor, United Jewish Appeal, the Islamic Center, and the National Conference of Christians and Jews.

- *Service*   This type of organization is a service organization or a group that is composed of members who work for service organizations. Examples of this group include: the American Red Cross, the League of Women Voters, United Services Organization (USO), the American Council to Improve Our Neighborhoods, and the Association of Junior Leagues, Boys Nation, and Girls Nation.

- *Environmental*   This type of organization or group is involved in environment protection based issues. Examples of this group include: National Wildlife Federation, League of Conservation Voters, Conservationist of the Year Award, and a group of leaders of national conservation organizations.

- *Other*   This type of organization or group does not fit neatly or clearly into one of the above eight designated categories. Examples of this group include: Organization of World Touring and Automobile Clubs, American Field Service Students, Consumers Advisory Council, and the National Council of Senior Citizens, the National League of POW/MIA Families, and the Black Watch Regiment.

After first classifying audiences according to their representation of mobilized interest groups, we then identify audiences within the broader class category according to their specific class position.

Table 2 shows the four class positions into which class-based groups have been sorted.

Table 2. *Class Positions*

POSITION
Capital
Labor
Professional
Mixed Audience

- *Capital*   This type of organization or group represents the owners of the means of production. Examples of this class location include: the US Chamber of Commerce, National Association of Manufacturers, a group of business executives, the National Alliance of Businessmen, Associated Milk Producers, the American Farm Bureau, the World Bank, and the International Monetary Fund.
- *Labor*   This type of organization or group represents members who sell labor-power. Examples of this class location include the AFL-CIO, United Steelworkers of America, a group of labor leaders, the International Federation of Ladies Garment Workers, the American Federation of Teachers, the National Education Association, United Auto Workers, the American Nurses Association, and the International Federation of Commercial, Clerical, and Technical Employees.
- *Professional*   This organization or group represents members of a profession, such as lawyers, physicians, journalists, architects, university professors, and so forth. Examples of this class location include: the American Medical Association, the American Bar Association, the American Institute of Architects, and the Fort Worth County Bar Association.
- *Mixed audience*   This group of people consists of a mixture of both members of *capital* and members of *labor*. This is typically observed when a president goes to a company plant or factory and addresses employees there. Examples of this class location include: employees of Rockwell International, employees of AccuPay Corporation, employees of Digital Equipment Corporation, and employees at the Chrysler Corporation.

Results and Findings

In the first phase of our analysis, audiences to whom minor presidential speeches are delivered are classified according to their representation of mobilized interests. Tables 3 and 4 show that class-based groups receive a strong plurality of presidential attention, comprising 36.4% of audiences for minor presidential addresses. Members of the next largest category – government officials and employees – receive less than one-third the level of attention directed toward class-based groups.

Table 3. *Raw Frequency of Interest Groups Receiving Minor Presidential Speeches by Presidential Party and Totals, 1953-2001*

DESIGNATION	DEMOCRATIC	REPUBLICAN	TOTAL
Class	262	391	653
Education/Scientific	41	59	100
Ethnic	62	71	133
Government	88	150	238
Media	53	97	150
Other	87	121	208
Religious	66	51	117
Service	55	118	173
Environmental	10	12	22
TOTAL	724	1070	1794

Table 4. *Percentage of Interest Groups Receiving Minor Presidential Speeches, 1953-2001*

DESIGNATION	FREQUENCY	PERCENTAGE
Class	653	36.4
Education/Scientific	100	5.6
Ethnic	133	7.4
Government	238	13.3
Media	150	8.4
Other	208	11.6
Religious	117	6.5
Service	173	9.6
Environmental	22	1.2
TOTAL	1794	100

Table 5 shows that the levels of attention directed toward the different interest group categories are strikingly similar for presidents from both major parties. This similarity in behavior across party lines suggests that institutional or structural forces, rather than radically contingent factors, are responsible for the consistently close contact between presidents and class-based groups.

Table 5. *Percentage of Interest Groups Receiving Minor Presidential Speeches by Presidential Party, 1953-2001*

Designation	Democratic	Republican
Class	36.2	36.6
Education/Scientific	5.7	5.5
Ethnic	8.6	6.6
Government	12.2	14
Media	7.3	9.1
Other	12	11.3
Religious	9.1	4.8
Service	7.6	11
Environmental	1.4	1.1
TOTAL	100	100

Tables 6 and 7 show that across myriad administrations from 1953-2001, speeches delivered to class-based organizations outnumber those directed toward other types of organized interest groups.

Table 6. *Raw Frequency of Interest Groups Receiving Minor Presidential Speeches, 1953-2001*

DESIGNATION	DDE	JFK	LBJ	RMN	GRF	JEC	RWR	GHWB	WJC	Total
Class	52	29	76	18	42	43	193	86	114	653
Ed./Scientific	6	4	14	1	5	2	16	31	21	100
Ethnic	6	3	4	2	9	25	35	19	30	133
Government	12	4	13	5	13	13	86	34	58	238
Media	9	4	12	9	13	19	47	19	18	150
Other	13	15	17	2	7	12	81	18	43	208
Religious	13	7	12	1	5	14	27	5	33	117
Service	15	4	22	14	17	7	34	38	22	173
Environmental	1	2	4	2	1	2	2	6	2	22
TOTAL	127	72	174	54	112	137	521	256	341	794

Table 7. *Percentage of Groups Receiving Minor Speeches by Presidential Administration, 1953-2001*

DESIGNATION	DDE	JFK	LBJ	RMN	GRF	JEC	RWR	GHWB	WJC
Class	40.9	40.3	43.7	33.3	37.5	31.4	37	33.6	33.4
Education/Scientific	4.7	5.5	8	1.9	4.5	1.5	3.1	12.1	6.2
Ethnic	4.7	4.2	2.3	3.7	8	18.2	6.7	7.4	8.8
Government	9.5	5.5	7.5	9.3	11.6	9.4	16.5	13.3	17
Media	7.1	5.5	7	16.7	11.6	13.9	9	7.4	5.3
Other	10.2	20.8	10	3.7	6.3	8.8	15.6	7	12.6
Religious	10.3	9.7	7	1.9	4.5	10.2	5.2	2	9.7
Service	11.8	5.5	12.8	25.8	15.2	5.1	6.5	14.8	6.5
Environmental	.8	2.8	2.3	3.7	.9	1.5	.4	2.3	.6
TOTAL	100	100	100	100	100	100	100	100	100

Also notable here is the fact that the variation in levels of attention paid to non-class groups was much greater than the variation in levels of attention paid to class groups. Speeches delivered to class groups vary from a low of 31.4% (Carter) to a high of 43.7% (Johnson). By contrast, speeches delivered to education/scientific groups range from 1.5% to 12.1%, religious groups from 1.9% to 10.2%, government groups from 5.5% to 17.2%, service groups from 5.1% to 25.9%, and so forth. These results suggest that presidents are much more consistent in their communication with class-based groups than with non-class groups. The data in Table 7 also allow us to conclude that the results shown in Table 4 are not driven disproportionately by a small number of outliers. Instead, there is a strong, observable pattern across all of the presidents under study here in terms of class-focused presidential communications.

The second phase of our analysis narrows the focus to include only class-based audiences and to locate them within one of four class positions: capital, labor, professional, or mixed audience. Determining which class or classes receive the balance of presidential attention will allow us to draw conclusions regarding the balance of class forces, vis-à-vis the communication priorities of U.S. presidents.

Table 8 reveals the extent to which capital dominates the attention of U.S. presidents. Nearly 3/4 of all minor presidential speechmaking is directed to groups or representatives of those who own means of production. Representatives of organized labor receive less than a 1/5 of these speeches.

Table 8. *Raw Frequency & Percentage of Class Groups Receiving Minor Presidential Speeches by Class Location, 1953-2001*

LOCATION	FREQUENCY	PERCENTAGE
Capital	468	71.7
Labor	108	16.5
Professional	29	4.4
Mixed	48	7.4
TOTAL	653	100

The partisan breakdown of presidential speeches delivered to representatives of mobilized classes is shown in Tables 9 and 10.

Table 9. *Raw Frequency of Class Groups Receiving Minor Presidential Speeches by Presidential Party, 1953-2001*

LOCATION	DEMOCRATIC	REPUBLICAN	TOTAL
Capital	143	325	468
Labor	87	21	108
Mixed	20	28	48
Professional	12	17	29
TOTAL	262	391	653

Table 10. *Percentage of the Class Locations of Groups Receiving Minor Presidential Speeches by Presidential Party, 1953-2001*

LOCATION	DEMOCRATIC	REPUBLICAN
Capital	54.6	83.1
Labor	33.2	5.4
Mixed	7.6	7.2
Professional	4.6	4.3
TOTAL	100	100

Republican presidents favor capital over labor by an overwhelmingly margin – 83.1% for capital to 5.4% for labor. Democratic presidents demonstrate similar tendencies in favoring capital over labor, but not nearly to the same degree as Republicans – 54.5% for capital to 33.2% for labor. Contrary to conventional wisdom, while Democratic presidents expend more speechmaking resources on representatives of labor than do Republicans, representatives of capital still receive the majority of their attention. As indicated in Table 9, mixed audiences (comprised of both members of labor and members of capital) and professional audiences show virtually identical levels of proportional frequency.

Tables 11 and 12 present both the raw frequencies and percentages for the four class locations broken down by individual presidents.

Table 11. *Raw Frequency of Class Groups Receiving Minor Presidential Speeches by Presidential Administration, 1953-2001*

LOCATION	DDE	JFK	LBJ	RMN	GRF	JEC	RWR	GHWB	WJC	TOTAL
Capital	43	17	44	11	35	25	165	71	57	468
Labor	5	12	28	5	3	18	6	2	29	108
Mixed	0	0	1	1	0	0	18	9	19	48
Professional	4	0	3	1	4	0	4	4	9	29
TOTAL	52	29	76	18	42	43	193	86	114	653

Table 12. *Percentage of Class Groups Receiving Minor Presidential Speeches by Presidential Administration, 1953-2001*

LOCATION	DDE	JFK	LBJ	RMN	GRF	JEC	RWR	GHWB	WJC
Capital	82.7	58.6	57.9	61.1	83.3	58.1	85.5	82.5	50
Labor	9.6	41.4	36.8	27.8	7.2	41.9	3.1	2.3	25.4
Mixed	0	0	1.3	5.6	0	0	9.3	10.5	16.7
Professional	7.7	0	4	5.5	9.5	0	2.1	4.7	7.9
TOTAL	100	100	100	100	100	100	100	100	100

Table 12 shows a consistent tendency by Democratic presidents to target capital groups between 50-60% of the time. Republican presidents demonstrate similar consistency in directing their remarks to capital between 80-85% of the time, with the curious exception of Richard Nixon. Labor organizations typically receive 26-40% of speeches directed toward class-based groups by Democratic presidents and 2-10% of similar speeches by Republican presidents (Nixon, again, standing as the lone exception). Also of note, here, is the fact that organized labor received the least amount of attention from Bill Clinton, as compared with other Democratic presidents. Intriguingly, our findings with regard to the class linkages of both Nixon and Clinton correspond well with the assessment that both were the only true triangulators among the modern presidents, able to succeed by co-opting elements of the opposing party's agenda. Despite these minor exceptions, the generally close and consistent variation of the results in Table 12 allow us to conclude that the patterns discernible in Tables 8 and 10 are not driven by one or two outliers, disproportionately skewing the results.

Conclusions

Our study suggests that both pluralists and post-Marxists have underestimated the salience of class struggle in contemporary politics. Contrary to the expectations of the pluralists, all interest groups are not created equal. Representatives of capital receive levels of access to and attention from U.S. presidents that are denied to representatives of labor. Contrary to the assumptions of the post-Marxist social movement theorists, class continues to loom large on the political landscape. The propensity of presidents to spend a disproportionate share of scarce time and attention on class-based organizations, as opposed to others, clearly indicates that for American heads of state, class struggle remains at the top of the agenda.

It may be that the tendency in recent years for social theorists to proclaim the death of class and class struggle stems from a type of category mistake. Visions of the post-industrial society and the rise of new social movements correspond closely with a precipitous decline in the number of U.S. workers organized by trade unions. If class struggle is understood to refer only to the political mobilization of workers, it has indeed fallen by the wayside since the early 1960s. If, however, class struggle is understood to include the political mobilization of owners of capital, our study suggests that it remains central to the life of the state.

Our study also lends empirical support to the contention that class struggle is a structural constraint or shaping force on the state and not a radically contingent one. All post-WWII presidents have given disproportionate attention to class-based organizations as opposed to others and all have given disproportionate attention to representatives of capital as opposed to those of labor. Yet, the precise nature of the structural constraint or shaping force producing this effect remains unclear. Is it that, as Domhoff suggests, political office-holders are shaped by and tied to the social networks of a ruling class?[19] Is the state itself an

---

[19] Domhoff 1967.

articulation of the class struggle, acting on behalf of capital, but not at its behest, as Miliband and Poulantzas contend?[20] Or is it, as Offe proposes, that in order to ensure its own survival, the state must maintain an environment conducive to capital accumulation?[21] The analysis of executive behavior alone cannot settle these questions, but the evidence provided by studies such as this one must play a part in the rebuilding of a theory of the contemporary capitalist state.

Selected Bibliography

Cicero, Marcus Tulius. *The Republic*. Trans. Niall Rudd. Oxford: Oxford University Press, 1998.

Cohen, Jean. "Strategy or Identity: New Theoretical Paradigms and Contemporary Social Movements." *Social Research* 52:4 (1985): 664-716.

Dahl, Robert. *Who Governs?* New Haven: Yale University Press, 1961.

Domhoff, G. William. *Who Rules America?* Englewood Cliffs: Prentice-Hall, 1967.

Gorz, Andre. *Farewell to the Working Class*. Boston: South End Press, 1982.

Hart, Roderick. *The Sound of Leadership*. Chicago: University of Chicago Press, 1987.

Hinckley, Barbara. *The Symbolic Presidency: How Presidents Portray Themselves*. New York and London: Routledge, 1990.

Hobbes, Thomas. *Leviathan*. Peterborough: Broadview Press, 2002.

Jones, Charles O. *The Presidency in a Separated System*. Washington DC: Brookings Institution Press, 1994.

Kernell, Samuel. *Going Public: New Strategies of Presidential Leadership*. 3rd ed. Washington DC: CQ Press, 1997.

Laclau, Ernesto and Chantal Mouffe. *Hegemony and Socialist Strategy*. London: Verso, 1985.

Locke, John. *Two Treatises of Government and A Letter Concerning Toleration*. New Haven: Yale University Press, 2003.

Lowi, Theodore. *The Personal President: Power Invested, Promise Unfulfilled*. Ithaca and London: Cornell University Press, 1985.

Madison, James. "Tenth Federalist Paper." Alexander Hamilton, James Madison, and John Jay. *The Federalist Papers*. Ed. Gary Wills. New York: Bantam, 1982.

Marx, Karl and Friedrich Engels. *The Communist Manifesto*. Ed. David McLellan. New York: Oxford University Press, 1998.

Miliband, Ralph. *The State in Capitalist Society*. London: Winfield and Nicholson, 1969.

---

[20] Miliband 1969; Poulantzas 1974.
[21] Offe 1975.

Morgan, David. "US Presidents and the Media." *Parliamentary Affairs* 48 (1995): 503-14.

Offe, Claus, "The Capitalist State and the Problem of Policy Formation." *Stress and Contradiction in Modern Capitalism.* Eds. Robert Alford, Colin Crouch, Leon. N. Lindberg, and Claus Offe. Lexington: Lexington Books, 1975.

Plato. *The Republic.* Trans. Raymond Larson. Arlington Heights: Harlan Davidson, 1979.

Poulantzas, Nicos. *Political Power and Social Classes.* London: New Left Books, 1974.

Ragsdale, Lyn. "The Politics of Presidential Speechmaking." *American Political Science Review* 78 (1984): 971-84.

Rockman, Bert. *The Leadership Question: The Presidency and the American System.* New York: Praeger, 1984.

Rousseau, Jean-Jacques. *Discourse on the Origins of Inequality.* In *The Basic Political Writings.* Trans. Donald A. Cress. Indianapolis: Hackett, 1987.

Stuckey, Mary E. *The President as Interpreter-in-Chief.* NJ: Chatham House Publishers, 1991.

The Public Papers of the Presidents of the United States. Annual, 1953-2001. Washington DC: Government Printing Office.

Touraine, Alain. *The Post-Industrial Society.* New York: Random House, 1971.

Truman, David. *The Governmental Process.* New York: Alfred A. Knopf, 1951.

Tulis, Jeffrey. *The Rhetorical Presidency.* Princeton: Princeton University Press, 1987.

Waterman, Richard W., Robert Wright, and Gilbert St. Clair. *The Image-Is-Everything Presidency: Dilemmas in American leadership.* Boulder: Westview Press, 1999.

Zernicke, Paul H. *Pitching the Presidency: How Presidents Depict the Office.* New York: Praeger, 1994.

Doctorow's *Ragtime:* Inserting Class in a Literary Discussion

Masood Raja (Kent State University)

> At just the time that we have begun to think small, history has begun to act big. 'Act locally, think globally' has become a familiar leftist slogan; but we live in a world where the political right acts globally and the postmodern left thinks locally. As the grand narrative of capitalist globalization, and the destructive reaction which it brings in its wake, unfurls across the planet, it catches these intellectuals at a time when many of them have almost ceased to think in political terms at all. ... The inescapable conclusion is that cultural theory must start thinking ambitiously once again – not so that it can hand the West its legitimation, but so that it can seek to make sense of the grand narrative in which it is now embroiled.[1]

After the decades of identity politics, culture wars, and the rise of the neoliberal global economic order, class, in its American context, can no longer be the prime signifier for the contest between the wretched of the earth and their more affluent counterparts within or without the metropolitan centers. Caught within the ever-fragmenting discourse of the postmodern, invoking class in itself becomes a sacrilege, as it intends to denote a sense of lateral solidarity across race, ethnicity and gender divide, the last ramparts of American liberalism against the global economic order in a world, both in its semiotic and material domains, so obviously obsessed with culturist solutions to all its problems.

The above cited passage from Terry Eagleton's *After Theory* is a most eloquent account of the dilemmas of postmodern thought: its distrust of grand narratives, exactly at a time when the world is caught within the most enduring and the most overpowering grand narrative of all, the neoliberal globalization. Under such circumstances, now compounded by the global war on terror that has replaced the old banners of progress with the new ones of freedom and prosperity for the global periphery, there is a need, at least, to consider the question of class in our classroom literary discussions. We must foreground class, if not for the proletarian revolution, then at least to create some consciousness about the texts we read and their very interaction with the tyranny of the market place. Using E. L Doctorow's *Ragtime* as a representative text, this essay attempts to articulate this class-conscious way of reading literary texts with an emphasis on the appropriation of literary texts by the market amidst the great debate between private and the public sphere. [2] While class will figure prominently in this discussion, the focus will, however, be on the material circumstances and ideologies that transform the very transgressive postmodernist literary texts into the tools of the global marketplace.

---

[1] Terry Eagleton, *After Theory* (New York: Basic Books, 2003) 73.
[2] E. L Doctorow, *Ragtime* (New York: Bantom/Random House, 1976).

In its beguilingly simple prose *Ragtime* captures the most important aspects of American history. Its characters consistently represent the epochal and
individual traits with the required degree of typicality that George Lukacs considered one of the important traits of a realist novel.[3] While Father and Mother
represent the typical American family of their time, Tateh and his daughter elucidate the plight of the immigrants during the narrative time of the novel. Present also in the novel is the American fascination with the frontier in Father's
journey to the Arctic; the life of the robber barons in the actions of J. P Morgan
and Henry Ford, and the heroic but tragic confrontation of the American racial
divide by Coalhouse. Due to its critique of the powerful – J. P Morgan and
Henry Ford – and its focus on the race, labor, and gender relations, *Ragtime* has
always been considered quite a transgressive text: it highlights and challenges
all major problems that formed part of American national history and even per-
sist in the twenty-first century America. If read within the paradigm of identity
politics and accessibility of the American dream, *Ragtime* becomes an ideal
pedagogical tool for teaching larger issues of American history. But considering
the changed economic paradigm, the most important aspect of the novel,
Tateh's move from the immigrant slum to a bourgeois suburb, tends to reinforce
the myth of the redemptive marketplace[4]. It is this particular aspect of the novel,
and the need to read it differently that forms the main emphasis of my inquiry.
This way of reading *Ragtime* is extremely important considering the novel's
popularity as a canonical text.

At least two major book-length works on postmodernist fiction make it a
point to include *Ragtime* amongst the most important late-modernist works.[5]
Linda Hutcheon in her brilliant work on postmodernism refers to *Ragtime* as a
novel that "moves the margins into the multiple 'centers' of the narrative, in
formal allegory of the social demographics of urban America."[6] Hutcheon's
treatment of the postmodern, however, is quite different from most other post-
modern theorists (McHale, for example). For her, "postmodernism is a contradictory phenomenon, one that uses and abuses, installs and then subverts, the

---

[3] George Lukacs. *The Historical Novel*. Trans. Hannah and Stanley Mitchell (Boston: Beacon Press,
1963)

[4] I am drawing on the idea of a redemptive marketplace as discussed by David Noble. He suggests
that in post WWII America a shift occurred in creating the new myth of American exceptionalism.
While the earlier myth was pastoral and invoked the open frontier as a redemptive place, the new
myth placed this redemptive power in the uplifting function of the capitalistic marketplace. For details
see David Noble, *Death of a Nation: American Culture and the End of Exceptionalism* (Minneapolis:
University of Minnesota Press, 2002).

[5] Brian McHale, *Postmodernist Fiction* (New York: Methuen, Inc. 1987) 88. While McHale places
Ragtime within the realm of late-modernist historical novels, Linda Hutheon (see works cited) treats it
as a Postmodernist text. Thus, *Ragtime* as a work of art defies a strict periodization and this ambiva-
lence is quite obvious in the way both these theorists deal with the text.

[6] Linda Hutcheon, *A Poetics of Postmodernism: History, Theory, Fiction* (New York: Routledge,
1988), 62.

very concepts that it challenges."[7] *Ragtime,* looked at from Hutcheon's perspective on the postmodern, gains prime importance under such a paradigm, for its attempts to subvert, challenge, and threaten the existing notions of history.

But a typical reading of the novel – a reading mediated through identity politics and the discourse of the margins – ends up appropriating the very transgressive strategies of *Ragtime* in the name of the neoliberal marketplace. It is this aspect of the critical reading of *Ragtime* that needs serious attention. If read from the perspective of race and gender relations alone, *Ragtime* ends up supporting the very norms of what Hutcheon calls moneyed capital and class distinctions of American society. Granted, the critic can retrieve quite a few peripheral, ex-centric histories narrated within the text, but our critical matrix must be stretched beyond this to include a critique of the modes of upward class mobility offered in the novel. If read within the context of global/American capitalism and its domination of the labor/artist population, *Ragtime* turns out to be a work that tends to favor the hierarchies and modes of upward mobility championed by the neoliberal global capital. In such a reading *Ragtime* ends, at least for Tateh and Mother, in a style clearly reminiscent of the Disneyfied fairy tales, an ending that in itself reinforces American exceptionalism in terms of upward social mobility. It is this exceptionalism with an emphasis on the individual rather than on the collective solidarity that has practically eliminated the question of class from mainstream American consciousness. Hence, by the end of the novel "Mother accepted him [Tateh] without hesitation. She adored him. They each relished the traits of character in the other. They were married in a judge's chamber in New York City" and, if I may add, lived happily ever after until the end of their days.[8] This wonderful, fairytale-like resolution would not have been possible if Tateh had not succeeded commercially as an artist. Thus, it seems, to achieve a "happily ever after" the artist must become (and there is no other alternative, no recourse to government/public support or lateral class alliance for upward mobility) a willing member of corporate capital.

To explain my attempt at reading the novel differently, I find it apt to introduce certain insights by Kenneth Saltman and Robin Goodman here whose work challenges the critical assumptions about works not only about the peripheral subjects, but also works by the writers of the periphery, works that because of their culturalist emphasis end up serving the very interests of the global capital that they aspire to contest. Their main argument is that under the guise of patronizing artistic production, for it makes the corporations look good, multinational corporations tend to reward the kinds of literary works that privilege the cult of the individual and escapist pastoral tendencies: hence, emphasizing a shift from the public collective action to the idea of freedom in the private sphere. In this context, while discussing Keri Helm's Maori novel *The Bone*

---

[7] Ibid., 4.
[8] Doctorow, 368.

People, which won the Pegasus Prize, Saltman and Goodman assert the following regarding metropolitan corporations' appropriation of the writers of the periphery:[9]

> While a text such as *The Bone People* is open to different interpretive frame-
> works, interpretations are hardly endlessly open-ended. The *Bone People* needs
> to be read in a way that shows how it affirms rather than challenges the activi-
> ties of multinational oil companies such as Mobil-Exxon that make corporate
> values into human values.[10]

In a nutshell, *The Bone People*, according to Saltman and Goodman, creates a
pastoral setting for the private troubles and dreams of its three main characters
couched in the language of private cultural identity. In this process violence,
alcoholism, and sexism is normalized in the name of cultural specificity while
no hope is offered in terms of collective action or public redemptive function of
the government. The individual is therefore sundered from the collective and
the public realm and therefore becomes the ideal subject for corporate
exploitation. Applying this insight to *Ragtime* will allow us to ascertain what
implicit agenda the novel might serve if read without a reference to the
exploitative tendencies of neoliberal global capital. There is no doubt that
Ragtime problematizes history and, in Douglas Fowler's words, attempts "to
depict the invasion, from below and within and without, of a smug and secure
American WASP family."[11] What does this invasion accomplish? Is it a
strategic repositioning of the silenced narratives, or is it just a cosmetic gesture
that unsettles nothing, but reasserts the same ideals of American exceptionalism
about the redemptive marketplace in a roundabout way?

Within the main plot of the novel, escape seems to be a major theme. Different characters seem to be searching for a way of escape out of their material
or spiritual predicaments. Thus, while Houdini seems to be practicing the art of
escape in its literal sense as an escape artist, Emma Goldman tries to accomplish the same through her politics, Evelyn Nesbit through her appeal as an object of desire, Father as a frontier pioneer, and Tateh through his art. On the
whole the novel clearly states that even fifty years after Houdini's death, the
"audience for escape is even larger."[12] There is only one successful escape from
material circumstances in the novel: Tateh's move from the immigrant slums to

---

[9] The Mobil Pegasus Prize for literature. For details see
www.magnolia.com/pegasus_prize/background.html. (Saltman and Goodman assert that certain
works by non-Anglo-American authors that were awarded the Pegasus Prize by the Mobil Corporation were chosen because they posit a positive view of multinationals by locating human agency in
the realm of the social and familial instead of the political.)
[10] Kenneth J. Saltman and Robin Goodman, *Strangelove: Or How We Learn to Stop Worrying and
Love the Market* (New York: Rowman & Littlefield, 2002) 95.
[11] Douglas Fowler, *Understanding E. L. Doctorow* (Columbia, SC: University of South Carolina
Press, 1992) 58.
[12] Doctorow, 8

Mother's house. It is this particular escape or upward movement that I find the most interesting, because it involves an important stage in the genesis of the myth of American exceptionalism. Before I discuss Tateh's class mobility in detail, I find it important to draw a comparison between Tateh and another artist from an earlier novel by a realist author, namely Hugh Wolfe of Rebecca Harding Davis's realist novel, *Life in the Iron Mills,* about the Irish immigrant experience of nineteenth century America.[13] This comparison helps in establishing the difference between the dominant redeeming forces represented in the two works. My contention is that while Davis's artist perishes after the unfulfilment of the desire created by the false promise of a visiting capitalist, the same capitalist system becomes an answer to Tateh's self realization and material fulfilment. Also, while in the first work religion is posited as the redeeming force, in *Ragtime* the same function has been appropriated by the myth of the redemptive marketplace. Both of these characters share quite a lot in common: they both are working class immigrants living in the urban slums, are both extremely poor, and are both artists. But what concerns me the most is not the commonalties of their plight, but rather, the means of upward mobility offered to them. While they both hope to use their art to achieve an escape from their material circumstances, the outcomes of their efforts are quite different. Wolfe is denied a chance of upward mobility because his would-be benefactor does not have the money and he is eventually lost because the church, the only instrument of reprieve at that time, cannot reach him in time.[14]

But the circumstances seem to have changed for Tateh: even though he lives in almost the same kind of immigrant ghetto, where the poor workers of the urban industry live, he is saved by the magic of the capitalistic marketplace. Thus, while Emma Goldman and her followers fight their rather comical and ineffectual battles for the labor rights, and while the government is posited as racist and unjust, the only saving grace seems to be a shrewd negotiation between the artist and the capitalistic order. The artist must sell his wares for profit to become successful, and this is the ultimate victory of the market as the place of the sacred in individual terms. Tateh's upward mobility suggests that the only way of improvement is through capitalism and corporate capital and that no public or social movement could achieve that. Only the market can make one succeed, if one is lucky enough to have something to sell. The possibility of a public discourse or lateral class alliance within the realm of the political is erased and replaced by an ethics of the market place. Thus, while Emma Goldman and her revolutionaries continue fighting for their rights, Tateh, who was never really interested in the movement, is the one who succeeds because the market takes care of him. Tateh's story, therefore, is the story of the success of the market place, which replaces any other forms of agency for

---

[13] Rebecca Harding Davis, *Life in the Iron Mills* (New York: Bedford Books, 1998).
[14] Davis, 56, 73.

upward mobility. An uncritical reading of this important aspect of the novel privileges the idea of a neo-liberal all-encompassing marketplace, the very agenda that only a class-conscious, public focused criticism can challenge. [15] Thus, while all other forms of resistance to the dominant order fail (including Coalhouse's challenge to institutional racism, Goldman's socialist politics, and Evelyn Nesbit's attempts at challenging the male paternalistic order) the regenerative capacity of market capitalism is overly emphasized. This comes across clearly in the way Tateh is able to transform his life after a chance encounter with a shop owner who has the capacity to mass produce his art work.

As stated earlier, the interventionist stance attributed to the peripheral subjects is rather cosmetic: a mere inclusion of the so-called silenced narratives does not necessarily grant *Ragtime* a spot within the pantheon of interventionist, ex-centric works. There has to be a level of agency made available to the peripheral subjects in order for the work to disrupt the master historical narratives. Even though some Doctorow critics take a mere insertion of the peripheral stories within the episteme of the center as an act of intervention, I do not think such a cosmetic gesture can offer any worthwhile resistance to the dominant notions of history. For Derek Wright, for example, Doctorow seems to be writing the silenced racial groups back into American history, but this mere inclusion does not accomplish an inversion of the master narrative from within. [16]

Compared with certain other postmodernist works, *Ragtime*, besides being a work that implicitly supports the corporate agenda, completely fails to measure up to the expectations of a work that posits itself as a reworking of history. Here, I would like to compare *Ragtime*, albeit briefly, to Ishmael Reed's *Mumbo Jumbo*.[17] As both these books were published in the mid seventies, and as both works are considered (late)-modern, this comparison would therefore elucidate my point. In *Mumbo Jumbo*, Reed problematizes history by asserting the eternal contest between Apollinian reason and Dionysian passion, in which he forwards the Dionysian order – the cultures of Africa and Caribbean – as the mainstream history as opposed to the Apollinian order of the White Anglo-Saxon culture. This rewriting of history subverts the very notion of dominant history and overwrites it with a fictionalized real history that had hitherto been silenced. McHale calls this treatment of history as "history as paranoiac conspiracy-theory."[18] Thus, Reed doesn't just tell his story by inserting peripheral

---

[15] By neoliberalism I mean the specific explanation of the term as discussed by John Rapley. In his view the present global economic order is neoliberal because it foregrounds Adam Smith's explanation of laissez-faire economics. In such paradigm the accumulative aspects of an economic regime are increased while the distributive function of an economy suffers drastically. Hence, a market economy model replaces the welfare state model. For further details see John Rapley, *Globalization and Inequality: Neoliberalism's Downward Spiral* (London: Lynne Rienner, 2004).

[16] Derek Wright, "*Ragtime* Revisited: History and Fiction in Doctorow's Novel," *International Fiction Review*, 20:1, 1993, 14.

[17] Ishmael Reed. *Mumbo Jumbo* (New York: Avon Books, 1972).

[18] McHale, 91.

subjects within the departmental narratives of the west, he intervenes to unsettle the official notion of history and reduces it to the level where the master narrative is transformed into a conspiracy to silence the real history. Reed's intervention may well be paranoiac, but it is certainly not cosmetic, and it clearly does not posit the dominant capitalistic order as the only true redemptive order. Compared to Reed's narrative, *Ragtime* turns out to be a text that can be easily appropriated in the name of the neoliberal global order.

My question here is that if *Ragtime* is read without a thorough knowledge of the current global economic paradigm, and the role of class in it, then whose particular agenda does it end up supporting? The answer is the narrative of the dominant corporate capital, for it does not offer any other successful alternative for vertical mobility other than that of the market economy model. After all is said and done, only access to the corporate marketplace can affect material change. While there are numerous references to the popular movements, the ultimate effect of such movements is rather tragicomic. Tateh is the only one who can accomplish some change, some happiness that "he'd constructed without help."[19] There is no major change in the over all political order; the Morgans and Fords can clearly sustain the petty challenges of Goldman and Coalhouse and through the coercive state machinery can sustain the dominant order, an order that may be challenged but cannot really be replaced. Thus, an uncritical reading of *Ragtime* instead of offering an alternative history ends up reinforcing the very notion of history, the apotheosis of the marketplace that we as critics must challenge.

The individual can only be successful through the benevolent mediation of corporations, and the government seems to lack any capacity to perform the public good. This neoliberal view of a hostile government and a benevolent corporation is the very paradigm that Saltman and Goodman challenge in their work referred to earlier, and this is the view of the government that *Ragtime* clearly foregrounds. What is elided in the process is the explicit notion of a benevolent government and a remunerative civic public relationship. The government is, of course, shown as clearly biased, inept and racist, a representation of government so enthusiastically popular with the supporters of globalization and neoliberalism. While this neoliberal view of an evil government is quite an accepted norm in postmodernist fiction, it is not necessarily a true representation. Actually, in recent American history, government, regardless of its ever-decreasing public service function, is the one institution that has reformed due to popular pressure. Thus, while not many legal forms of governmental discrimination exist, the corporate world, in the name of private capital, still maintains quite a number of discriminatory practices. We need only think of racially exclusive country clubs, religiously affiliated universities with discriminatory

---

[19] Doctorow, 300.

hiring policies, and golf clubs like Augusta, which discriminate on the bases of gender.

In Tateh's flight from the city, Doctorow takes him through two of the earliest myths of American exceptionalism. This is how Doctorow describes Tateh's flight to the end of the railroad tracks:

> The great wooden car swayed from side to side. The wind flew in their faces. They sped along the edges of open fields from which birds started and settled as they passed. The little girl saw herds of grazing cows. She saw brown horses loping in the sun. [...] The car threatened to jump off the tracks. It banged from side to side and everyone laughed. Tateh laughed. He saw the village of his youth going by now, some versts beyond the meadow. [...] He looked around at the riders on the trolley and for the first time since coming to America he thought it might be possible to live here.[20]

The imagery of the above passage clearly invokes the myth of the redemptive landscape as opposed to the exhausting city life that Tateh seems to be escaping. But this passage should not just be read for the beauty of its pastoral imagery; there is something much deeper embedded within the very innocent lines of this passage – the very myth of the pastoral landscape as a universal sacred. Here is how David Noble elaborates the creation of this early myth of American exceptionalism by Frederick Jackson Turner[21]:

> Turner wrote about the ability of the frontier, the west, to free Europeans from their ancestral cultures. To become Americans, adult Europeans crossing the Atlantic forgot their pasts and became as children. Then they were able to be born again. They were given new identities by the sacred national landscape.[22]

Even though Tateh is not the typical European immigrant Turner had imagined, and he is definitely not moving to a real frontier, for frontiers within the historical context of Tateh's journey had already been closed, Tateh's move from the city to the end of the railroad and thus to a more pastoral landscape is still imbued with a definite trace of Turner's myth.[23] Thus, implicitly, Tateh's route to personal happiness does pass through one myth and culminates into the other: the promise of delivery through industry. Noble explains this myth of American exceptionalism as following:

---

[20] Doctorow, 106.

[21] Turner is famous for his work *The Frontier in American History* (New York: H. Holt, 1920).

[22] Noble, 7.

[23] According to David Noble it was only people who could fit the paradigm of "history as progress" who could be redeemed by this national landscape, Since Jews and Catholics were considered people without history, they could not find a new self on the frontier; Tateh, being Jewish, would not have qualified as someone capable of creating a new self on the frontier in Turner's views.

The uniform culture imagined by Beard[24] in 1914 was different from that of Bancroft and Turner because he saw it as the expression of an urban-industrial rather than a pastoral landscape. He imagined, therefore, that the democratic people in the United States were in harmony with the productive forces of industrialism. It was possible, then, for the democratic people in the United States to share this universal international with democratic people in other industrialized nations[25].

But Tateh, as evidenced from the text, does not fare well within this urban-industrial national universal. *Ragtime* clearly demystifies this important American myth. The following passage clearly displays Tateh's plight as a worker:

> This same winter found Tateh and his daughter in the mill town of Lawrence, Massachusetts. [...] Tateh stood in front of a loom for fifty-six hours a week. His pay was just under six dollars. The family lived in a wooden tenement on a hill. They had no heat. They occupied one room overlooking an alley in which residents customarily dumped their garbage. He feared she would fall victim to the low-class elements of the neighborhood. He refused to enrol her in school – it was easier here than in New York to avoid the authorities – and made her stay home when he was not there to go out with her.[26]

If there is no national landscape to invigorate Tateh, and if the urban-industrial labor becomes yet another instrument of oppression, then what other institution can transport him to the promised land of success? As *Ragtime* contains no redemptive attributes of the government, there is therefore no possibility of a regenerative public domain, nor is there any chance of an effective working class mobilization. The government, as the text makes clear, is controlled and manipulated by the J.P Morgans and Fords of the world. The only possible escape for Tateh is consequently the marketplace. Hence Tateh moves through the earlier redemptive myths of American exceptionalism and reaches the ultimate and the most enduring one – the myth of the sacred marketplace.

In Saltman and Goodman's words, this sacred marketplace reveals that "collective action, worker solidarity, or political action as a response to threatening labor conditions. [...] never appear as an option to the protagonist."[27] This can be clearly applied to Tateh's situation: under repressive labor conditions he leaves yet again in the middle of a labor strike to seek his destiny as an individual. Hence, the very importance of worker solidarity – which historically won most of the freedoms and protections enjoyed by the workers in America – is elided and replaced by the ethics of an idealized individual freedom within a market economy. At this juncture Tateh seems ready to finally redeem himself

---

[24] Charles A. Beard and his wife Mary R. Beard are most famous for their work in generating the myth of industrial America. For details see their *American Citizenship* (New York: MacMillan, 1914).
[25] Noble, 22.
[26] Doctorow, 137.
[27] Saltman and Goodman, 194.

and his daughter through the unplanned, but timely, intervention of capitalism and a benevolent marketplace. Tateh's negotiation of the capitalistic market and his eventual success resonates with the very myth of capitalism as envisaged by Hofstadter, which David Noble explains as follows:

> In 1970, however, [Hofstadter] described capitalism as creating a pluralistic so-ciety in which there were no clear-cut class divisions. Under capitalism, history as unmanageable conflict had ended; history as chaos would cease when people no longer tried to escape history. The future, for Hofstadter in 1971, was a capi-talistic one in which a spirit of pragmatic compromise would sustain a harmo-nious human experience within the inevitable flow of time.[28]

The resemblance between Tateh's personal success and the above mentioned theorization of global capital is quite striking, for he does succeed financially and ends up marrying the very heart of the WASP family – mother. The ques-tion arises once again: What is wrong with such a representation? It is, after all, possible. My problem with this representation is that the novel ends up privileg-ing the neoliberal version of the capitalistic myth to redeem Tateh. In this ver-sion, as stated earlier, politics becomes redundant and the market is expected to eliminate all barriers towards upwards mobility, which does not really happen in the real-life global marketplace. In other words, the novel posits the same view of marketplace as that of Hofstadter, in which "the marketplace could ful-fil the failed promises of the national and international landscape."[29]

Now, of course, it is evident that the novel is quite critical of the capital-ists, the government, and the factory owners. Hence, my criticism of this repre-sentation of Tateh might seem out of place. But I consider this new questioning of the text a very important exercise in terms of current global capitalistic ten-dencies. Texts, especially when seen as representative of the periphery, do have the power to mold public consciousness. There is, therefore, a need to de-emphasize the myth of individualism and foreground the importance of solidar-ity. One way of doing this involves reading canonical texts differently. In the grand class struggle between the wretched of the earth – whose numbers keep increasing – and their affluent counterparts, nothing short of a global solidarity of the poor would affect any change, certainly not the romanticized view of lo-cal resistances to global pressures. While it may not be possible to invoke class in its classic Marxian sense, it is imperative to keep consciousness of class alive in our literary discussions.

I would not be wrong in suggesting that a seemingly radical narrative, which is implicitly neoliberal could have devastating effects on readers trying to clearly understand the political implications of the current global capitalistic or-der. The destructive power of such an effect cannot be denied, which makes it

---

[28] Noble, 49.
[29] Noble, 50.

imperative for critics to read *Ragtime* within the current political paradigm that has changed drastically since the publication of the novel.

Within the current stage of neoliberal globalization, the need for a viable public sphere is much greater than before. While the corporate media are constantly producing the images of family as the only place of a valid agency, and governments are cutting down on welfare while expecting the family to function as a sustaining locus for the individual, it is necessary to reemphasize the need for a viable class solidarity. Hardt and Negri assert the following about globalization:

> Our political task, we will argue, is not simply to resist these processes but to reorganize and redirect them towards new ends. The creative forces of the multitude that sustain Empire are also capable of autonomously constructing a counter-Empire, an alternative political organization of global flows and exchanges. The struggles to contest and subvert Empire, as well as those to construct a real alternative, will thus take place on the imperial terrain itself – indeed, such new struggles have already begun to emerge. Through these struggles and many more like them, the multitude will have to invent new democratic forms and a new constituent power that will one day take us through and beyond Empire.[30]

I am, of course, not suggesting anything as colossal as the above, but maybe that global process will start with small efforts such as reading a text differently, and that is what I have tried to accomplish. As stated above, the current political order, and our perception of it, needs a drastic overhaul that cannot be undertaken only within the limited space of individual agency or within the confines of the family. Hence, the need for a larger public sphere and class alliances becomes instrumental in creating a world in which not one but most of the Tateh's of the world succeed.

Selected Bibliography

Davis, Rebecca Harding. *Life in the Iron Mills*. New York: Bedford Books, 1998.

Doctorow, E.L. *Ragtime*. New York: Bantom/ Random House, Inc., 1976.

Eagleton, Terry. *After Theory*. New York: Basic Books, 2003.

Fowler, Douglas. *Understanding E. L. Doctorow*. Columbia, SC: University of South Carolina Press, 1992.

Goodman, Robin T. and Kenneth J. Saltman. *Strangelove: Or How we Learn to Stop Worrying and Love the Market*. New York: Rowman & Littlefield, 2002.

Hardt, Michael and Antonio Negri. *Empire*. Cambridge, MS: Harvard University Press, 2000.

---

[30] Michael Hardt and Antonio Negri, *Empire* (Cambridge, MS: Harvard University Press, 2000) xv.

Hutcheon, Linda. *A Poetics of Postmodernism: History, Theory, Fiction.* New York: Routledge, 1988.

McHale, Brian. *Postmodernist Fiction.* New York: Methuen, 1987.

Noble, David W. *Death of a Nation: American Culture and the End of Exceptionalism.* Minneapolis: University of Minnesota Press, 2002.

Reed, Ishmael. *Mumbo Jumbo.* New York: Avon Books, 1972

Wright, Derek. "Ragtime Revisited: History and Fiction in Doctorow's Novel." *International Fiction Review* 20:1(1993): 14-16.

Gendered Dreams and the Hollywood Cross-Class Romance

Wuming Zhao (Doshisha University, Kyoto)

In this essay I intend to examine America's class issues through Hollywood's representation of the American Dream in gender related variations, paying special attention to the narrative pattern of cross-class romance often known as the Cinderella story, because I believe class involves not only material social existence but also cultural value systems, and class is entangled with other categories such as gender. I hope to expand the understanding of the complexity of class in America by exploring how the ideology in the quintessential Dream of success affects the practice and understanding of class, how the prevalent cross-class romance in America contributes to the gender-specific disposition of the supposedly gender-free Dream, and how movies, or popular culture products in general, provide, however covertly or unintentionally, important sites for constructing and negotiating possible visions of the American Dream at the intersection of class and gender.

Among various remarks concerning class in America, the following two often appear in my mind side by side. One is from a much-quoted speech by U.S. President George H. W. Bush: "Class is for European democracies or something else – it isn't for the United States of America. We are not going to be divided by class."[1] The other is from a letter to the editor of the New York Times. Responding to social critic Benjamin DeMott[2]'s article "In Hollywood, Class Doesn't Put up much of a Struggle,"[3] which criticizes movies for obfuscating or even hiding the class realities in America, reader Marcia C. Spires writes

> There's nothing wrong with Benjamin DeMott's premise. It's just that the audience for these popular 'feel good' movies is way ahead of him. We don't need to have subtle differences explicated or belabored. We spend all day making instantaneous assessments of CQ (class quotient). Egad, even buying a plane ticket is complicated. Which of four or five classes do you – and your budget – fit into? So sometimes it's pleasant to relieve the tedium of trying to maintain a foothold in this society by watching a modern fairy tale.[4]

These two apparently contradictory remarks reveal some intriguing features of class in America.

---

[1] Quoted in both Benjamin DeMott, *The Imperial Middle: Why Americans Can't Think Straight about Class* (New Haven and London: Yale University Press, 1990) 9-10, and Paul Kalra, *The American Class System: Divide and Rule* (Pleasant Hill, CA: Antenna, 1995).

[2] Benjamin DeMott is Mellon Professor of Humanities at Amherst College and a popular commentator on America's social and political issues.

[3] *The New York Times*, late edition, Sunday Jan 20, 1991, sec. 2, Arts & Leisure Desk, 1.

[4] *The New York Times*, late edition, Sunday Feb 10, 1991, sec. 2 Arts & Leisure Desk, 4.

Rather than trying to prove which of the two reflects the reality of socio-economic inequality, I see them depicting different forms or aspects of class, and therefore representing different ways of understanding class. In the U.S. president's usage, class presumably refers to a social system with strict and explicit rules for and formations of class, such as that in Britain, from which the United States from its beginning strove to depart. Such depiction evokes the popular belief that because America was founded in deliberate opposition to the system of kings/queens and titled aristocrats, Americans are equal individuals and should be able to pursue their betterment in an open system that provides them with opportunities for free mobility across socioeconomic strata. In this sense, though statistics show that the lot of the wealthy and the poor in America have become more and more polarized,[5] it is possible for the president to claim that America is a classless society, and for most Americans, including many from the most affluent and the poorest fifths, to feel that they all belong to the inclusive normative middle class.[6] However, class in the reader's letter denotes not a remote, foreign system but a ubiquitous existence, unavoidable in people's daily life. Not only airfares, but almost everything can be classified so as to convey the possessor or consumer's status. From their various and multiple positions within the social matrix, people classify each other and themselves with the unwritten rules of social classification.[7]

Whereas in the rigid class society class is a system that divides people, their rights, and worth into different levels according to birth and heritage, in an open society such as America's, class as a social system is denounced, but the social and ideological hierarchies differentiating people function to the same effect. The operation of such hierarchies depends, as in Social Darwinism, largely on naturalizing the divisions based on biologic traits and personal attributes. Since Marxist class theory dissected the exploitative mechanism of capitalism, further contemporary studies have explored other forms of naturalized social differentiation based on race, gender, ethnicity, sexuality, age, region, etc., to recognize, categorize and denaturalize these socially and culturally constructed and maintained hierarchies sustaining the social inequalities.

To sum up, the term "class" here designates at least three different but related meanings: a strictly stratified social system, the lived experience of socioeconomic differences, and a lens or critical tool we use to examine and analyze the phenomena and causes of socioeconomic inequality.

---

[5] Various data are synthesized and discussed in William H. Frey, Bill Abresch, and Jonathan Yeasting, *America by the Numbers: A Field Guide to the U.S. Population* (New York: The New Press, 2001), and Robert Perrucci and Earl Wysong, *The New Class Society: Goodbye American Dream?* (Lanham: Rowman & Littlefield, 2003) among others.

[6] Frey, 90-91.

[7] Pierre Bourdieu, *Distinction: A Social Critique of the Judgement of Taste* (Cambridge: Harvard University Press, 1984).

Once beyond the apparent contradiction between the earlier two remarks defining class as a fixed social system and as the lived experience of socioeconomic differences, it may become more obvious that these two forms of class are interrelated phenomena. Many have long pointed out that the discourse of the open class system, with its advocacy of individualism and material success, in a way actually makes class or class mobility a central issue in people's lives. Without clear lines between classes or obvious signs (such as titles) of social standing, it is difficult for people to see and be sure of their positions and achievement. Anxiety and pressure are therefore constant. Since the discourse of an open class system presumes to provide freedom of social mobility, the efforts of individuals become the decisive factor for people's achievement and success. If individuals cannot make it, it is somehow a proof of their deficiency rather than the fault of the system. People are responsible for their own failures.

Essential to the notion that people can move freely across the borders between classes, I would add, is the assumption that people all desire to do so. While discarding the inherited and fixed class positions, "classless," or open class capitalism fosters not social and economic equality among people but an ideology of individual-based success. The talk of openness implies an unmistaken expectation of its members' desire to move up and get ahead of others. If monetary and material accumulation and consumption often showcase a person's success, the desire for and devotion to gaining success indicates a person's legitimacy in society. With their efforts to achieve upward mobility, or even merely, in the words of Spires' letter, to "maintain a foothold" in such a society, people are actually constantly demonstrating their possession of such a desire and determination, as well as their effort and ability to realize that desire. To "maintain a foothold" means not only to keep oneself from falling across the open class borders, it also means to prove that one is not a "loser," but a worthy member of the society. It is in such a sense of legitimacy, worthiness and respectability supported by a broadly shared value system that the real power of domination over the less powerful lies. As in a formulation of capitalism in which people's value is often measured by their monetary and material possession and consumption, for people like Spires, class is in the socioeconomic differences appearing in any and all forms: from what kind of clothes one wears to what class of air ticket one buys, from what car one drives to where one resides; education, recreational activities, manners, taste and even body type can all be markers of class.

Although the questions of how, what, or whether various theories and concepts of class are useful or crucial for understanding and characterizing post-industrial capitalist phenomena are still under heated debate[8], the way people's

---

[8] See Erik Olin Wright, ed. *Approaches to Class Analysis* (Cambridge: Cambridge University Press, 2005); Perrucci and Wysong; Janeen Baxter and Mark Western, eds. *Reconfigurations of Class and Gender* (Stanford: Stanford University Press, 2001) among others.

lives are affected by the injustice embedded in such a system has been docu-
mented and examined. Class can and has been studied as a subject of political
economics; however, class should also be studied through how the socioeconomic inequality is understood, and how the understandings are formed. For an
open class society, researchers can divide or group the population into different
classes according to income levels, professions, and other factors to grasp,
through statistics, the formation and transformation of class existence. However,
in order to trace how people's understanding of class or socioeconomic inequality, as ways of thinking and cultural practices, are formed and transformed, we
need to go to the sites where such actions and practices are carried out, but are
overlooked or neglected.

One such site is film. To a great extent, America's class formation and
transformation are, as Robert Sklar and others have discussed, realized with the
production and consumption of movies, and people's understanding or misun-
derstanding of class as well as other issues are influenced by the cultural myths
and dreams they encounter on the screen.[9] For various reasons, however, film
and class has not been a favorite connection for many. On the one hand, audience members like Spires, who expect movies to entertain and to take them
away from the hassles of class and such, do not or prefer not to see class in movies. On the other hand, there are also critics who steer away from films when
dealing with class because they generally believe that Hollywood products do
not reflect but rather obscure social reality and are therefore not hard, factual
materials proper/suitable for such purposes. Then there are those who stay away
from class when dealing with film because they have found a more immediate
need to focus on issues of gender, race, etc.

Since the 90s, more attention has been paid to the issues of class in film. As
in his aforementioned *New York Times* article, Benjamin DeMott, in his 1990
book, *The Imperial Middle: Why Americans Can't Think Straight about Class*
critically discusses how various forces, including Hollywood, have produced the
myth of classless America. Exploring the recent versions of yesterday's rags-to-
riches story patterns on both big and small screens – patterns emphasizing the
discovery of the classlessness of American society, the *upendings* of social hierarchies and the reversal of status, and the *renunciations* of the temptation of ascension – he concludes that these stories together dismiss or erase America's reality of high stratification.[10] These arguments are reconsidered by Carolyn Anderson in "Diminishing Degrees of Separation: Class Mobility in Movies of the
Reagan-Bush Era." (1996)[11] Her examination of dozens of '80s films indicates

---

[9] Robert Sklar, *Movie-Made America: A Social History of American Movies* (New York: Random House, 1975), and Steven J. Ross, *Working-Class Hollywood: Silent Film and the Shaping of Class in America* (Princeton: Princeton University Press, 1998).

[10] Benjamin DeMott, *The Imperial Middle*, 51-70.

[11] Carolyn Anderson, "Diminishing Degrees of Separation: Class Mobility in Movies of the Reagan-Bush Era" in Paul Loukides and Linda K. Fuller eds., *Beyond the Stars 5: Themes and Ideologies in*

that the messages of class therein are more complex and mixed than mere dismissal. Even when class issues are reduced to individuals' problems, the individual characters are not without their senses of class belongings.

Also appearing in 1996 is a significant collective effort entitled *The Hidden Foundation: Cinema and the Question of Class*.[12] This collection of 12 essays explores new and effective ways to establish class as a main framework for film analysis and to combine class with the ongoing agenda of race and gender in various aspects. Two years later one of the contributors, Steven J. Ross published his research on working class audiences, the worker film movement, and depictions of class during Hollywood's silent era in *Working-Class Hollywood: Silent Film and the Shaping of Class in America* (1998). Dealing with class along with other central categories of race, gender and sexuality in movies from the silent era to the present, Harry Benshoff and Sean Griffin's *American on Film: Representing Race, Class, Gender, and Sexuality at the Movies* (2004) provides an introduction to themes of social mobility, the American Dream, class difference, class conflict, and others in different periods of Hollywood history and in movies of various genres.

Two other works of particular interest here are Thomas E. Wartenberg's *Unlikely Couples: Movie Romance as Social Criticism* (1999) and Christopher Beach's *Class, Language, and American Film Comedy* (2002). As the titles indicate, these works are devoted to examining the often-present class issues in two durable and often overlapping Hollywood genres. Though the cross-class relationships Beach studies have been a comedy staple since the beginning of film and difference of social positions are among the major obstacles Wartenberg's unlikely romantic couples confront, romance and comedy are traditionally even less associated with discussions of class than other genres. Movies in these genres are often regarded as escapist fantasy, sentimental indulgence, or farce, at best entertaining. But their embedded and thus less explicit involvement with serious issues such as class can become somewhat hidden in the entertainment, and is easily overlooked. Wartenberg and Beach's works are especially valuable because they tackle these kinds of movies and provide close readings of how they on different levels represent class, question social orders, critique social system, while simultaneously, in bringing the couples together, smooth over class differences and dismiss social reality.

Like most recent works, Wartenberg and Beach's books do not limit their discussion to a single category, but connect class with race, gender, sexuality, and ethnicity in order to explore the complex functions of intensification and/or disruption among these social factors. To extend this effort, I will examine a few groups of movies same as or similar to what they have dealt with, nevertheless

---

American Popular Film (Bowling Green: Bowling Green State University Popular Press, 1996), 141-163.

[12] David E. James and Rick Berg, eds. *The Hidden Foundation: Cinema and the Question of Class* (Minneapolis: University of Minnesota Press, 1996).

focusing on the themes of social mobility and gender relationship as depicted in the movies' cross-class narratives. The story of a poor or mistreated girl and a man of a higher social position (the genders are occasionally reversed) is a familiar and frequently recycled narrative in American culture, often referred to as the Cinderella story. Its adaptations and variations can be found not only in Hollywood movies but also among various other popular culture products. Having grown up in socialist China, I am more accustomed to two other narrative patterns concerning gender relationships, both rejecting the cross-class structure, yet for quite different reasons. One is based on old, feudal teachings: Ideal couples were expected to have well-matched social and economic status, and therefore girls particularly were to be content with their lot and not dream of things beyond that. The other narrative pattern developed from the then new, socialist ideologies: Poor girls were encouraged to unite their strengths to destroy the exploitative rich class and improve their socioeconomic condition *collectively*; if two people from opposite classes become a couple, it would most probably happen when the girl had, with her love and class consciousness, first changed the young man from the politically-denounced old rich class into a working, self-supporting equal.[13] Worth noting here is that not only does the girl not move up, actually even the wealthy class is not necessarily considered "upper" in this framework. The broad and lasting popularity of cross-class Cinderella narratives in America thus offers an intriguing contrast and provides another site, a peculiar one, to understand class and gender in American (and at the same time my own) culture.

The Cinderella story is sometimes casually referred to as the female American Dream. This equation, while suggesting the similarity and connection between the two narratives, neglects some fundamental differences between them. Even though movies are not necessarily expressly made as American Dream or Cinderella stories, and genres sometimes do merge, for my purpose it is important to distinguish the two at this stage. The conventional American Dream usually grants success and wealth to a poor or underprivileged yet diligent and determined person (mostly male), whereas the Cinderella story most often unites in love a poor or underprivileged girl and a man from a higher social position, and elevates her to his level. The most obvious similarity the two narratives share is that they both provide upward mobility for their protagonists. Some of the differences are obvious: The protagonists in the American Dream are often depicted as self-made men working their way up, while the protago-

---

[13] Although there are few Cinderella heroines in Chinese culture, there do exist some "CinderFella" narratives in old Chinese stories, such as a poor scholar gets to marry the emperor's daughter after winning the first place in the Imperial Examination. However his mobility depends first of all upon his own effort and ability, as with the conventional American Dream heroes, and the marriage strengthens his position. In socialist China, social stratification does not necessarily accord to economic classes, and social mobility also takes different forms. I explore these issues in some of my cross-cultural comparative projects.

nists in the Cinderella stories are usually shown as women rescued by their heroes.

Such gender specific routes for mobility – the male working his way up and the female marrying her way up – can be summarized by the popular belief in America that "even a poor boy can grow up to become president," and its "unliberated corollary" that "even a poor girl can grow up and become the president's wife."[14] The presidency serves as the ultimate symbol of success and power, but in reality as well as in movies successful mobility is expressed more often in comparatively terms of increased wealth, fame, status, or respectability. Any of those successful protagonists, president or otherwise, can be candidates for the poor girl's Prince Charming.

Throughout the history of film countless heroes have realized their American Dream on the screen. In the business world, we find the young clerk of a department store in the silent comedy *Safety Last* (1923), making his way up by climbing to the top of the 12-story department store to attract customers; in *Trading Places* (1983) and *The Hudsucker Proxy* (1994) the little guys in the corporate jungle outwit and turn the tables on their villainous bosses. In the political arena, decent common men (including deep-down decent con-men) stand up to the corrupt system and build careers in Congress in *Mr. Smith Goes to Washington* (1939) and *The Distinguished Gentleman* (1992). On stage or on the dance floor, the working class young men fulfill their aspirations through dance in *Saturday Night Fever* (1977) and *Dirty Dancing* (1987). And in the ring, boxers from Italian and Irish immigrant neighborhoods fight and succeed against all odds to prove their worth and to support their loved ones in *Rocky* (1976) and the recent *Cinderella Man* (2005).

On the other hand, just as the cinder girl in Disney's animated *Cinderella* (1950) achieves emancipation through her union with the Prince, numerous heroines in various modern variations secure their upward mobility through love and marriage with their bosses (*It*, 1927; *Flashdance*, 1983), their masters or "creators" (*Sabrina*, 1954 and 1995; *My Fair Lady* 1964), millionaires (*How to Marry a Millionaire*, 1953; *Pretty Woman*, 1990), princes (*The Prince and the Showgirl*, 1957; *The Prince and Me*, 2004) and kings (*The King and the Chorus Girl*, 1937), or politicians (*Maid in Manhattan*, 2002).

The gender-specific routes toward the American Dream discursively provided in these films clearly have their roots in the patriarchal ideology that assign men and women separate spheres in life. A conventional, simpler picture of the good life promised by the American Dream would show a happy couple, with their kids, living in a beautiful house in the suburbs, all achieved with the husband's income, and sustained by the wife's work in the home. To make possible the happy picture requires not only the successful heroes in the American

---

[14] Jane Yolen, "America's Cinderella" in *Cinderella: A Casebook*, ed. Alan Dundes (Madison: University of Wisconsin Press, 1988) 294-306.

Dream but also the domesticated heroines of the Cinderella story. The important role of Cinderella in America up until a few decades ago can be seen as a complement to the more male-oriented and individual effort-based American Dream. While it is understandable that the narratives of the American Dream and Cinderella together should create the most harmonious picture of the happy life, the picture itself is problematic and therefore unstable. One problem with this happy picture is that although it requires the efforts of both man and woman, the man is often regarded as the provider and the woman the beneficiary, because toil in the workplace is highly valued while housework in the home is systematically and culturally devalued.

Do films give us any indication then, that it is possible for women to improve their social standing by adopting the same route as men? Though limited in number, there do exist some memorable female rags-to-riches stories: *A Star Is Born* (1937, 1954, 1976), *All About Eve* (1950), *Funny Girl* (1968), *New York, New York* (1977), *Coal Miner's Daughter* (1980), *Working Girl* (1988), *Up Close and Personal* (1996), *Erin Brockovich* (2000). Even though their accomplishment still sometimes requires help from the men above them (the aspiring young singers in the three versions of *A Star Is Born* break into show business with the aid of the male stars who will become their husbands; in *All About Eve*, the young actress literally uses all the men and women around her on her way to the top; the secretary in *Working Girl* rises from the secretarial pool through her own effort and her male partner's devoted support and trust; discovered and tutored by a veteran newsman, the young woman from a small town develops into a major network anchor in *Up Close and Personal*), the heroines in these movies all start from very humble backgrounds and work their way up to stardom or executive positions (as in *Working Girl* and *Erin Brockovich*) through their talents and determination like their male counterparts.[15]

A closer look at the aforementioned male and female success narratives and at how the protagonists are rewarded or what is included in their success will reveal that the heroes (the male protagonists) do not just gain success, they obtain happiness, whereas female access to class advancement in the public sphere is not necessarily desirable because the advancement is often an obstacle preventing her from having an ideal happy life. At the end of each movie when the hero prevails he is always seen with his woman by his side as the purpose or the effect of his struggle. When the young clerk in *Safety Last* reaches the top of the building, waiting for him there are the $1000 reward and his sweetheart; in *Trading Places*, *The Hudsucker Proxy*, and *Mr. Smith Goes to Washington*, the heroes, while fighting their way up, also win the hearts and support of the

---

[15] In addition to these rags-to-riches stories, the list may also include stories of successful personal development, such as *Gone with the Wind* (1939), *Alice Doesn't Live Here Anymore* (1974), *Norma Rae* (1979), *Silkwood* (1983), *Baby Boom* (1987), *G.I. Jane* (1997), *Music of the Heart* (1999), *Million Dollar Baby* (2004), *Ice Princess* (2005), *Beauty Shop* (2005). All but one made since the early 70s, these movies feature various strong-willed leading women tenacious in their own pursuits.

women first sent to destroy them; the con man in *The Distinguished Gentleman* finally finds an honorable man in himself and his true love and camaraderie in a female political activist; with sweat and grace, the two dancers in *Saturday Night Fever* and *Dirty Dancing* become the stars on the dance floor and receive respect, admiration and love from their dance partners; and Rocky's and Braddock's (*Cinderella Man*) victories in the ring bring themselves glory and their loved ones hope and joy.

When compared to movies depicting the failed Dream, it becomes more apparent that the romantic love in the above-mentioned narratives is not mere decoration but an essential element of success. The TV network executive in *The Man in the Grey Flannel Suit* (1956) realizes that his success at work takes away from his time with his wife and children, alienates him from his family, and threatens their wellbeing. He gives up further promotion that would lead to the top position at the network to be a good husband and father for the sake of a happy family. The hero in *The Great Gatsby* (1974) is a self-made millionaire, but his Dream turns tragic because no matter how much money he accumulates or spends, he cannot win the romantic love he has longed for since his impoverished childhood. These Hollywood narratives of the failed American Dream seem to demonstrate that success without happiness is empty, meaningless, and even destructive. The ultimate goal of all *men* in mainstream conservative Hollywood narratives is the pursuit of happiness, sanctified in the Declaration of Independence, and the formula for happiness most often includes not only success in material terms, but also the fulfilment provided by (heterosexual) romantic love.

When evaluated against Hollywood's own formula for success/happiness, the female success stories show a critical difference in their treatment. What women have to face is a "double bind"[16] situation: In order to achieve their goals in the public sphere they must sacrifice a happy personal life. The common consequence of their success is that they lose their loved ones. The birth or rise of a female star often parallels the decline of her husband's career, as in *A Star Is Born*, *Funny Girl*, *New York, New York*, and *Up Close and Personal*. In these and other movies, such as *Coal Miner's Daughter*, *Erin Brockovich*, *Norma Rae*, *Silkwood*, etc., the woman's success outside the home almost always causes friction in the couple's relationship. The heroine in *Gone with the Wind* is depicted as capable but unattainable, which results in her losing both her child and her husband. The naïve-looking ambitious actress in *All about Eve* coldbloodedly steps on others on her way to superstardom and arrives there without friends and without love. Their successes lead them, not toward the unproblematically happy version of the Dream, but away from it. *G.I. Jane* portrays, positively, a very special and strong female character. However, she has to prove her

---

[16] Molly Haskell, *From Reverence to Rape: The Treatment of Women in the Movies* (Chicago & London: University of Chicago Press, 1987) 173.

worth by becoming male; at the climax of a series of hard training scenes, when she finally gains the acceptance and respect of her male fellows, the first female navy seal proclaims her triumph to her opponent: "Suck my dick!" But her symbolic dick, representing her acquired physical and mental masculinity, does not seem to qualify her for the romantic happy ending typically accompanying male American Dreamers. She stays strong till the end, and alone. As for *Million Dollar Baby*, whereas her ring brothers bring home championships and new lives to their loved ones, what awaits the tough and determined female boxer is not great victory but a future of unbearable loss.

With the shortage of male labor during WW II, the surging need and desire for consumer goods from the 50s on, and the development and spread of feminist ideologies in the past decades, women in the paid American labor force increased in great number. [17] Working single women have become more or less the norm, and working wives and mothers have become common in the work places outside the home. Nevertheless, the popular imagination toward women's new rolls in achieving the American Dream through career and profession as represented in Hollywood is still very limited. During the last three decades, there have appeared some movies that begin to extend the traditional happy Dream formula to women. Among the movies concerning female success discussed earlier, we can see that in *Alice Doesn't Live Here Anymore* (1974), *Norma Rae* (1979), *Baby Boom* (1987), *Working Girl* (1988), *Music of the Heart* (1999), *Ice Princess* (2005), and *Beauty Shop* (2005), the female protagonists are depicted somewhat optimistically, as making progress in dealing with the double bind dilemma. A caring male partner has been offered as a key factor in the change.

While the list of the female American Dream movies is very short, we can easily find more to include in the list of Cinderella (love/marriage-based American Dream for women) movies. The cross-class romance seems to be as popular as ever, if not more so today. During the first few years of the new century there have appeared, *The Wedding Planner* (2001), *Kate and Leopold* (2001), *Two Weeks Notice* (2002), *Maid in Manhattan* (2002), *Sweet Home Alabama* (2002), *A Cinderella Story* (2004), *Ella Enchanted* (2004), *The Prince and Me* (2004).[18]

The contrast poses a question. Why is the Cinderella story, a story virtually branded as patriarchal since the publication of *The Cinderella Complex: Women's Hidden Fear of Independence* in 1981, so prevalent in America?[19] Denouncing the narratives as mere backlash against feminism is not helpful in investigating the complexity of the issue. In *Transforming the Cinderella Dream:*

---

[17] Susan Van Horn, *Women, Work, and Fertility, 1990-1986* (New York: New York University Press, 1988) 145, and Frey, 104-105.

[18] Hollywood's modern Cinderellas for the last three decades in the 20th century include: *Love Story* (1970), *An Officer and a Gentleman* (1982), *Flashdance* (1983), *Coming to America* (1988), *Working Girl* (1988), *Pretty Woman* (1990), *White Palace* (1990), *Sabrina* (1995), *Evita* (1996), *You've Got Mail* (1998), *Ever After* (1998), *Bulworth* (1998).

[19] Colette Dowling, *The Cinderella Complex: Women's Hidden Fear of Independence* (New York: Summit Books, 1981).

From Frances Burney to Charlotte Bronte, a study of the Cinderella theme in the British novel, Huang Mei points out that in addition to patriarchal elements, the ideology of individualism for self-realization is also embedded in the Cinderella story, and is often taken for granted.[20] Recognition of one's inner Self, and the desire to prove one's self-worth through upward mobility in Cinderella echo what the American Dream expects from its dreamers. My study of a group of modern Cinderella renditions in 1980s Hollywood indicates that unlike most male versions of the American Dream, the Cinderella narrative provides a venue for women's upward social mobility at the intersection of gender and class.[21] In other words, women are urged to desire ascent as individuals but the uplift has to rely on their relationship with men. Whereas the dependence is romanticized as part of the ultimate happiness, the concept of romantic love requires a basic equal relationship between the couple. This discourse logic indicates a strong patriarchal influence but also shows that patriarchy does not have a monopoly on the story of Cinderella. Women's dream of success on screen or other media of popular imagination has been built upon a continuous tension between two competing themes; one romanticizing a domesticated, subordinate woman, and the other encouraging an aspiring female social climber.

From the beginning, Hollywood, like other mass-mediated forms of popular culture, has been complementing the male-oriented American Dream narrative with the female-targeted Cinderella. In a culture that prioritizes individuality, self-reliance and personal success, it was inevitable that women would feel the desire to achieve what had been conventionally reserved for men, when the concept of "men" had changed from the white, male, property owner in the *Declaration of Independence*, and begun to include any gender, racial, and class others. However, the female success narratives that follow conventionally male-oriented paths have posed great challenges to the early harmonious picture. Theoretically, women, like their male counterparts, should be able to both assume responsibilities and enjoy fulfilments of both public and private spheres. In reality, however, the social system is not immediately compatible with such change. It is not hard to see that this shift would seriously destabilize the gender hierarchy and transform family structure. In order for women *Growing up in the Shadow of the American Dream* to have it all, a redesign or revision of the whole blueprint of the conventional male-centered American Dream is necessary and unavoidable. [22]

The American Cinderella narratives can be regarded as an effort to deal with this crisis. By offering women the Cinderella-styled upward social mobility

---

[20] Huang Mei, *Transforming the Cinderella Dream: From Frances Burney to Charlotte Bronte* (New Brunswick: Rutgers University Press, 1990).

[21] Wuming Zhao, "The Cinderella Narrative in Eighties' Hollywood," *Doshisha American Studies*, 39, 2003, 93-108.

[22] Ruth Sidel, *On Her Own: Growing up in the Shadow of the American Dream* (New York: Penguin, 1990).

through cross-class romance, these narratives address and satisfy women's urge for success and attainment, and also tactically channel that desire into a marriage-based uplift that pairs with the male American Dream. Moreover, regardless of whether or not the female effort-based American Dream can replace the marrying-up Cinderella narrative, the transformation of the Cinderella narrative itself or the possible merging of the two is already underway. Though, granted, the male protagonists still hold superior position in terms of social status and economic condition, the female protagonists in *Flashdance, Working Girl, Evita, You've Got Mail, Ever After, The Wedding Planner, Two Weeks Notice, Maid in Manhattan, Sweet Home Alabama, A Cinderella Story, Ella Enchanted, The Prince and Me* all demonstrate their capability, determination and other virtues required for the Dream. In this process, female characters have become more and more active and self-reliant, while the men's role in the heroines' success stories has shifted from essential to instrumental. These movies allow us to argue basing on their narratives that women can be and are men's equal, and that men and women both need help from each other. The gender relation of domination and subordination is moving toward interdependence.

Regarding popular entertainments, including film, some, like Benjamin DeMott, criticize them for not engaging class, and others, like Marcia Spires, believe they are not supposed to. Except for a very limited collection of movies concerned with such overt topics as unions and the struggle of the working class, movies, particularly romances, have been considered mostly unsuitable for serious subject matter such as class. However, as they entertain with stories of individual success and social ascension or chill with depictions of failure and social descent, movies actually deal with our understandings of issues concerning class without speaking the word. In our daily lives as well as in the realm of cultural representation, class interlocks with other categories; moreover, class problems are often translated into or replaced by gender, racial, ethnic, sexual, regional, or more individualized problems. Focusing exclusively on the category of class reduces our ability to examine different forms of social inequality. Yet neglecting class prevents us from grasping the problems caused by the capitalist system. Scrutinizing patterns in Hollywood success narratives through the lenses of class and gender can enable us to see the transformation and reconfiguration of gender and class at their intersection. Gender facilitates peculiar routes of class crossing, and class divisions can lessen or heighten the effect of gender hierarchy.

Popular culture products may not reflect social realities in the ways some of us might like; nonetheless, their representations shape some of our understanding of the realities around us. The messages that movies deliver, or rather the interpretations we make from them, are multiple and fluctuating. Though it offers some opportunities for breaking class borders, the ideology of the American Dream, by requiring us to desire mobility to a higher level, actually reinforces the structure of socioeconomic hierarchies. The Cinderella narrative can still function as a patriarchal instrument to domesticate and subordinate women, but it can also serve as a popular site for women to negotiate their roles and goals in the realization of their own dream of success.

Selected Bibliography

Anderson, Carolyn. "Diminishing Degrees of Separation: Class Mobility in Movies of the Reagan-Bush Era." *Beyond the Stars 5: Themes and Ideologies in American Popular Film*. Eds. Paul Loukides and Linda K. Fuller. Bowling Green: Bowling Green State University Popular Press, 1996. 141-63.

Baxter, Janeen et al, eds. *Reconfigurations of Class and Gender*. Stanford: Stanford University Press, 2001.

Bourdieu, Pierre. *Distinction: A Social Critique of the Judgement of Taste*. Transl. Richard Rice. Cambridge, Massachusetts: Harvard University Press, 1994 [1984].

Demott, Benjamin. *The Imperial Middle: Why Americans Can't Think Straight About Class*. New Haven: Yale University Press, 1990.

Frey, William H., Bill Abresch, and Jonathan Yeasting. *America by the Numbers: A Field Guide to the U.S. Population*. New York: The New Press, 2001.

Huang, Mei. *Transforming the Cinderella Dream: From Frances Burney to Charlotte Bronte*. New Brunswick: Rutgers University Press, 1990.

James, David E., and Rick Berg, eds. *The Hidden Foundation: Cinema and the Question of Class*. Minneapolis and London: University of Minnesota Press, 1996.

Kalra, Paul. *The American Class System: Divide and Rule*. Pleasant Hill, CA: Antenna, 1995.

Perrucci, Robert, and Earl Wysong. *The New Class Society: Goodbye American Dream?* 2nd ed. Lanham: Rowman & Littlefield Publishers, 2003.

Ross, Steven J. *Working-Class Hollywood: Silent Film and the Shaping of Class in America*. Princeton: Princeton University Press, 1998.

Sidel, Ruth. *On Her Own: Growing up in the Shadow of the American Dream*. New York: Viking, 1990.

Sklar, Robert. *Movie-Made America: A Social History of American Movies*. New York: Random House, 1975.

Wright, Erik Olin, ed. *Approaches to Class Analysis*. New York: Cambridge University Press, 2005.

Zhao, Wuming. "The Cinderella Narrative in Eighties' Hollywood." *Doshisha American Studies*, 39 (2003): 93-108.

PART III

CLASS AND INSTITUTIONS

Social Class and the Education of Adults[1]

Tom Nesbit (Simon Fraser University)

Economic, social, and cultural factors profoundly influence how we live and what we do. The societies we live in, the relationships we have and create with other people, the ways we accommodate or resist unfairness and oppression, and the ways we choose to think about these phenomena are both limited and enabled by our place in the economic structure of society. Whether we like it or not, at individual, community, and societal levels, everything we believe and everything we do is influenced by our place in an economic and social order.

Thus, education, as a major arena of social activity, operates within a set of social, cultural, and economic relations and is shaped by cultural and economic influences.[2] Education also shapes how we experience social, cultural, and economic forces. It's through education that we first come to understand the structures of society and the ways that power relations permeate them. It's also through education that we learn the strategies and approaches that help us either accommodate or resist power relations in our personal and public lives. Educational systems are thus one of the most important vehicles for *hegemony,* the process by which a society inculcates and maintains dominant ideas by portraying them as natural and normal. Because of this, groups and individuals regularly use the systems, institutions, policies, approaches, and practices of education to perpetuate positions of privilege and power. Two ways to do this are to favor technical rather than emancipatory knowledge and skills[3] and to socialize people into accepting particular economic systems and cultural traditions. In doing so, dominant groups reproduce existing patterns of social relations and reinforce unequal distribution of power and privilege. Ironically, the education system also legitimates its role in social reproduction by deflecting attention away from the process. However, education can also counter hegemony by helping people understand how they might resist and challenge social structures and by suggesting ways to do so.

Such notions are particularly appropriate to the education of adults: that aspect of educational provision that involves all education and learning after compulsory schooling. Adult education takes place in many diverse settings and caters to a wide variety of learners. Here I use the term to encompass not only the learning that takes place in the formal settings of education and training col-

---

[1] An earlier version of this paper appears in *Class Concerns: Adult Education and Social Class*, ed. Tom Nesbit (San Francisco: Jossey-Bass, 2005).

[2] See Louis Althusser, "Ideology and Ideological State Apparatuses," in *Lenin and Philosophy*, ed. Ben Brewster (London: New Left Books, 1971) 127-186; Antonio Gramsci, *Selections from the Prison Notebooks*, ed. and trans. Quintin Hoare and Geoffrey Nowell Smith (New York: International Publishers, 1971).

[3] Jürgen Habermas, *Knowledge and Human Interests* (Portsmouth: Heinemann, 1972).

leges, universities, literacy centers, private companies etc., but also in the informal settings of social movements, workplaces and community groups.

Whatever its particular focus, approach, or clientele, adult education is an
essentially social and political endeavor. The struggles for power – who has it,
how they use it, and in whose interests – lie at the heart of the adult education
enterprise.[4] Concerned with identity and personal and social change, adult education seeks to provide the knowledge, skills, and attitudes for people to engage
more fully in their individual and social worlds. And it's in the political realm,
encompassing both the individual and the social, that the effects of class are
most clearly visible.

These social and political relations establish the environments for adult
education. As Habermas also indicated, education is a moral and political endeavor as much as it is a technical practice, and it is thus affected by its role in
maintaining or challenging the social order. Do educational policies and practices reproduce existing relations of dominance and oppression? Alternatively,
do they contribute to social as well as personal change? Answering such questions involves exploring the extent to which adult education intersects with notions of class and the related demands of capitalist ideology.

In other words, the relationships between class and educational policies and
practices can be made visible by examining the approaches of adult education.
In this chapter, I outline these various relationships. I first explore how ideas
about class inform educational practices in general. Next, in focusing specifically on discussions of class in adult education, I discuss several arenas of adult
education practice and show how they inform and are informed by notions of
class. Finally, I suggest several reasons for a continued attention to class and
adult education.

Class and Education

Education is generally intended to inculcate dominant values, not confront them.
Because educational institutions are generally a middle-class domain, their policies and practices are weighted strongly in favor of middle-class values.[5] So
capitalist societies, in which class operates as the primary structuring of social
inequality, usually ignore or bury class perspectives in their educational institutions. As such, many adult educators are uncertain about how their work reflects
underlying political structures, let alone economic systems. Observing the effects of power and privilege is far easier than determining their causes. Yet a
number of studies explore how education reproduces existing patterns of power.
Economists Samuel Bowles and Herb Gintis demonstrated how educational sys-

---

[4] Ronald M. Cervero, Arthur L. Wilson, and Associates, *Power in Practice* (San Francisco: Jossey-
Bass, 2001).
[5] Michael W. Apple, *Education and Power* (London: Routledge, 1995).

tems are part of a system of broader capitalist class relations.[6] Their correspondence theory explains how, in general, schools reproduce the social relations that capitalist production requires. As Bowles and Gintis describe, capital requires two things: workers of specific types and relative social stability and ideological acceptance of class relations. The capitalist class thus has a broadly shared set of interests pertaining to educational systems and the capacity to promote such interests.

Some find the correspondence theory too mechanistic or reductive; it allows little agency for those involved. One less-deterministic approach came from Pierre Bourdieu who suggested that education serves the interests of the privileged by structuring learners' access to and uses of various forms of social and cultural capital.[7] Others have introduced notions of struggle and resistance into this process. Most notably, Paul Willis showed how several working-class teenage lads consciously resisted and rebelled against school and classroom authority.[8] Tellingly, however, this resistance worked better within school than outside it: when the lads left school, they remained unable to find anything but unskilled and unstimulating jobs. The work of Peter McLaren and Michael Apple also shows how individuals can resist and contest social and cultural oppression in educational settings.[9] They document the complex relationships between cultural reproduction and economic reproduction and explore how class interrelates with the dynamics of race and gender in education.

All these studies indicate the essential role of education in promoting and maintaining the social relations required for capitalist production. Further, they suggest that we can fully understand education only as part of a broader capitalist class system. Although we now recognize that the relationships between educational practices and political structures are much more complex than correspondence theory suggests, adult educators who work in such areas as Adult Basic Education, literacy, vocational education, and the pernicious welfare-to-work programs will recognize how often their work, the policies about it, and the textbooks and curricula they use are still much more closely tied to employers' needs than to their adult or working-class students' interests.[10]

---

[6] Samuel Bowles and Herbert Gintis, *Schooling in Capitalist America* (New York: Basic Books, 1976).

[7] Pierre Bourdieu and Jean Claude Passeron, *Reproduction in Education, Society, and Culture* (Thousand Oaks, CA: Sage, 1977).

[8] Paul Willis, *Learning to Labour* (Farnborough, England: Saxon House, 1977).

[9] Peter L. McLaren, *Critical Pedagogy and Predatory Culture* (New York: Routledge, 1995), and Michael W. Apple, *Cultural Politics and Education* (New York: Teachers College Press, 1996).

[10] Deborah D'Amico, "Race, Class, Gender, and Sexual Orientation in Adult Literacy: Power, Pedagogy, and Programs," in John Comings, Barbara Garner, and Christine Smith (eds.), *Review of Adult Learning and Literacy,* vol 4: *Connecting Research, Policy, and Practice,* (Hillsdale, NJ: Erlbaum, 2004) 17-69. Joe L. Kincheloe, *How Do We Tell the Workers? The Socioeconomic Foundations of Work and Vocational Education* (Boulder, CO: Westview Press, 1999). Mike Rose, *Lives on the Boundary: The Struggles and Achievements of America's Underprepared* (New York: Free Press, 1989).

Focusing on Adult Education

Together with its K–12 counterpart, adult education is now firmly established as central to the smooth functioning of economic systems and societies. As such concepts as lifelong learning and the knowledge society gain prominence, education and training become key vehicles for preparing people to be adaptable to economic changes in society. Even though the aim of adult education is generally to ameliorate the social disadvantages that class and background produce, nowadays adult education often serves merely to exacerbate those disadvantages.

Ironically, adult education scholars have left the study of social class and its effects relatively under-explored, especially in North America. For example, although ideas of class clearly inform several of the contributions to the two most recent editions of the major reference handbook of the field, overall, the handbooks treat the topic only tangentially.[11] Further, when we compare studies of class with the related analytic vectors of gender and race, we again see that scholars do not explore class so rigorously. Recent searches of the major American educational database (ERIC) combining the descriptors *adult education* with *gender, race,* and *social class* produce totals of 533, 324, and 86 hits, respectively. Assuming that the number of references roughly correlates with researchers' interests, why do researchers so significantly less acknowledge class than its counterparts? Why is class so underrepresented in social and educational theory? Why is class ignored as the elephant in the room?[12]

Most of the North American studies referenced in the ERIC database focus on the consequences or experiences of class and explore such issues as the participation, access, and attainment of different groups. In documenting how social class affects participation in adult education programs, those studies consistently underscore how far social class remains a key determinant of adult participation in organized learning. To give just one recent example, Sargent and Aldridge indicate that upper- or middle-class adults are twice as likely to engage in some sort of learning activity than are those from the working class.[13]

However, although such studies detail that class is a major factor affecting adult education participation, most do not really explore how class works. From a conceptual perspective, they add little to Jack London's classic study which explored the important contribution that adult education makes to larger society, specifically for those deemed "less educated and less skilled."[14] London and his

---

[11] Arthur L. Wilson and Elisabeth R. Hayes, (eds.) *Handbook of Adult and Continuing Education* (New Edition) (San Francisco: Jossey-Bass, 2001); Sharan B. Merriam and Phyllis M. Cunningham, (eds.) *Handbook of Adult and Continuing Education* (San Francisco: Jossey-Bass, 1989).

[12] bell hooks, *Where We Stand: Class Matters* (New York: Routledge, 2000).

[13] Naomi Sargent and Fiona Aldridge, *Adult Learning and Social Division* (Leicester, England: National Institute of Adult Continuing Education, 2002).

[14] Jack London, Robert Wenkert, and Warren O. Hagstrom, *Adult Education and Social Class* (Berkeley: University of California, Berkeley Survey Research Center, 1963).

colleagues found a strong connection between social class and people's abilities to prosper in a rapidly changing world. Class not only affected participation in adult education activities but was also closely related to such other facets of social life as jobs, vocations, and leisure pursuits. Anticipating the subsequent debates about lifelong learning, London's report called for adult education and training to "become a continuing part of everyone's life," providing "both education for work and education for leisure."[15] Perhaps more seriously, the majority of the studies listed in the ERIC database do little to further class awareness or address what Allman, McLaren and Rikowski describe as a chasm between class as social inequality and class as a constitutive element of the world of struggle.[16]

This concentration on the interactions between adult education and class rather than on any underlying mechanisms is perhaps understandable. Individuals tend to internalize the conflicts within hierarchical systems, especially those individuals without much power. Also, people usually closely experience class at the same time as other, more recognizable forms of oppression. These factors, when combined with the scarcity of class scrutiny, ensure that people do not always have readily available concepts to identify – let alone analyze – the class aspects of their experiences. So most people, scholars included, continue to overlook class in their everyday lives and theoretical analyses.

Class can also be difficult to discern; we can usually only examine it through its consequences or outcomes. And, as it's not easy to identify or operationalize on an individual level, it's much better suited to macro- rather than micro-analyses. Even when it's acknowledged, class still tends to be regarded as an individual characteristic or an entity rather than a constituent social relationship. Thankfully, educational systems are so central to the functioning of advanced industrial societies that they can provide fertile ground for the investigation and analysis of class. If one looks closely, class can be seen at work in most aspects of adult education.

As might be expected, sophisticated explorations of class and adult education are more readily found outside the USA. Several authors provide rich empirical and theoretical examinations of how adult education practices are linked to social class and the increasingly globalized nature of capitalism.[17] To give a

---

[15] Ibid, 148, 153.

[16] Paula Allman, Peter L. McLaren, and Glenn Rikowski, "After the Box People: The Labour-Capital Relation as Class Constitution and its Consequences for Marxist Educational Theory and Human Resistance," in *Capitalists and Conquerors,* ed. Peter L. McLaren (Lanham MD: Rowman and Littlefield, 2005), 135-165.

[17] See for example Paula Allman, *Critical Education against Global Capitalism* (New York: Bergin & Garvey, 2001). Michael Collins, *Critical Crosscurrents in Education* (Malabar, FL: Krieger, 1998). Nelly P. Stromquist, *Literacy for Citizenship* (Albany, NY: SUNY Press, 1997); Jane Thompson, *Women, Class and Education* (New York: Routledge, 2000); Shirley Walters, (ed.) *Globalization, Adult Education and Training* (London: Zed Books, 1997); Michael R. Welton (ed.) *In Defense of the*

flavor of such work, I now explore how others have addressed issues of class in several different arenas of adult education practice: approaches to learning and teaching, adult education's role in social movements, and the related fields of higher education and working-class studies.

Learning and Teaching

A distinguishing feature of adult education is its strong emphasis on learning. In his study of workers learning computing, Peter Sawchuk[18] provides one of the best recent analyses of the inter-relation of class and learning. Sawchuk identifies a distinctive working-class learning style that operates independently of formal training and centers around informal workplace and community networks. This learning style is collective, mutual, and solidaristic: people exchange knowledge and skills, hardware and software and they use each other's differences, which then become group resources. And so they develop an expanding learning network: a powerful working-class resource that stands opposed to the trajectory of dominant forms of workplace and institutionalized education that individualize and commodify learning. Although most research on adult education and class focuses on how working-class people are excluded and help to exclude themselves from formal education, Sawchuk's research shows that working-class adults bring rich cultural resources to their learning.

How such learning is (or is not) acknowledged is a central concern of pedagogical approaches in adult education. It's now commonly understood that teaching approaches influence learners' attitudes towards education, learning, themselves, and society at large. So, just as teaching can disguise and obfuscate, it can also promote a greater understanding of class through the way it is conducted. Two components are particularly useful here. The first is *praxis* – the cycle of critical reflection and practice that connects our daily activities with broader theoretical analyses. For example, a class perspective on teaching considers its dominant approaches as activities for socialization and social reproduction. Acknowledging this can aid the exploration of the relationships between ideology, power, culture, and knowledge and the asking of such questions as what counts as knowledge and knowing? How is such knowledge produced and distributed? Do certain forms legitimate one set of interests above others? Whose interests get downplayed or ignored? How might alternate forms be considered?

Second, through the use of such questions, teaching can extend learners' knowledge and experience into social critique. Regardless of course or program, most curricula are alien to working class adult learners: usually divorced from

---

Lifeworld: Critical Perspectives on Adult Learning (Albany, NY: SUNY Press, 1995); Frank Youngman, *The Political Economy of Adult Education* (London: Zed Books, 2000).

[18] Peter H. Sawchuk, *Adult Learning and Technology in Working-class Life* (New York: Cambridge University Press, 2003).

any social and historical context, foreign to their experiences and culture, and imposed upon them. Pedagogy that ignores learners' experiences and culture is often a form of ideological imposition that reflects a particular balance of political and social power. So, although "starting where the students are" is a familiar adult education approach, it requires far more than simple pedagogic devices or mere lip service.

A class perspective on teaching never unquestioningly endorses dominant approaches to teaching but regards the capacity to unsettle and irritate as important. Instead of ironing out complexity, it celebrates it, problematizes it, and makes it critical. So, a class perspective on teaching regards learners' knowledge and experience and their development of critical awareness as key parts of the curriculum itself. One of the leading adult educators who has written about class and teaching is Frank Youngman, whose *Adult Education and Socialist Pedagogy* is one of the best attempts in English to consider adult education from a Marxist perspective – specifically that it should be analyzed within its economic and political context. [19] For Youngman, the aims of a socialist pedagogy should be "to challenge the ideology and culture of capitalism and create a counter-hegemony and to develop the general knowledge and technical expertise necessary to reorganize production and society in a fully democratic way."[20]

Social Movements

Adult education deliberately links the personal with the social. A class perspective reminds us that lasting social change comes about through people acting together. So, learning about previous battles for social justice can provide resources and hope to those involved in current struggles. Many others have fought for adult education to play a role in class struggles and the broader movements for social change. Particularly, the biographies of such educators as Myles Horton, Moses Coady, bell hooks, and Paulo Freire all offer connections to a wider set of ideas about adult education for social change.[21] More theoretical discussions of the role of adult learning and education in social movements are provided by John Holst and Griff Foley.[22] Basing their work on the ideas of Freire, Gramsci, and Marx, they each explore the idea that radical adult educators can help build civil society through social movements. Two aspects of their work are particularly important to an appreciation of adult learning. First, "learning in such situations is tacit, embedded in action and often not recognized

---

[19] Frank Youngman, *Adult Education and Socialist Pedagogy* (London: Croom Helm, 1986).

[20] Ibid, 197.

[21] Myles Horton with Judith Kohl and Herbert Kohl, *The Long Haul* (New York: Doubleday, 1990). Michael R. Welton, *Little Mosie from the Margaree* (Toronto: Thompson Educational, 2001); bell hooks, *Where We Stand: Class Matters* (New York: Routledge, 2000); Moacir Gadotti, *Reading Paulo Freire: His Life and Work,* transl. J. Milton, (Albany: State University of New York Press, 1994).

[22] John D. Holst, *Social Movements, Civil Society, and Radical Adult Education* (New York: Bergin & Garvey, 2002). Griff Foley, *Learning in Social Action* (London: Zed Books, 1999).

as learning."[23] Second, the notion of learning in and through struggle. Foley again: "people's every day experience reproduces ways of thinking and acting support which support the, often oppressive, status quo, but [can also] enable people to critique and challenge the existing order."[24]

One key social movement that has clearly adopted an educational perspective informed by class is that of the labor movement. Most American histories tend to ignore or downplay the part played by working people and histories of adult education are no exception.[25] One exception is Fred Schied's exploration of the radical working-class traditions in Nineteenth Century Chicago and the role that immigrant German socialists played in creating the labor movement there.[26] Schied affirms how the educational forms and approaches that took place in workers' clubs, reading rooms and debating societies were not separate activities but an integral (albeit transitory and informal) part of a broader radical working-class culture that had its own goals and traditions. Non-formal educational institutions have also occasionally tapped into these resources. Probably the best-known example of this in the USA is the Highlander Education and Research Center in Tennessee where Myles Horton and his colleagues taught working-class people to analyze their experiences critically.[27] The Highlander pedagogy was firmly based on participants' needs, interests, and principally working-class culture. Other useful accounts of adult educators developing with working-class learning include Richard Altenbaugh's description of the American labor colleges of the 1920s and 1930s and the once extensive but now all-but-forgotten Jefferson School of Social Science, which flourished in New York City during the 1940s and early 1950s.[28]

Higher Education and Working-Class Studies

Although higher education has not normally been considered part of the adult education enterprise, universities and colleges are increasingly recognizing that they need to pay more attention to and accommodate adult and other "non-traditional" learners. Several studies provide analyses of how universities treat adult learners from different class backgrounds and how working-class students

---

[23] Foley, 3.

[24] Ibid., 3-4.

[25] Cyril O. Houle *The Literature of Adult Education* (San Francisco: Jossey-Bass, 1992); Malcolm S. Knowles, *A History of the Adult Education Movement in the United States* (2nd ed.) (Malabar, FL: Krieger, 1977); M. S. Welton, "Historical Inquiry," in Leona M. English (ed.) *International Encyclopedia of Adult Education* (New York: Palgrave Macmillan, 2005) 283-286..

[26] Fred M. Schied, *Learning in Social Context* (DeKalb, IL: LEPS Press, 1993).

[27] Myles Horton and Paulo Freire, *We Make the Road by Walking: Conversations on Education and Social Change* (Philadelphia: Temple University Press, 1990).

[28] Richard J. Altenbaugh, *Education for Struggle: American Labor Colleges of the 1920s and 1930s* (Philadelphia: Temple University Press, 1990); Marvin E. Gettleman, "'No Varsity Teams': New York's Jefferson School of Social Science, 1943–1956," *Science & Society, 66* :3, 2002, 336–359.

experience university-level education.[29] They also explore how curricula and pedagogy in several disciplines reflect class-based interests,[30] how to challenge the status quo and democratize classroom practices,[31] and how academic institutions might change to better accommodate the needs and interests of working-class and adult learners.[32]

The emergent field of working-class studies has also reinvigorated discussion of the intersections of class, adult learning, and institutional practices in North America.[33] Acknowledging that working-class learners now constitute a significant proportion of students enrolled in institutions of higher education, this body of work incorporates a sensitivity to students' working-class roots while suggesting curricular and pedagogic innovations informed by an awareness of class culture. Several recently published books detail the travails of academics from working-class backgrounds.[34] All contain powerful autobiographical and analytic essays that address the personal, professional, and ideological issues in the experiences of working-class teachers and students in higher education. Although it will come as no great shock to most university-based adult educators, "many current higher education practices [still] pose barriers to [adult] participation which include a lack of flexibility in calendar and scheduling, academic content, modes of instruction and availability of learning services."[35]

The studies mentioned above all provide rich theoretical analyses on the relationships between class and various aspects of the education of adults. For example, many explore the notion that working-class learners who enter formal educational environments experience what Sennett and Cobb call *status incongruity*.[36] Here, the differences between the culture and language of students' working-class backgrounds and the academic environments they enter can create discomfort and uncertainty. Working-class learners can become unsure of their

---

[29] Vivyan C. Adair and Sandra L. Dahlberg (eds.) *Reclaiming Class: Women, Poverty, and the Promise of Higher Education in America* (Philadelphia: Temple University Press, 2003); Michelle M. Tokarczyk, "Promises to Keep: Working-class Students and Higher Education" in *What's Class Got to Do with It?*, ed. Michael Zweig (Ithaca: Cornell University Press, 2004), 161-167.

[30] Eric Margolis (ed.), *The Hidden Curriculum in Higher Education* (New York: Routledge, 2001).

[31] Ira Shor, *When Students Have Power* (Chicago: University of Chicago Press, 1996).

[32] Mike Rose, *Lives on the Boundary: The Struggles and Achievements of America's Underprepared* (New York: Free Press, 1989).

[33] Sherry L. Linkon (ed.), *Teaching Working Class* (Amherst: University of Massachusetts Press, 1999); Janet Zandy (ed.) *What We Hold in Common: An Introduction to Working-class Studies* (New York: Feminist Press at CUNY, 2001).

[34] C. L. Barney Dews and Carolyn L. Law (eds.) *This Fine Place So Far from Home: Voices of Academics from the Working Class* (Philadelphia: Temple University Press, 1995); Jake Ryan and Charles Sackrey, *Strangers in Paradise: Academics from the Working Class* (Boston: South End Press, 1984); Michelle M. Tokarczyk and Elizabeth A. Fay, *Working-class Women in the Academy: Laborers in the Knowledge Factory* (Amherst: University of Massachusetts Press, 1993).

[35] Commission for a Nation of Lifelong Learners, *A Nation Learning: Vision for the Twenty-First century* (Albany, NY: Regents College, 1997) 3.

[36] Richard Sennett and Jonathan Cobb, *The Hidden Injuries of Class* (New York: Vintage, 1972).

own identity, feel out of place and marginalized, and experience what Ryan and Sackrey tellingly call "the sense of being nowhere at home."[37] Such work also dispels the myth that the working-class pursuit of adult and higher education is always a rejection of or an escape from one's culture and the often harsh and demeaning living and working conditions that shape it. Neither is it, as some maintain, an accommodation to middle-class values or a capitulation to bourgeois cultural hegemony. Rather, it represents for many a compelling act of resistance against the repression of a system that damages the spirit as well as the body. Although for too many working-class learners, education is still "about failure; about being 'found out,'"[38] it can also provide opportunities for upward mobility and a greater understanding of and interaction with one's self, community and society.[39] Because much of working-class life and culture is already marked by struggle anyway, many working-class learners view their education as a continuance of their personal and collective struggles for a better world – not just for themselves but often for everyone else as well.

Finally, such attention to class in adult education offers two other benefits. First, it helps "subvert the tendency to focus only on the thoughts, attitudes, and experiences of those who are materially privileged." [40] Second, it benefits learners. As Linkon claims, "the more we can recognize and understand working-class culture, the more clearly we can recognize the strengths of our working-class students and, more important, the better our chances of engaging and inspiring them."[41]

The Importance of a Class Perspective

Class can mean different things to different people: a theoretical device for analyzing the social world; shared social conditions; or a set of particular orientations, beliefs, and life practices. Popular understandings of class still describe it in terms of jobs, income, wealth, the lifestyles that people can buy, or the power that accrues from ownership. Yet, class is less a possession than a dynamic: a relationship between different people and groups divided along axes of power and privilege. So class differences play out in power relations. And adult education as conventionally constituted plays a critical role in forming and mediating these relations: providing opportunities for personal mobility while legitimating social inequality. Thus, adopting a class perspective on adult education does two things: it draws clear links between educational institutions, the world of work, and the economic system that underpins them; and it highlights how educational

---

[37] Ryan and Sackrey, 119.
[38] Diane Reay, "Finding or Losing Yourself? Working-class Relationships to Education," *Journal of Education Policy,* 16:4, 2001, 333–346.
[39] Tokarczyk, "Promises," 161-167.
[40] hooks, 185.
[41] Linkon, 6.

institutions function to maintain and inculcate societal ideology and values.

Many adult educators find such a perspective overwhelming and off-putting. Others question the extent to which adult educators should critique dominant social systems and the prevailing capitalist system. Yet the many and varied ways that class shapes adult education continue to demand our attention. First, as many have cogently argued, adult education is a function of the state and is therefore regulated according to certain economic, political, and cultural interests and pressures. Second, educational institutions are situated in historical and social contexts that suggest that adult education is intimately linked with maintaining particular cultural and social arrangements. Capitalist societies structure these arrangements around inequalities, because capitalism foundationally depends on a labor force of differing levels of skill. Educational institutions, by creating and maintaining a steady supply of workers with these differing levels, ensure that existing and future workforces can adapt to changes in investment, production, and trade circumstances. They do this through complicated systems involving financing, credentialing, selection criteria, curricula, pedagogies, cognitive classification, rewards, and assessment. Thus, by transmitting, sustaining, and legitimizing particular systems of structured inequality, educational systems uphold the characteristics of a particular order of social relations.

Third, adult educators should closely consider class because of how it plays out in everyday educational situations and practices. For example, consider teaching: what educators teach and how they teach are choices made from a wider universe of knowledge and values. Such choices always benefit and privilege some while ignoring, downplaying, or deprivileging others. Curricular and pedagogical choices reflect different ways of understanding and responding to social relations. Fourth, political choices permeate the adult education profession itself, leading to struggles over autonomy, respect, wages, job security, and evaluation. Educational practices reflect the ways people and societies think about the transmission of ideologies and cultures. Must we assume that adult educators are always neutral, objective, and benevolent agents of the state? Is their job only to impart basic information necessary for learners to survive and prosper within an economic system? Must it always support a particular social order? Or are there alternative ways to think and behave? For educators with a commitment to social class, such questions raise several key issues: How do they negotiate or internalize dominant ideologies and relations of ruling? How might alternative ones be developed? How can marginalized people, silenced by social, economic, and cultural relations of power, recover their voices and the right to be heard? What part can education and educators play in that process?

Conclusion

Many have argued that the idea of class has outlived its usefulness. The complexities of modern society have effaced the antagonisms that Marx described;

the word *class* itself has little or no value; the indicators are unreliable.[42] In spite of this, "the fiction that class has ceased to exist is being spread in a world in which inequality has never been greater."[43] Examining the intersections of class and adult education can alert us to the unexamined patterns of behavior through which society produces and reproduces social classes in the dynamics between educational activities and the wider cultural politics of societies. It can also expose to thoughtful scrutiny the superficiality of a variety of currently prescribed educational reforms: the individualizing of educational opportunities, increased commercial involvement determining educational goals, privatization of schools and colleges, a return to so-called basics, the streaming of learners of all ages into cultural or functional literacies or core competencies, and the increasing pressures to work harder and longer.

To be truly effective, adult educators must provide their students with the tools necessary to attain a critical understanding of the social and economic order. I have argued that this must include incorporating class perspectives into adult education. As educators, they should also resist and challenge (and help others to do so) what Allman calls the postmodern condition: "skepticism, uncertainty, fragmentation, nihilism, and incoherence."[44] This is no easy task. The totality of capitalism renders it difficult to challenge. However, it also underscores the necessity of doing so if we want to create a fairer and safer world built on more than economic values.

Nowadays people often regard approaches that focus on class and other forms of oppression as misguided or even sinister. Instead, some encourage us to accept limited and partial integrations into and accommodations to social orders based on systemic inequalities. Yet we are not bystanders to political contexts but vital and essential members of them. Educators of adults have a responsibility to raise important and challenging questions and to build upon their students' lived experiences about how inequalities play out in communities, lives and workplaces. They must also challenge the current directions that capitalist education is taking and resist all attempts to confine adult education to the production and maintenance of human capital. Above all they must reassert a class-based approach to adult education that is grounded in the struggles of those who seek to build a fairer, safer and more democratic society for all.

---

[42] Peter Calvert, *The Concept of Class: An Historical Introduction* (London: Hutchinson, 1982).

[43] Jeremy Seabrook, *The No-nonsense Guide to Class, Caste and Hierarchies* (Oxford: New Internationalist Publications, 2002) 8.

[44] Paula Allman, *Critical Education against Global Capitalism. Karl Marx and Revolutionary Critical Education* (New York: Bergin & Garvey, 2001) 209.

Selected Bibliography

Adair, Vivyan C. and Sandra Dahlberg, eds. *Reclaiming Class: Women, Poverty, and the Promise of Higher Education in America.* Philadelphia: Temple University Press, 2003.

Allman, Paula. *Critical Education Against Global Capitalism. Karl Marx and Revolutionary Critical Education.* New York: Bergin & Garvey, 2001.

Allman, Paula, Peter L. McLaren, and Glenn Rikowski. "After the Box People: The Labour-capital Relation as Class Constitution and its Consequences for Marxist Educational Theory and Human Resistance." *Capitalists and Conquerors.* Ed. Peter McLaren. Lanham MD: Rowman and Littlefield, 2003. 135-165

Altenbaugh, Richard. J. *Education for Struggle: American Labor Colleges of the 1920s and 1930s.* Philadelphia: Temple University Press, 1990.

Althusser, Louis. "Ideology and Ideological State Apparatuses." *Lenin and Philosophy.* Ed. B. Brewster.London: New Left Books, 1971. 127-186

Apple, Michael. W. *Cultural Politics and Education.* New York: Teachers College Press, 1996.

Apple, Michael W. *Education and Power.* London: Routledge, 1995.

Bourdieu, Pierre and Jean Claude Passeron. *Reproduction in Education, Society, and Culture.* Thousand Oaks, CA.: Sage, 1977.

Samuel Bowles and Herbert Gintis. *Schooling in Capitalist America.* New York: Basic Books, 1976.

Calvert, Peter. *The Concept of Class: An Historical Introduction.* London: Hutchinson, 1982.

Cervero, Ronald M., Wilson, A. L. and Associates. *Power in Practice.* San Francisco: Jossey-Bass, 2001.

Collins, Michael. *Critical Crosscurrents in Education.* Malabar, FL: Krieger, 1998.

Commission for a Nation of Lifelong Learners. *A Nation Learning: Vision for the Twenty-First Century.* Albany, N.Y.: Regents College, 1997.

D'Amico, Deborah. "Race, Class, Gender, and Sexual Orientation in Adult Literacy: Power, Pedagogy, and Programs." *Review of Adult Learning and Literacy: Connecting Research, Policy, and Practice* 4 (2004). Eds. J. Comings, B. Garner, and C. Smith Hillsdale, N.J.: Erlbaum, 2004. 17-69.

Dews, C. L. Barney, and Carolyn Leste Law, eds. *This Fine Place So Far from Home: Voices of Academics from the Working Class.* Philadelphia: Temple University Press, 1995.

Foley, Griff. *Learning in Social Action.* London: Zed Books, 1999.

Gadotti, M. *Reading Paulo Freire: His Life and Work.* Trans. J. Milton. Albany: State University of New York Press, 1994.

Gettleman, Marvin. E. "'No Varsity Teams': New York's Jefferson School of Social Science, 1943–1956." *Science & Society,* 66.3 (2002): 336–359.

Gramsci, Antonio. *Selections from the Prison Notebooks.* Trans. and ed. Quintin Hoare and Geoffrey Nowell-Smith. New York: International, 1971.

Habermas, Jürgen. *Knowledge and Human Interests.* Portsmouth, N.H.: Heinemann, 1972.

Holst, J. D. *Social Movements, Civil Society, and Radical Adult Education.* New York: Bergin & Garvey, 2002.

hooks, bell. *Where We Stand: Class Matters.* New York: Routledge, 2000.

Horton, Myles and Paulo Freire. *We Make the Road by Walking: Conversations on Education and Social Change.* Philadelphia: Temple University Press, 1990.

Horton, Myles, with Judith Kohl and Herbert Kohl. *The Long Haul.* New York: Doubleday, 1990.

Houle, Cyril. O. *The Literature of Adult Education.* San Francisco: Jossey-Bass, 1992.

Kincheloe, Joe. L. *How Do We Tell the Workers? The Socioeconomic Foundations of Work and Vocational Education.* Boulder, Colo.: Westview Press, 1999.

Knowles, Malcolm. S. *A History of the Adult Education Movement in the United States* (2nd ed.). Malabar, FL: Krieger, 1977.

Linkon, Sherry. L., ed. *Teaching Working Class.* Amherst: University of Massachusetts Press, 1999.

London, Jack, Robert Wenkert, and Warren O. Hagstrom. *Adult Education and Social Class.* Berkeley: University of California, Berkeley Survey Research Center, 1963.

Margolis, Eric, ed. *The Hidden Curriculum in Higher Education.* New York: Routledge, 2001.

McLaren, Peter L. *Critical Pedagogy and Predatory Culture.* New York: Routledge, 1995.

Merriam, S. B., and Cunningham, P. M., eds. *Handbook of Adult and Continuing Education.* San Francisco: Jossey-Bass, 1989.

Nesbit, Tom, ed. *Class Concerns: Adult Education and Social Class.* San Francisco: Jossey-Bass, 2005.

Reay, Diane. "Finding or Losing Yourself? Working-Class Relationships to Education." *Journal of Education Policy* 16.4 (2001): 333–346.

Rose, Mike. *Lives on the Boundary: The Struggles and Achievements of America's Underprepared.* New York: Free Press, 1989.

Ryan, Jake, and Charles Sackrey, eds. *Strangers in Paradise: Academics from the Working Class.* Boston: South End Press, 1984.

Sargent, Naomi and Fiona Aldridge. *Adult Learning and Social Division.* Leicester, England: National Institute of Adult Continuing Education, 2002.

Sawchuk, Peter. H. *Adult Learning and Technology in Working-Class Life.* New York: Cambridge University Press, 2003.

Schied, Fred M. *Learning in Social Context*. DeKalb, IL: LEPS Press, 1993.
    Seabrook, Jeremy. *The No-Nonsense Guide to Class, Caste and Hierarchies*. Oxford: New Internationalist Publications, 2002.
Sennett, Richard, and Jonathan Cobb. *The Hidden Injuries of Class*. New York: Vintage, 1972.
Shor, Ira. *When Students Have Power*. Chicago: University of Chicago Press, 1996.
Stromquist, Nelly. P. *Literacy for Citizenship*. Albany, NY: SUNY Press, 1997.
Thompson, Jane. *Women, Class and Education*. New York: Routledge, 2000.
Tokarczyk, Michelle. M. "Promises to Keep: Working-Class Students and Higher Education." *What's Class Got to Do with It?* Ed. M. Zweig. Ithaca: Cornell University Press, 2004. 161-167.
Tokarczyk, Michelle. M. and Elizabeth A. Fay, eds. *Working-Class Women in the Academy: Laborers in the Knowledge Factory*. Amherst: University of Massachusetts Press, 1993.
Walters, Shirley, ed. *Globalization, Adult Education and Training*. London: Zed Books, 1997.
Welton, Michael. R., ed. *In Defense of the Lifeworld: Critical Perspectives on Adult Learning*. Albany, NY: SUNY Press, 1995.
___. *Little Mosie from the Margaree*. Toronto: Thompson Educational, 2001.
___."Historical Inquiry." *International Encyclopedia of Adult Education*. Ed. Leona M. English. New York: Palgrave Macmillan, 2005. 283-286
Willis, Paul E. *Learning to Labour*. Farnborough, England: Saxon House, 1977.
Wilson, Arthur. L., and Elisabeth R Hayes, eds. *Handbook of Adult and Continuing Education* (new edition). San Francisco: Jossey-Bass, 2001.
Youngman, Frank. *Adult Education and Socialist Pedagogy*. London: Croom Helm, 1986.
Youngman, Frank. *The Political Economy of Adult Education*. London: Zed Books, 2000.
Zandy, Janet, ed. *What We Hold in Common: An Introduction to Working-class Studies*. New York: Feminist Press at CUNY, 2001.

Achieving Social Class Diversity Throughout the Workforce: A Case Study of TIAA-CREF

Ken Oldfield (University of Illinois, Springfield)

Shaw's Challenge

In his thought-provoking *The Intelligent Woman's Guide to Socialism and Capitalism*, Shaw proposes that society be reformed so everyone earns the same annual income. While his idea is unlikely to receive a serious hearing in America anytime soon, at one point Shaw writes profoundly and eloquently about the virtues of equality and the pernicious effects of unearned standing. He explains,

> Between persons of equal income there is no social distinction except the distinction of merit. Money is nothing: character, conduct, and capacity are everything. Instead of all the workers being leveled down to low wage standards and all the rich leveled up to fashionable income standards, everybody under a system of equal incomes would find her and his own natural level. There would be great people and ordinary people and little people: but the great would always be those who had done great things, and never the idiots whose mothers had spoiled them and whose fathers had left them a hundred thousand a year; and the little would be persons of small minds and mean characters, and not poor persons who had never had a chance. That is why idiots are always in favor of inequality of income (their only chance of eminence), and the really great in favor of equality.[1]

Not that long ago, women were prohibited from voting, serving on juries, and attending medical school, to name only a few conspicuous insults to our nation's equal protection ideals. Fortunately, today, the press extensively covers news about the struggle for women's equality, ranging from near enactment of the Equal Rights Amendment, to passage of "equal pay for equal work" laws, to Title IX, to insisting we use male and female pronouns in everyday conversations and writings. In short, the mainstream media have become far better attuned to the sexual chauvinism prevalent in our culture. There is widespread concern for gender equity. Similarly, our mainstream culture has opened itself to examining the harmful effects of racism. For instance, television shows about slavery, segregated schools, and black voting patterns are now commonplace. February is Black History Month. Countless other groups have stepped forward demanding equal treatment under law, ranging from the physically challenged, to the elderly, to the lesbian, bisexual, gay and transgender community, to name only a few examples.

---

[1] George Bernard Shaw, *The Intelligent Woman's Guide to Socialism and Capitalism* (London: Constable and Company LTD, 1928) 71.

Interestingly, our mainstream culture still does not apply similar concerns and standards of fairness to contrast the inherent advantages and disadvantages of people's family socioeconomic backgrounds. As hooks says, "Class is the elephant in the room – as a nation we are afraid to have a dialogue about class."[2] Consider, for example, that rarely does anyone in the mainstream media challenge the unfairness intrinsic to, say, two white American females born into families of highly different socioeconomic circumstances. The two daughters' race and gender are mentioned here only to avoid any confounding considerations that might, for now, distract us from the point. Perhaps one girl's parents are both neurosurgeons and the other girl's parent is a single mother, with an eighth grade education, working at a fast food restaurant, earning minimum wage, and having no health benefits.

If it were possible, and all other things being equal, certainly most people, if they could, would choose the neurosurgeons as their parents. Obviously, we cannot select our mother and father any more than we can choose our race or gender. Still, today, few Americans ever ponder whether a child born to a fast food worker in the lower class is *really* the equal of a child born to two neuro- surgeons. While the popular culture constantly discusses how, for instance, ra- cism and sexism limit people's opportunities, even shock announcers rarely, if ever, consider whether two people born into grossly unequal socioeconomic cir- cumstances really have similar chances at the good life.

Much like Shaw, our national ideology says accomplishment should only derive from merit. It is assumed we should all earn our way by being the best- qualified candidate for a job, a university course of study, and so forth. Ironi- cally, despite what we say about such matters, most Americans want to give their children a home environment and life experiences that will assure them as big an advantage as possible over all future competitors. This preoccupation with enabling their kids includes, hopefully, leaving them a substantial inheri- tance. Of course, few of us weigh the contradiction between meritocracy and giving children as big a head start as possible. Nor do most parents fear that a large financial bequest will stifle their children's will-to-succeed, although they know it will kill the motivation of the recipient if given as welfare to "those lazy undesirables," the ne'er-do-wells who want something for nothing. Mythologies can get confusing when you really start thinking about them.

Another essential ingredient of the American mythology involves taking a lottery attitude toward significant upward social mobility. Consider how news- paper advertisements for state lotteries show smiling people who have won large prizes. The ads never show those who have lost large sums playing the lot- tery, nor do they cite the odds of winning the various amounts listed. Mean-

---

[2] Gary Younge, quoting hooks, in "America is a Class Act," *Guardian* (January 27, 2003) http://www.guardian.co.uk/comment/story/0,3604,882935,00.html. Also, see bell hooks, *Where We Stand: Class Matters* (New York: Routledge, 2000).

while, our early schooling teaches how people like John D. Rockefeller and Andrew Carnegie worked very hard to overcome the long odds in gaining their fantastic fortunes. As Gary Younge says, "America prides itself on being a country where anyone who works hard enough can make it, a nation of taut bootstraps and rugged individualism."[3] Seldom, if ever, does our early schooling encourage us to challenge the fairness of allowing Rockefeller and Carnegie to will unearned advantages to their offspring. Nor, as with the lottery ads, do most Americans ponder the chances that people of humble origins will attain high social standing in their lifetimes,[4] versus the odds for children born of well-to-do families. In sum, as long as a few lower socioeconomic status people move far up the status hierarchy during their lifetimes, most Americans are reluctant to apply the same fairness criteria to social class disadvantage as they do when judging race and gender equity. As long as a few people win the class lottery, it seems the system is working well.

Of course, this is not to say the media should ignore racism, sexism and other discriminatory practices that restrict individual opportunities. These stories warrant telling and retelling. But why have Americans still not developed the same level of consciousness toward how birth circumstances dramatically affect what people become? Why do so few Americans recognize the effects of "parentism," if you will? Why is there still no popular reform movement directed against the problem of wildly unequal starts? Admittedly, there are programs for the "disadvantaged," but these do not require us to question why they are needed in the first place. We end up treating the symptoms and not the causes of social class inequalities.[5] Meanwhile, our country's recognition of other forms of discrimination have led to both a deep concern about their malicious effects and, consequently, public policies to remedy their causes. Yet, while America has advanced on other social equity fronts, progress against unequal starts has gone backwards, as the country's wealth and income become concentrated in fewer hands. According to Collins and Yeskel, in 1976, ten percent of the population owned 49% of all wealth.[6] By 1999, ten percent owned 73% of all wealth.[7] Younge explains one of the harmful effects of viewing social equity too narrowly. He writes, "For it is in addressing the plight of the poor, white or black, that America can honestly examine its own self-image. So long as those who wish to have an honest debate about equal opportunities confine themselves to race, they will only understand inequality as an aberration in

---

[3] Younge, "Class Act."

[4] Richard H. DeLone, *Small Futures: Children, Inequality, and the Limits of Liberal Reform* (New York: Harcourt Brace Jovanovich, 1979).

[5] See William Ryan, *Blaming the Victim* (New York: Vintage Books, 1971).

[6] Chuck Collins and Felice Yeskel, *Economic Apartheid in America* (New York: The New Press, 2000) 55.

[7] Ibid. Also, see Kevin P. Phillips, *Wealth and Democracy* (New York: Broadway Books, 2002).

the normal order of things. Only once they wed it to class does it become a systemic flaw which underpins the order of things."[8]

This reluctance to discuss social class and mobility does not derive from a dearth of relevant research and analysis. There is a vast and growing body of literature showing how social class matters throughout our lives. Just about all the good things we can have correlate with social class, ranging from longevity,[9] to dental health,[10] to mental health.[11] Likewise, a mounting body of research shows that family origins play an especially prominent role in determining one's eventual standing in the social class hierarchy. Kahlenberg[12] and DeLone,[13] for example, present an exhaustive review of the literature relating to class and mobility in America. Both authors cite numerous studies showing how parental status significantly enhances or restricts a child's social opportunities, including, as you might expect, most aspects of formal schooling, ranging from whether people go to college, where they attend, whether they complete their degrees, and so on. DeLone summarizes his findings on the overall effects of social class origins as follows:

> In the United States, as elsewhere, it is a penalty to be born poor. It is a compounding penalty to be born to parents with little education. It is a further penalty to be born to parents who are frequently unemployed and whose employment opportunities are limited to relatively uninteresting, dead-end jobs. Some of the penalties are immediate – the physical deprivation of poor nutrition, poor health, poor housing, inadequate medical care; some accumulate slowly, influencing the development of adult skills, spirations, and opportunities. Together, they produce the odds that make Bobby's [the child of higher social class parents] probable future a vista rich with possibilities and Jimmy's [the child of lower social class parents] probable future a small door into a small room.[14]

Hart and Risley produced an especially compelling examination of how social class origins affect language acquisition and, therefore, one's subsequent chances of success in life.[15] These authors studied child-rearing practices among three household categories, including: "welfare [AFDC]," "working-class," and "professional." The research involved meticulously measuring both the input

---

[8] Younge, "Class Act."

[9] Nancy E. Adler and Joan M. Ostrove, "Socioeconomic Status and Health: What We Know and What We Don't," *Annals of the New York Academy of Sciences*, 896, 1999, 3-15.

[10] Noelle Lalley Huntington, Elizabeth A. Krall, Raul I. Garcia and Avron Spiro, III, "SES and Oral Health Status in an Elderly Population." *Annals of the New York Academy of Sciences* 896 (1999): 451-54.

[11] Margaret J. Lundberg, *The Incomplete Adult: Social Class Constraints on Personality Development* (Westport Connecticut: Greenwood Press, 1974).

[12] Richard D. Kahlenberg, *The Remedy* (New York: Basic Books, 1996).

[13] DeLone, *Small Futures*.

[14] Ibid., 4.

[15] Betty Hart and Todd R. Risley, *Meaningful Differences in the Everyday Experiences of Young American Children* (Baltimore: Paul H. Brookes Publishing Co., 1995).

(number and variety of words received; number of imperative v. interrogative sentences addressed to the child, and so forth) and output sides (such as, self-esteem, confidence, motivation, scores on the Stanford-Binet IQ test, among others) of language acquisition in a child's initial years.

The effects of social class were consistent and striking, and usually far more important than other variables one might have thought relevant. In her Foreword to the book, Bloom offers a particularly gripping and concise summary of Hart and Risley's findings and conclusions. She writes:

> We have long known that children differ greatly in when they begin to learn language and how fast they learn once they begin. The children in this study did indeed differ. Some began to learn words with a learning trajectory that took off like a small rocket. But other children, who may even have begun to say words at about the same age, were much slower to get off the ground, and their trajectories were forever in the shadow of the other children. Why? That is the central question in this book.[16]

> In answering the question, Hart and Risley discovered that some things don't matter. For example, race/ethnicity doesn't matter; gender doesn't matter; whether a child is the first in the family or born later also doesn't matter. But what does matter, and it matters very much, is relative economic advantage.[17]

Contrary to what we might commonly perceive about such things, some investigators report that social mobility in America is *decreasing*. Wysong, Perrucci, and Wright, for example, studied 2,749 fathers and their sons from the 1970s to the 1990s to measure the effects of class background on the offspring's odds for upward mobility. Based on their analysis, these authors conclude,

> First, compared with the 1970s, our study reveals much less upward mobility, far more downward mobility, and a higher percentage of sons replicating their fathers' rankings in 1998. Second, compared with the 1970s, in 1998 a greater proportion of the upper SES ranks appear to be occupied by sons from upper SES [socioeconomic status] backgrounds. Third, compared with the recent past, [...] the U.S. class structure today appears less likely to accommodate upward mobility across generational lines – especially from lower and mid-level ranks into the highest rank.[18]

Interestingly, although he is best known for his role in the Civil Rights Movement, in his later years, Martin Luther King, Jr. was steadily evolving toward seeing how economic inequality accounts for many social problems commonly associated with race alone. By the end of his life, King had become more fo-

---

[16] Hart and Risley, x.

[17] Ibid.

[18] Earl Wysong, Robert Perrucci and David W. Wright, "Organizations, Resources, and Class Analysis: The Distributional Model and the U.S. Class Structure." A paper presented at the American Sociological Association Conference in Chicago, Illinois, August 16, 2002, 32.

cused on the well-being of lower and working class people of all races. Based on his world travels, King concluded, "The bourgeoisie – white, black, or brown – behaves about the same the world over."[19] According to Kahlenberg, "in the last four years of his life, King's commitment to class-based solutions grew stronger and stronger."[20] That so few people know about this part of King's philosophical evolution is perhaps further testament to the enduring power of American ideology to distract us from recognizing the effects of socioeconomic status. Even all these years after King's death, class remains a "taboo" subject in most circles, especially conversations about unearned advantages, both monetary and cultural.[21]

Finally, in 2003 the U.S. Supreme Court ruled on the constitutionality of the University of Michigan's efforts to increase campus "diversity" by recruiting more students of color. The majority decision stated that although race or ethnicity can be considered as one factor among many in deciding admissions, neither can be used as the only criterion for deciding student acceptances. In other words, the University was prohibited from admitting or rejecting qualified applicants by race or ethnicity alone, but school officials could give these characteristics some additional weight when deciding which students to accept; race or ethnicity could be a factor but not the single factor in choosing among applicants. The considerable and oftentimes rancorous debate surrounding this decision mostly disregarded how the same entrance programs granted special status to "socioeconomically disadvantaged" applicants.[22] Ironically, despite Americans not knowing much about the odds of social mobility, such class-based plans are both popular and clearly lawful; the courts have consistently recognized and upheld the constitutionality of weighing socioeconomic considerations when deciding admissions.[23] According to Kahlenberg, "while race has been and remains a suspect classification, class is clearly not."[24] He further shows that the courts have never rejected a statute or action because it discriminates according to class.

The Present Study

So far, most arguments for class-based diversity have included extending more professional educational opportunities to disadvantaged students, especially applicants to college and professional schools, such as law and medicine. Despite

---

[19] Martin Luther King, Jr., *The Autobiography of Martin Luther King, Jr.*, ed. Clayborne Carson (New York: Warner Books, 1998) 125.
[20] Kahlenberg, 10.
[21] Robert Perrucci and Earl. Wysong, *The New Class Society* (Lanham, Maryland: Rowman and Littlefield Publishers, Inc., 2003) 44.
[22] *Gratz v. Bollinger*, 539 U.S. 244, 286 (2003).
[23] Kenneth Oldfield and Richard F. Conant, "Professors, Social Class, and Affirmative Action: A Pilot Study," *Journal of Public Affairs Education*, 7:3, 2001, 171-185.
[24] Kahlenberg, 108.

the legal precedents and popular sentiment about class-based diversity programs, the social equity movement still pays little attention to achieving greater
diversity among full-time personnel, including organization leaders and workers. Given that those from disadvantaged backgrounds suffer a lifetime of limitations, this omission is puzzling. Perhaps it further evidences the power of ideology to exclude certain questions from the public debate. Still, it seems logical
to say that one of diversity's primary justifications – bringing different perspectives to the discussion – should apply to all personnel and thus include social
class origins.[25]

Presumably, if only one prestigious organization implemented a class-
based diversity plan to hire and promote both full-time employees and their su-
periors, this would bring considerable attention to the situation of unequal life
starts and the need for remediation. The social equity movement could then use
this program to publicize further the issue of inherited inequalities and possible
means of redress. Most reform movements start with consciousness-raising.
Once acquired, this new awareness becomes the foundation for recruiting more
volunteers to the cause. In other words, people must first understand how an
inequality that until now has been considered "natural," is, in fact, not so, and,
therefore, worthy of remedy. The present project details such a reform plan for
unequal social origins.

The present project is a case study showing how a well-respected organization can operationalize a class-based diversity plan for its entire workforce. This
investigation focuses on the Teachers Insurance and Annuity Association – College Retirement Equities Fund (TIAA-CREF). In particular, this research examines social class diversity among the TIAA-CREF Board of Directors. This
highly concentrated approach is used simply for reasons of economy. It gathers
all the necessary data at minimum cost, versus surveying everyone at the organization. While only addressing one tier of TIAA-CREF employees, both the
methodology and research rationale is applicable workforce wide. Finally,
TIAA-CREF was chosen as the object of analysis because of its impressive record in achieving gender and racial diversity throughout the organization. It sets
a high standard for recruiting and placing individuals from such previously underrepresented groups. Furthermore, TIAA-CREF has made numerous public
pronouncements about its commitment to diversity and how a heterogeneous
mix of employees improves operations. TIAA-CREF has won awards for recruiting and hiring more women and minorities. In summary, given its accom-
plishments and well-publicized philosophy, TIAA-CREF is a logical candidate
to lead such a social class diversity movement. The present analysis details both

---

[25] C. L. Barney Dews and Carolyn Leste Law, eds., *This Fine Place So Far From Home: Voices of Academics from The Working Class* (Philadelphia: Temple University Press, 1995); Alfred Lubrano, *Limbo: Blue-Collar Roots, White-Collar Dreams* (Hoboken, New Jersey: John Wiley and Sons, Inc., 2004); and Jake Ryan and Charles Sackrey, eds., *Strangers in Paradise: Academics from the Working Class* (Boston: South End Press, 1984).

the means and justification for initiating this bold step. The next several paragraphs outline the history, goals, and management philosophy of TIAA-CREF.

The Teachers Insurance and Annuity Association-College Retirement Equities Fund is a "group of companies that offers educators, researchers, their families, and the public a range of products and services to help them save for retirement and other goals."[26] TIAA-CREF is over 80 years old. While TIAA and CREF are usually mentioned together and have similar goals and functions, they have separate governing boards. Nevertheless, to understand what follows, there is no need to explain any differences between the two organizations' objectives and operations.

Periodically, TIAA distributes a brochure, accompanying letter, and a ballot relating to a pending election for the organization's Board of Directors. For example, a late 2002 letter read, in part:

> Enclosed is your ballot for the five nominees to the TIAA Board of Trustees [...] Although, under TIAA's charter, the TIAA Board of Overseers elects the TIAA trustees, the Overseers believe it is important that TIAA participants contribute to the election process by expressing their preferences for those nominated and by recommending future candidates.[27]

> This year's nominees are listed on the following pages, together with brief biographies [...] To enable you to consider the nominees in the context of the entire TIAA Board of Trustees, the nine continuing members are also listed, followed by the members of the TIAA Board of Overseers.[28]

Dr. Stanley Ikenberry, Emeritus President of the University of Illinois, and "President, TIAA Board of Trustees," signed the letter. Dr. Ikenberry does not explain what he means by "consider the nominees in the context of the entire TIAA Board of Trustees," but the brochure suggests he wants voters to weigh these factors:

First, the leaflet shows the TIAA governing board's size and arrangement. Of the 20 people listed, nine were "TIAA Trustees Continuing in Office," seven were on the "TIAA Board of Overseers," and five were "Nominees for the TIAA Board of Trustees." (One person was listed on both the "Board of Overseers" and "Continuing in Office." Thus, the sum of the just-mentioned numbers exceeds twenty.) (Hereafter, all people listed in the brochure, whether nominees or people serving, are simply called "the board," "board members," or "members.") *Second*, because each biography has an accompanying picture, readers can see there are: 1) fourteen males and six females, and 2) four African-Americans and sixteen Euro-Americans. *Third*, this is a seasoned group.

---

[26] "Governing TIAA-CREF," http://www.tiaa-cref.org/pubs/html/governance/. Consulted July 3, 2003.
[27] TIAA-CREF Ballot, October 13, 2003.
[28] Ibid.

The average age is 65 years, with a standard deviation of 5.7 years, and a range of 53 to 75 years. *Fourth*, all but one person held at least an undergraduate degree and a web search revealed this individual "attended" a public university.[29] Based on "highest degree obtained," the list contains eleven Ph.D.s, five attorneys, four people with masters' degrees, and the just-mentioned "attended college." (One person had a law degree and a Ph.D., which explains why there are more than 20 degrees noted.) *Finally*, a very high percent of the group had at least one diploma from a prestigious private college. In particular, sixteen of the twenty members – 80% – had at least one degree from an Ivy League institution. Thus, on average, this group had experienced some very expensive instruction.

The definition of "context" has changed over the years. Seemingly, in the early days the board's racial and gender mix was deemed unimportant, given that the first woman was not appointed until 1940 and no African-Americans served before 1957.[30] Changes in these race and gender facts combined with the just-mentioned brochure information suggest TIAA-CREF accepts the contemporary interpretation of "diversity." Assumedly, the board should represent a rich mix of demographic categories so it can make wiser and more acceptable policies; having a representative number of minorities and female board members guarantees more rational policy-making and greater buy-in from constituent groups. As the TIAA-CREF website claims:

> Although trustees are not selected as formal representatives of a specific constituency or an institutional category, every effort is made to include individuals who, in addition to their professional qualifications, are from diverse backgrounds. This brings different perspectives to board deliberations.[31]

> Because it's unlikely that any one individual will possess all or even most of this knowledge, the boards seek strength through diversity.[32]

Elsewhere we read:

> TIAA-CREF takes the lead on issues concerning corporate management practices and board independence, diversity, and effectiveness. [...] In keeping with our belief that board diversity promotes better corporate governance, almost 25 percent of TIAA and CREF trustees are women, and 20 percent are minorities...[33]

---

[29] "Our Team," http://www.advmedicine.com/about-team-bod.php?detailID=17. Consulted July 4, 2003.

[30] TIAA-CREF, "Board Composition," http://www.tiaa-cref.org/governance/board_comp.html. Consulted July 3, 2003.

[31] Ibid.

[32] "Governing TIAA-CREF," http://www.tiaa-cref.org/pubs/html/governance. Consulted July 3, 2003.

[33] "A Leader in Corporate Governance," http://www.tiaa-cref.org/pubs/html/built_Foundation/corp_gov.html. Consulted 03.06.2003.

Historically, the TIAA and CREF boards have had more women and minority trustees than virtually any public corporation.[34]

TIAA-CREF categorizes its other workers by ethnicity and gender. *Fortune* lists the following 2002 workforce figures:

TABLE 1: TIAA-CREF WORKFORCE RACIAL COMPOSITION		
CATEGORY	MINORITY	NON-MINORITY
Board of Directors:	21.4%	78.6%
Top-Paid Employees:	8%	92%
Officials and Managers	27.2%	72.8%
New Hires	50%	50%
Total Workforce	46.8*	53.2%
*Workforce Percentages	Asian = 9.0%, Black = 27.5%, Hispanic = 10.2%, Native American = 0.0%	
Source: Jonathan Hickman, "America's 50 Best Companies for Minorities," *Fortune* 146, 1 (July 8, 2002): 110-120.		

According to Hickman, "The percentage of minorities hired jumped from 42% to 50% at the pension and mutual fund company in 2001. Three-quarters of the firm's 48 interns last year were minorities too."[35] Finally, TIAA-CREF has been formally recognized for its diversity efforts:

> In the trillion-dollar retirement industry, TIAA-CREF is an exceptional leader and has received citations for initiatives in workplace diversity and flexibility by publications that include: 1) Fortune - America's Best Companies for Minorities; 2) Hispanic - The 100 Best Companies for Hispanics; 3) Working Mother - 100 Best Companies for Working Mothers; 4) Computer World - One of the Best Places to Work.[36]

Despite this recognized public commitment to diversity, the TIAA brochure says nothing about what the board members' parents did for a living or how far they went in school. Evidently, "context" excludes socioeconomic origins. The TIAA brochure does not tell constituents at what point the various candidates started life's race.

Because the TIAA brochure says nothing about any member's class origin, the 20 people listed on the board were surveyed regarding their family backgrounds. All 20 received a postcard with two types of questions. First, they were asked to check a box indicating their parents' highest education levels, and, second, they were asked to describe their parents' occupations. There were four survey waves, one per month over four months. Thirteen of the 20 members responded, a 65% return rate.

---

[34] "TIAA and CREF Board of Trustees," http://www.tiaa-cref.org/libra/govern/boardoftrustees.html Consulted July 4, 2003.

[35] Hickman, 144.

[36] "Hot Jobs," A Yahoo Company, http://hotjobs.yahoo.com/careers-7398-TIAA_CREF. Consulted June 30, 2003.

The responses were reviewed with two goals in mind. First, they were checked for which board candidates were of humble origins. Second, the overall sample results were compared with the U.S. population. If the board were disproportionately drawn from the highest social classes, these findings would justify saying TIAA should become as concerned about social class diversity as it has been with increasing representation by women and minorities. The sample v. U.S. population calculation involved three steps.

First, it was determined that the average board member was born in 1937 (the brochure date of 2002 – 65 years = 1937). In the late 1930s, few Americans had a high school diploma. Thus, it was assumed that if a large number of respondents indicated their parents had attended college, the board would be judged highly unrepresentative of the national population and therefore in need of greater social class diversity. To control for age, the survey results were compared against the 1940 Census figures, the year closest to the average board member's birth date.

Second, until recently men were more likely than women to attend college. Given this difference, it was deemed important to see if there was a significant discrepancy between the U.S. population and the questionnaire results for family origin when controlling for gender. Thus, the present study made separate comparison between the sample's fathers and mothers versus the 1940 Census figures broken down by gender.

Finally, the Nam-Powers[37] socioeconomic scale (hereafter, "NP") was used to gauge each parent's relative occupational status. NP assigns rankings ranging from 1% to 100% for each U.S. Census occupation category using a formula weighing the income and education of people doing such work. For instance, attorneys (98%) and veterinarians (95%) are among the highest rated vocations, while boilermakers (59%) and bakers (50%) fall in the middle ranges, and housemaids (7%) and bootblacks (2%) are among the lowest ranked.

NP was first applied to the 1950 Census figures; thus each respondent's parental occupation was coded using that year's scale. The occupational scores do not vary much between censuses and given the general nature of the respondents' answers (mostly high ranking professionals), it was assumed this coding strategy would provide a sound estimate of the group's overall standing. (Incidentally, the just-mentioned rankings for attorneys, boilermakers, etc. come from the 1950 NP scale.)

---

[37] Charles Nam and Mary Powers, "Changes in the Relative Status of Workers in the United States, 1950-1960," *Social Forces*, 47, 1968, 158-170.

FINDINGS

Tables 2 and 3 present the survey results.

TABLE 2: TIAA PARENTAL EDUCATION V. U.S. POPULATION 25 YEARS OLD AND HIGHER (1940 Census)*					
EDUCATION LEVEL	ALL TIAA	ALL US	TIAA FATHERS	U.S. MALES	TIAA MOTHERS	U.S. FEMALES
High School	15.4%	75.5%	15.4%	77.3%	15.4%	73.7%
High School	11.5%	14.3%	7.7%	12.2%	15.4%	16.4%
Some College	15.4%	5.5%	7.7%	4.9%	23.1%	6.1%
College or +	57.7%	4.6%	69.2%	5.5%	46.2%	3.8%
Total	100%	99.9%**	100%	99.9%*	100.1%**	100%
N =	26	73.73***	13	36.87***	13	36.86***

* Table only includes U.S. respondents who listed education. Non-respondents were as follows: 1.4% of U.S. population, 1.6% of U.S. men and 1.2% of U.S. women.
** Does not equal 100% due to rounding.
*** in Millions
Source: "Table 1: Persons 25 Years and Over, By Years of School Completed, Race, and Sex, For the United States, Urban and Rural: 1940," http://www.census.gov/population/socdemo/education/p10-8/tab-01.pdf (Consulted July 3, 2003.)

TABLE 3: TIAA PARENTS' NP LEVELS	
NAM-POWERS RANGE	ALL TIAA PARENTS
< 50%	11.8%
51 – 79%	11.8%
80-89%	35.3%
90% - 100%	41.2%
Total	100.1%
N =	17

In all cases, the sample education levels far exceed those for the U.S. population. In 1940, when ten percent of Americans were attending or finishing college, almost three-quarters (73.1%) of the sample parents had at least gone to college. Over half had a four-year degree or more. The ratio of college educated board parents to the U.S. population is nearly 13 – 1. The survey findings show when controlling for gender, 69% of the sample fathers had a college degree or more compared to the nation's 5.5%, again about a 13-1 ratio. Meanwhile, nearly half (46.2%) of the sample mothers had at least finished college, compared to 3.8% of the U.S. population, roughly a 12 – 1 ratio. The average board member's parents were far more educated than the U.S. population. The occupational status comparisons revealed similar results. Over three-quarters of the parents were ranked in the top 20% of all occupations. More than one-third fell in the top ten percent. Fewer than 12% came close to being of lower and working class status. In sum, the survey results show TIAA respondents are highly unrepresentative of the U.S. population for socioeconomic status and educational attainment. Thus, it is reasonable to argue that "context of the entire TIAA Board of Trustees" should include social class origins.

Detailing a Remedy

If TIAA really is making "every effort to include individuals who, in addition to their professional qualifications, are from diverse backgrounds [because t]his brings different perspectives to board deliberations," it should ensure its leadership is more reflective of the national population for social origins, versus having only token representation of people with lower and working class beginnings; if the race and gender composition of the board should roughly equal the U.S. population, why not also its members' social class roots?[38]

Based on the present findings and discussion, TIAA should consider adopting six policies to monitor and increase its class diversity. *First*, TIAA should revise its website language to include discussion about needing greater diversity based on socioeconomic origins. The organization should seek to attract more people who were raised in lower and working class households, as it now does in seeking to increase the number of female and minority employees.

Second, when writing bibliographies, TIAA should encourage its leadership to acknowledge their own socioeconomic origins. This background information should be listed in all brochures distributed to constituents, so voters can weigh these facts when considering the current board's "context."

Third, and related to point two, TIAA should implement a class-based diversity plan so its whole workforce is more heterogeneous, including interns. The company should survey all its workers about their social origins, as it now counts and publicizes information about its employees' gender and ethnicity. Surely, if TIAA members see that those of humble birth are significantly underrepresented in the workforce, it will be easier for organizational leaders to justify recruiting and hiring more people who were raised in lower and working class homes. If TIAA can change its attitudes about race and gender, certainly it can reconsider how it views – or better to say, does not view – social class beginnings.

Just by implementing such a plan, TIAA would help its member's appreciate the problem of unequal starts. The publicity flowing from this intrepid move would show the world this organization really is a diversity leader, and more awards would surely follow. Certainly, given its well-promoted commitment to fair play and social justice, few, if any, TIAA leaders or staffers would refuse to acknowledge their parents' occupations and educational attainments. Instead, it is expected that the suggested policy will be like most other progressive ideas, where each succeeding generation becomes more committed to the change and eventually it will seem odd not to do things as proposed here.

---

[38] TIAA-CREF, "Board Composition."

Fourth, TIAA should inform its members that there is precedent for including social class considerations in a diversity plan, even in certain of the institutions with which these representatives have been affiliated. One board member is an emeritus professor at the University of Arizona (UA), and that school's website says:

> Clearly, diversity has an almost endless scope and offers fertile ground for many definitions, agendas, philosophies, and initiatives. In a large, complex, research and land-grant institution such as the UA, diversity includes, and can be examined through the lenses of student and employee characteristics, curriculum, learning and teaching styles, gender, ethnicity, sexual orientation, physical and cognitive abilities, family status, age, *socioeconomic status*, and community relations (emphasis added).[39]

Fifth, TIAA officials should explain that class-based diversity is consistent with meritocracy, contrary to what some critics might say. Just by qualifying for consideration as TIAA personnel, whether as regular employees or board members, people who come from humble origins will have already shown they have the "right stuff."[40]

Finally, TIAA should inform its members that the proposed changes are soundly based in law. As Taylor says, it is "legally unassailable" to use socioeconomic considerations in diversity plans.[41]

One TIAA respondent's survey postcard offered the following comment:

> For your information, I am extremely proud of my parents. Neither my father nor my mother had the advantage of receiving any education whatever. They were both teenage immigrants who arrived in the U.S. determined that their children would have the education they were denied. Three of their children, of four, earned graduate school degrees. A typical American Story, wouldn't you say?

Of course, the evidence suggests this is not the "typical American story." This person is extraordinary, the proverbial social class lottery winner. Probably what is more common is the lesson that because people do not know the data, the myth remains in the popular consciousness.

One has to question whether this comment is not *prima facie* evidence of how our national ideology fosters prejudice against lower status people. That is, why does this respondent feel moved to say, "I am extremely proud of my parents"? Would the child of two physicians write: "Although they were both medical doctors, I am extremely proud of my parents"? As noted, conscious-

---

[39] "Diversity Action Plan Fall 2002," http://uanews.opi.arizona.edu/diversityreport.html Consulted July 7, 2003.
[40] See Lubrano; and Oldfield and Conant.
[41] Stuart Taylor, "A Case for Class-Based Affirmative Action," *Connecticut Law Tribune*, 17:38, September 3, 1991, 18.

ness-raising is the first step toward policy reform. After seeing the data and reading the accompanying discussion, perhaps the author of this survey note will become the strongest advocate for having TIAA adopt the ideas being suggested here.

In sum, the lesson should be that the real meaning of "typical" involves the *chances* of social ascension. Interesting, in this country, with its rags-to-riches self-image, our government excludes social mobility odds from the well-publicized monthly economic data it releases, including, for example, inflation figures, first time claims for unemployment, consumer confidence, and so forth. Why do these reports omit the likelihood of someone being the child of a boot-black and a housemaid and becoming, say, a TIAA board member, versus the odds of a neurosurgeons' child doing so? The idea of providing such information is not that far fetched. Our government distributes statistics showing the socioeconomic conditions of minorities and women. With enough political will, we could easily include mobility odds in our list of "economic indicators."

Before concluding, it is important to acknowledge and address a final classist assumption about social mobility in America. Surely, some critics will rely on this supposition to reject the present proposal out-of-hand. Namely, it is customarily believed that once those of humble origin gain higher standing, they forsake every lesson from their early years. For parvenus, the past is suddenly irrelevant to understanding how they think and act as grown-ups; while most other groups in our country are encouraged to study and remember their histories, class risers are simply assumed to forget theirs.[42] Rather than being considered exceptional, they are presumed to have become "one of us" in all manner of action and thought.

This "forget-the-past" reasoning rarely applies in reverse. When wealthy people divorce they can sue their spouses to "maintain a lifestyle to which they had become accustomed." On the other hand, if people move *up* the status ladder several rungs, they supposedly replace all the values and beliefs of their youth with the mindset of their new class. In short, it is assumed the higher situated will cling to their old ways and ideas even after they can no longer afford them, at least not without help from a former spouse, but presumably those who ascend the status hierarchy more than a few steps will forget where they came from. There seems to be a double standard that reads, "Only fallers – not risers – are assumed to remember their past."

The lessons of upward mobility are not a zero-sum game, where every new idea learned automatically replaces an old one. Better to say that risers have the advantage of understanding two perspectives instead of one; they carry the lessons of their underclass days plus what they know from being of higher status.

---

[42] See, for example, Dews and Law; Lubrano; Oldfield and Conant; and Ryan and Sackrey.

Therefore, it is reasonable to say that if TIAA truly seeks heterogeneity because it "brings different perspectives to board deliberations,"[43] where justified by research emulating the methods used here, this organization should actively recruit more people of humble origins. In so broadening its membership, both among board personnel and throughout the workforce, TIAA would assure itself of having a *true* diversity of worldviews.

Conclusion

At the end of Inheritance and Wealth in America, Miller and McNamee say: "Barring fundamental ideological change, the best practical advice for getting ahead in America remains as it has always been – choose your parents *very* carefully."[44] The present findings suggest the same logic applies to becoming a TIAA leader. At the same time, this paper recommends ways to achieve the "fundamental ideological change" needed to assure that (at least) this group and the rest of TIAA is representative of the U.S. population for class origins. As with every social equity movement, other writers and activists will surely add their own suggestions to this list. The main objective here is to move more people toward thinking differently about this issue.

Given that TIAA has already achieved significant race and gender equity in its various operations, it is only logical to insist that these diversity efforts include socioeconomic origins. If TIAA did this, certainly someday it would be viewed as having that rare and enviable capacity for seeing far beyond the prejudices of its time by seeking to make the American Dream truly typical for every citizen, even those who choose the wrong parents. Finally, by adopting the proposed reforms, TIAA would take a monumental step forward in acknowledging "the elephant in the room."[45] Every long journey requires a beginning, and TIAA now has both a strategy and rationale for leading the way toward greater class equity throughout its workforce. If we expect that the old ways of thinking will change without such guidance, we can only be disappointed, for, as Younge says about these matters, "[b]itter experience shows us that time and tide will not do it alone."[46]

---

[43] TIAA-CREF, "Board Composition."

[44] Robert K. Miller, Jr. and Stephen J. McNamee, *Inheritance and Wealth in America* (New York: Plenum Press, 1998) 211. Emphasis in original.

[45] Younge, "Class Act." Also, see hooks, 2000.

[46] Younge, "Class Act."

Selected Bibliography

Adler, Nancy E. and Joan M. Ostrove. "Socioeconomic Status and Health: What We Know and What We Don't." *Annals of the New York Academy of Sciences* 896 (1999): 3-15.

Collins, Chuck, and Felice Yeskel. *Economic Apartheid in America.* New York: The New Press, 2000.

De Lone, Richard H. *Small Futures: Children, Inequality, and the Limits of Liberal Reform.* New York: Harcourt Brace Jovanovich, 1979.

Dews, C.L. Barney and Carolyn Leste Law, eds. *This Fine Place So Far From Home: Voices of Academics from the Working Class.* Philadelphia: Temple University Press, 1995.

"Diversity Action Plan Fall 2002," University of Arizona. http://uanews.opi.arizona.edu/diversityreport.html. (Consulted July 7, 2003.)

Gratz v. Bollinger. 539 U.S. 244; 123 S. Ct. 2411; 156 L. Ed. 2d 257, 2003.

Hart, Betty and Todd R. Risley. *Meaningful Differences in the Everyday Experiences of Young American Children.* Baltimore: Paul H. Brookes Publishing Co., 1995.

Hickman, Jonathan. "America's 50 Best Companies for Minorities." *Fortune* 146. 1 (July 8, 2002): 110-120.

hooks, bell. *Where We Stand: Class Matters.* New York: Routledge, 2000.

"Hot Jobs." http://hotjobs.yahoo.com/careers-7398-TIAA_CREF. (Consulted June 30, 2003.)

Huntington, Noelle Lalley, Elizabeth A. Krall, Raul I. Garcia and Avron Spiro III. "SES and Oral Health Status in An Elderly Population." *Annals of the New York Academy of Sciences* 896 (1999): 451-54.

Kahlenberg, Richard D. *The Remedy.* New York: Basic Books, 1996.

King, Martin Luther. *The Autobiography of Martin Luther King, Jr.* Ed Clayborne Carson. New York: Warner Books, 1998.

Lubrano, Alfred. *Limbo: Blue-Collar Roots, White-Collar Dreams.* Hoboken, New Jersey: John Wiley & Sons, Inc., 2004.

Lundberg, Margaret J. *The Incomplete Adult: Social Class Constraints on Personality Development.* Westport Connecticut: Greenwood Press, 1974.

Miller, Robert K. Jr. and Stephen J. McNamee. *Inheritance and Wealth in America.* New York: Plenum Press, 1998.

Nam, Charles and Mary Powers. "Changes in the Relative Status of Workers in the United States, 1950-1960." *Social Forces* 47 (1968): 158-170.

Oldfield, Kenneth and Richard F. Conant. "Professors, Social Class, and Affirmative Action: A Pilot Study." *Journal of Public Affairs Education* 7.3 (2001): 171-185.

Perrucci, Robert and Earl Wysong. *The New Class Society.* Lanham, Maryland: Rowman and Littlefield Publishers, Inc., 2003.

Phillips, Kevin P. *Wealth and Democracy*. New York: Broadway Books, 2002.

Ryan, Jake, and Charles Sackrey, eds. *Strangers in Paradise: Academics from the Working Class*. Boston: South End Press, 1984.

Ryan, William. *Blaming the Victim*. New York: Vintage Books, 1971.

Shaw, George Bernard. *The Intelligent Woman's Guide to Socialism and Capitalism*. London: Constable and Company LTD, 1928.

Taylor, Stuart. "A Case for Class-Based Affirmative Action." *Connecticut Law Tribune* 17, 38 (September 3, 1991) 18.

Theravance. "Our Team," http://www.advmedicine.com/about-team-bod.php?detailID=17. (Consulted July 4, 2003.)

TIAA Ballot, October 13, 2003.

TIAA and CREF, "Board Composition." http://www.tiaa-cref.org/about/governance/corporate/topics/board_composition.html. Consulted July 3, 2003.)

TIAA-CREF. "Governing TIAA-CREF," http://www.tiaa-cref.org/pubs/html/governance/. (Consulted July 3, 2003.)

TIAA-CREF, "A Leader in Corporate Governance." http://www.tiaa-cref.org/pubs/html/built_foundation/corp_gov.html. (Consulted June 3, 2003.)

U.S. Census Bureau: http://www.census.gov/population/socdemo/education/p10-8/tab-01.pdf. (Consulted June 30, 2003.)

Wysong, Earl, E., R. Perrucci and David W. Wright. "Organizations, Resources, and Class Analysis: The Distributional Model And The U.S. Class Structure." Paper presented at the American Sociological Association Conference, Chicago, Ill., August 16, 2002.

Younge, Gary. "America is a Class Act." *Guardian* (January 27, 2003). http://www.guardian.co.uk/comment/story/0,3604,882935,00.ht

PART IV

NARRATIVES OF CLASS

The Stories We Tell

Irvin Peckham (Louisiana State University)

The genre of working-class narratives may be said to have begun in 1984 with the publication of *Strangers in Paradise*, a collection of stories by largely disaffected working-class academics coming to terms with the difficulties they faced when crossing into the intellectual fraction of the middle class. Through writing about it, many of the working-class academics seem to have gotten in touch with an unacknowledged anger, a consequence perhaps, of their not having understood the nature of the new game they were playing.

In 1995, C.L. Barney Dews and Carolyn Laws edited another collection of narratives by working-class academics, *This Fine Place So Far From Home.* The title echoes *Strangers in Paradise*, but with a twist. Noting that paradise is far from home is not the same as remaining a stranger there – and the tone of the writers in this later collection reflects that different perspective. Although one wouldn't want to characterize the working-class academics in *This Fine Place* as full-fledged citizens, most of them seem to have lost the bitter edge characteristic of *Strangers*. Something had happened in the intervening decade to the social class conflict that made *Strangers* by comparison read like a raw wound.

It has been a little over ten years since the publication of *This Fine Place*. In those years, we have seen several collections of working-class narratives both inside and outside the academy: *Getting By*; *Coming to Class*; *Teaching Working Class*; *Writing Work: Writers on Working-Class Writing*; *Reclaiming Class: Women, Poverty, and the Promise of Higher Education in America*; and *Those Winter Sundays: Female Academics and Their Working Class Parents*. In the United States, we have three working class listserves that I know of, a Special Interest Group at the Conference of College Composition and Communication,[1] and at least two conferences – one annual (Working-Class Academics Conference) and one biennial (Working-Class Studies Conference).[2] It's almost as if class had become cool.

Being an academic with working-class origins,[3] I have been interested in the evolution of working-class studies and in the stories we working-class aca-

---

[1] The Conference on College Composition and Communication is the national conference for postsecondary writing teachers in the United States. Special Interests Groups (SIGs) form around themes such as Computers and Writing, or Working Class issues. These SIGs meet in the evenings.

[2] Many people have contributed to this development, but four people in the United States stand out: Ira Shor for his early focus on class issues and for creating the Working Class Studies SIG at CCCC, Janet Zandy for her rescue of so many working-class stories, and Sherry Linkon and John Russo for their Center for Working Class Studies.

[3] "Working-class academic" is a vexed label for a social group. A sub-theme of this essay explores the contradiction within the term. I will use it, however, because of its currency. When I refer to myself as a working-class academic, I do not mean that I still consider myself to be a member of the working

demics tell about ourselves in order to make sense of our social class trajecto-
ries. By hearing the narratives of academics who have made similar journeys, I
have been able to understand a little more of mine. And through hearing their
stories, I have also learned how to tell my own.

In part, this essay continues the working-class narrative genre, but I want
to change the contours of the genre in response to the evolving transformation
of the nexus between the social groups working-class academics straddle. As in
most narratives of working-class academics, I will focus on the dissonance between our working-class origins and the middle-class territory we try to cross
into, but I want to explore a feature of this dissonance that reaches across the
social class differences between us and our middle-class colleagues. I am interested here in the stories that I think many of us tell about ourselves, no matter
what social class we come from. Although I will be approaching these stories
from a working-class perspective, I hope that through this lens my middle-class
friends will also be able to see themselves and the parts they play in a larger
drama, the theme of which is the use of words to escape labor. In my case, they
were simply my escape from the working class. Or at least, that's the story I
tell.

Staging

I am approaching this essay with a split desire, a common enough phenomenon
for anyone who has been raised in one social group and migrated to another
characterized by attitudes in conflict with the first. One half of my desire is to
write out thoughts without paying attention to how they will be received. As I
review my academic career, I admit to this continuously suppressed desire to
lay things bare. I have been writing for decades, but I have this nagging perception that I have never gotten close to the core of what I mean.

The other half is my instinct to dissemble. Dissemble might be an overly
strong verb – I could say it lies in my desire to stage myself. When I am writing
to you, I am thinking of your various – if you will forgive me – subject positions, which is what makes me want to leave my unadorned self behind the cur-
tains while someone more *present*able walks on-stage. The spotlight is on this
staged self; he speaks through the mike to an audience that he sees only
vaguely. He does his best to create an illusion of identity with the off-stage self,
but the mere fact of being on-stage disrupts his timing and accent.

Of course most people see through my staged identity: they know I am not
really middle-class and perhaps even that I am not in control of my words –
which might amount to the same thing. The literature of social class stratification frequently mentions that working-class migrants are always recognized as

---

class. It means I came *from* the working class. I am also aware of the self-privileging that goes with
being *from*.

pretenders. Theorists have called us parvenus,[4] late-comers,[5] authentic l
ners,[6] border-crossers,[7] and straddlers.[8] Natives of the middle-class ter
have an instinctive recognition of people who have not been born to their social
group. Knowing that we never really "pass" imbues us with the impostor syndrome, which reads like a mantra in working-class narratives. On the other side
of the coin, we working-class people recognize each other, no matter how long
we have been living middle-class. Our social class origins are in our speech,
how we carry our bodies, how we dress, how we manage ourselves in conversations with others. I suspect we recognize each other by how we mis-stage ourselves. Unsurprisingly, we are drawn toward each other like immigrants.

The Differences

I have in this overly-reflexive introduction elided the problematic issues of social classes and identity. I have referred to social classes as if they have an objective existence in a one-dimensional hierarchy when I know they are conceptual, multi-dimensional, and significantly shaped by our socio-economic points
of view. Working-class people think of social class differently than middle-class
people do. Actually, since I have become a (working)/middle-class academic, I
no longer think of social classes, although I will use that phrase as a shorthand
for multi-dimensional social groups in line with Pierre Bourdieu's concept of
social spaces dependent on various kinds of capital. That being said, I know
there is a significant difference between the working class that I come from and
the middle class in which I live. There's a gap as wide and deep as the Grand
Canyon, and it's not easy to cross. That's why even at this late stage in my life,
my middle-class wife has trouble getting along with my working-class parents.

These two social groups have seriously conflicting values. They are usually represented as dichotomies. These are so well-known in the literature, that I
am going to place them in a paired listing without undue elaboration.

Working	Middle
Geographically bound	Geographically open
Close extended family	Loose extended family
Provincial	Sophisticated

---

[4] Pierre Bourdieu, *Distinction: A Social Critique of the Judgement of Taste*, trans. Richard Nice (Cambridge MA: Harvard UP, 1984).

[5] James Paul Gee, *Social Linguistics and Literacies*, 2d ed. (Bristol PA: Taylor & Francis, 1996).

[6] James Paul Gee, "Learning Language as a Matter of Learning Social Languages within Discourses" in *Language Learning and Teacher Education: A Sociocultural Approach*, ed. Margaret R. Hawkins (Clevedon, UK: Multilingual Matters, 2004) 13-31.

[7] Henry Giroux, *Border Crossing: Cultural Workers and the Politics of Education* (New York: Rout-ledge, 1991).

[8] Alfred Lubrano, *Limbo: Blue-Collar Roots, White Collar Dreams* (Hoboken, N.J.: John Wiley & Sons, Inc., 2004).

Practical	Theoretical
Concrete	Abstract
Subjective	Objective
Emotional	Rational
Authoritarian	Democratic
Rule bound	Situational
Clarity	Ambiguity
Manichean	Relativistic
Monologic	Dialogic
Child/Adult separation	Child/Adult integration
Heavily gendered	Loosely gendered
Communal	Individual
Collaborative	Competitive
Existential/local	Systemic/global
Implicit language	Explicit language
Straight talk	Circumlocution

In specific situations, these oppositions are shaded and sometimes act against each other, but they present guidelines by which one could identify a person's social class orientation. If you meet a man who rarely travels, has his primary relationships with his extended family, has a generally narrow point of view, doesn't read a lot of different kinds of books or listen to different kinds of music, is practical, believes in law and order, likes to know where he stands, doesn't talk with a lot with other people, draws a firm line between the worlds of adults and children, believes in significantly different male and female roles, likes to align himself with people like himself and those he grew up with, works well with his close friends, relies on gestures as much as words, fixes things himself, and doesn't beat around the bush, then chances are he's working class. I have referred here to the male working class, because working-class women, in line with the heavily gendered roles, tend to be different in their orientations. Bourdieu claims that working-class women will be more inclined to adjust to the demands of legitimated language, a subclass of the world of symbolic goods.[9] Valuing symbolic goods over material goods shifts women, on several counts, to the middle-class set of values in the dichotomies I have listed above, particularly those dichotomies connected with literacy and language. It is no accident that in the narratives of working-class academics, it is generally the women in the family who encouraged the child to read and *change* his or her language from "ain't" to "isn't."

With a few variations, the terms on the left side define my social class of origin and quite explicitly my family, dominated by my father. The terms on the right side describe my assumed middle-class values, the values of my middle-

---

[9] Pierre Bourdieu, *Language and Symbolic Power*, ed. John B. Thompson, trans. Gino Raymond and Mathew Adamson (Cambridge, MA: Havard UP, 1991) 50.

class wife, and the ones that have become the home values of our children. This is the difference between the working class I have known and the middle class in which I live. It is also the difference between my parents (my father, in particular) and my children. My children could never be called working-class.

Identity is the second problematic I have skipped over by imagining a real and a staged self, as if there were only two of me. Postmodern theory has identity slipping all over the place. I acknowledge the gist of identity slippage, but there is a certain point at which all the subject position rhetoric gets tiresome, particularly for working-class academics who have grown up in cultural environments predicated on stable identity formation. I know very well that there is an internal me that even my wife and children don't know; there is a private me, the self I present to my wife and children, a self that knows a censor but without a stage manager; and there is the staged me – the one that goes to work and is active in the community. I think of these three categories of self within the framework of prototype theory.[10] Prototype theory explains language as being largely constituted of categories that carry meaning for speech communities sharing a generally typical idea of categories dominated by prototypes (like robin rather than emu for bird). But meanings get fuzzy as the signifier points toward instances that lie toward the edge of what people mean, for example, by a "nation." People get in fights over these fuzzy meanings.

Linked to prototype theory is Wittgenstein's theory of meaning, based on family resemblances – words have meaning as a consequence of shared attributes among instances in which the words are used, but meanings may not necessarily have a stable set of attributes. If A, B, and C are related meanings, what's common between A and B may not be common between A and C. But A and C are referred to by the same word as a consequence of shared attributes between B and C. Meanings shade into other meanings depending on how the words are used. Within this framework, I can imagine a prototype interior me, a prototype family me, and a prototype public me – the staged one. In this essay, I am blurring the first two prototypes into the category of real self and everything else into the staged self. These two selves are shorthand for a more comprehensive paradigm of identity formation. My working- and middle-class selves work the same way.

When I'm lucky – and this has happened – I have reached a near-consonance between these two selves as if I had plucked a B and a D string and played myself in the key of G. I have been aiming all my life for this consonance between my real and staged selves – or between all of the possible variations on the theme. I can imagine that some people live that way; in fact, as the years slide by, I feel as if I am getting closer, most likely because I have less to

---

[10] See George Lakoff, *Women, Fire, and Dangerous Things: What Categories Reveal About the Mind* (Chicago: University of Chicago Press, 1987); Eleanor Rosch, "Principles of Categorization," in *Cognition and Categorization*, ed. Eleanor Rosch and Barbara Lloyd (Hillsdale NJ: Lawrence Erlbaum Associates, 1978) 25-49.

lose. But I remember that when I was first went to college, the dissonance between these two selves was like the sound of a braking freight train.

Putting the Blame Elsewhere

But working-class academics haven't cornered the market on dissonance. No
matter what social class you come from, you are bound for dissonance because
identity dissonance is the nature of a communal being. James Paul Gee describes the origin of the dissonance as the difference between your primary and
secondary Discourses (by capital D, he means the conglomerate of attributes
that define your social communities, like Bourdieu's *habitus*);[11] in one of my
favorite books, Peter Berger and Thomas Luckmann describe the dissonance as
the conflict between primary and secondary socialization.[12] The primary so-
cialization/Discourse is your home and local community; the second is the public arena, and most notably, school. Although people from privileged classes
like to imagine that the dramatic disparity in educational achievement among
social groups is a consequence of I.Q. (a notion constructed by male, middle-
class Anglos), stratification and social reproduction theories attribute a good
deal of the difference to the dissonance between primary and secondary socializations. There are all sorts of variations, such as educational level, the kind of
school one attends, one's social class fraction (economic or intellectual),[13] race,
and gender, but the general relationship remains: the higher one's social class,
the less the dissonance between one's primary socialization and school – an inverse relationship that becomes more pronounced at increasingly higher levels
of education, which is in turn a function of the social class origins of those who
teach.

   An extensive list of books documents the working-class dissonance.
Shirley Brice Heath's *Ways with Words*,[14] Basil Bernstein's *Class, Codes, and
Control*,[15] Samuel Bowles and Herbert Gintis' *Schooling in Capitalist Amer-
ica*,[16] Paul Willis' *Learning to Labor*,[17] Mike Rose's *Lives on the Boundary*,[18]

---

[11] Gee, *Social Linguistics and Literacies*, 131-32.

[12] Peter Berger and Thomas Luckmann, *The Social Construction of Reality* (New York: Anchor
Books, 1967) 140-41.

[13] See Bourdieu, *Distinctions*, chapter 5. Any attempt to summarize Bourdieu's interpretations of social categories is doomed from the start because for Bourdieu, they are three-dimensional, ever-
shifting, and dynamic, one group gaining definition by how it is positioned in its relationship to other
groups. One could say there is an overarching opposition between those who value cultural capital
and those who value economic capital, as if you have to spend one to get the other (Bourdieu calls
this "conversion"). Each social class fraction, say the lower middle class, is similarly bifurcated into
those who value cultural capital and those who value economic capital.

[14] Shirley Brice Heath, *Ways with Words: Language, Life, and Work in Communities and Classrooms*
(New York: Cambridge UP, 1983).

[15] Basil Bernstein, *Class, Codes, and Control*, vol 1 (London: Routledge & Kegan Paul, 1971).

[16] Hebert Bowles and Samuel Gintis, *Schooling in Capitalist America* (New York: Basic Books,
1976).

James Paul Gee's *Social Linguistics and Literacies*, and Lilia Bartolomé's *The Misteaching of Academic Discourse*[19] are some of the more important ones. Of special note is Annette Lareau's recent book, *Unequal Childhoods*,[20] a report on ethnographies of several families with nine- and ten-year-old children. Lareau describes in detail the child-rearing practices of twelve families divided along class, race (White verses Black), and gender lines. The major class division was between the working and middle classes, but the working class was subdivided into the poor and the working classes. One middle-class family was toward the lower end of the middle-class category and one in the upper middle class. All families were in the economic fraction of their respective social classes. Although Lareau's report focused on these twelve families, her generalizations were also drawn from a larger study of eighty-eight families.

Lareau's work substantiated (with the caveat that she resists over-generalizing) that working-class and school environments were in conflict in important ways, whereas the middle-class home environments were essentially prep schools for institutionalized educational settings – and for professional workplaces. With some apologies for the values embedded in the metaphors, she characterized the working-class home environments as dominated by a concept of *natural growth* and the middle-class home environments by a concept of *concerted cultivation*. The parents in working-class environments tended to construct borders (like behavioral and geographical fences) around their children within which the children were free to grow; middle-class parents worked without borders – behavior was subject to negotiation and the children typically travelled frequently and far. Within this generally ambiguous and negotiated environment, middle-class parents prepared their children for middle-class, professional worlds characterized by fluid, ambiguous situations requiring sophisticated negotiating skills through language. The middle-class children were raised to move almost seamlessly between their private and public worlds. They were made to feel as if they belonged in school and in professional spaces, creating what Bourdieu called the "entitlement" effect.[21] They would assume, for instance, they would *naturally* go on to college and very likely get advanced degrees. That's their birthright. Working-class kids think they're lucky to get to college – and when they do, they know they're strangers.

The inverse relationship of dissonance and social class is predictable. Working-class parents train their children for the worlds they know, in which

---

[17] Paul E. Willis, *Learning to Labor: How Working-Class Kids Get Working-Class Jobs* (Westmead, England: Saxon House, 1977).
[18] Mike Rose, *Lives on the Boundary* (New York: Penguin Books, 1990).
[19] Lilia Bartolomé, *The Misteaching of Academic Discourses: The Politics of Language in the Classroom* (Boulder CO: Westview Press, 1998).
[20] Annette Lareau, *Unequal Childhoods: Class, Race, and Family Life* (Berkeley, CA: U of California P, 2003).
[21] Bourdieu, *Distinctions*, 23.

people have to accommodate themselves to taking orders and being alienated from their labor. Middle-class parents train their children for their worlds, which are markedly different from those of the working class. Middle-class parents enjoy a greater degree of workplace autonomy and have greater ownership of their labor. These workplace conditions shape their respective world views, which they tend to reproduce in the home. In *Work and Personality*, Melvin Kohn and Carmi Schooler have put together a fascinating collection of reports on empirical research into the relationship between workplace environment and worldviews. Reporting on a survey of 1500 males in five social classes ("Stratification, Occupation, and Orientation,") they say that "the higher the fathers' social-stratification positions, the more they value characteristics of self-direction and the less they value characteristics indicative of conformity to external authority."[22] Elaborating on those values, Kohn and Schooler point out that one's workplace environment and social class shape whether one locates authority internally or externally. It should be clear as to which vision will be most consonant with the ethos of the university, which itself is a consequence of middle-class professors' dialectical relationship with their workplace environment. It's almost as if members of the professoriate have been trained to reward their own children for cognitive characteristics that the professors would like to imagine are class-neutral.

These social class reproduction mechanisms are not the consequence of intention but rather a manifestation of any social group's subliminal urge to reproduce itself through, as Bourdieu puts it, "structuring structures" that gain their power through misrepresentation.[23] Professors do not consciously weed out – to take us back to Lareau's agronomical metaphor – working-class students on the basis of the dissonance between their primary and secondary Discourses, but that's what happens. The social class reproductive system works most effectively when these weeding mechanisms are disguised from the weeds, flowers, and gardeners. Thus, language is imagined as class neutral – it is either correct or incorrect. Abilities to challenge, question, negotiate, and substantiate are likewise imagined as class neutral – but they ain't, as anyone who has grown up working-class but tried to slip into academia well recognizes. This veiling of criteria is what lies behind Bourdieu's concept of allodoxia, which is essentially the social practice of putting the blame elsewhere.

The Escape

Like most working-class academics, I wanted to escape the working class. This disarmingly simply motivation is fraught with complications, not the least of

[22] Melvin L. Kohn and Carmi Schooler. "Stratification, Occupation, and Orientation" in *Work and Personality: An Inquiry into the Impact of Social Stratification*, ed. Melvin L. Kohn and Carmi Schooler (Norwood NJ: Ablex, 1983) 8.

[23] Bourdieu, *Language*, 165-66.

which is social class betrayal. The narratives of working-class graduate students, in particular, reflect the struggle of escape, perhaps because graduate school is the time when working-class academics come face-to-face with what they are doing. More so than in undergraduate school, they find themselves in a social group dominated by people with middle-class origins because the higher working-class students go, the more their working-class peers have been weeded out. In addition, graduate students in the arts and humanities will very likely read scholars who write about social reproduction mechanisms, bringing to light precisely what these graduate students are experiencing in real time. Most of them get a sense of being behind (a consequence of, in Gee's phrasing, being "true" rather than "false beginners."[24] They realize they don't have voices and the language of authority. They know they don't belong, that they don't know how to slip into seminar conversations, that they don't recognize cues for speaking, how to hold the floor and demonstrate what little legitimated cultural capital they have. They don't know how to cede to other speakers and return to the conversation, how to keep a distance from issues and arguments through a fine sense of irony, which always mocks those who get caught up and tangled in their own thoughts. They don't wear the right clothes, have the right physical gestures or straight teeth. They also know that the very fact of their presence in the vestibule to the academic community represents social class betrayal – that they are trying to gain entrance into the community their home community has distrusted, populated by the "stupid rich bastards," as Laurel Johnson Black's father memorably called them.[25] They pretend (as they have been taught to pretend) they are only on a search for knowledge or social justice, but at a perhaps deeper and unacknowledged level, they have gone to school to escape their class of origin.

Social class betrayal is complicated. Because I am wrapped in it myself, I can't adequately describe the phenomenological contortions working-class academics put themselves through in order to justify what they are doing. The fact that our trajectory would even be known as social class betrayal reveals the twists involved in our prototypical American desire to make "a better life for ourselves." The game usually begins with a double gesture from our parents. On the one hand, one or both of them want us to get out of the working-class condition. On the other, they recognize the escape means leaving them behind, geographically, emotionally, linguistically, and intellectually. A prototypical narrative will have a parent (for me, it was my grandmother) being a cook, maintenance person, or bricklayer in the university the social class traitor attends. Richard Rodriguez' *Hunger of Memory* was perhaps the first book documenting

---

[24] Gee, "Learning," 14-15.

[25] Laurel Johnson Black, "Stupid Rich Bastards," in *This Fine Place So Far from Home: Voices of Academics from the Working Class*, ed. C. L. Barney Dews and Carolyn Leste Law, 15 (Philadelphia: Temple UP, 1995).

the contradictory desire of a parent's wish for his or her child.[26] I hated that book when I first read it decades ago. I was in graduate school and didn't want to recognize the degree to which I was playing Rodriguez' game.

I can track my sense of the game to when I was in first grade in a one-room rural schoolhouse. As if on film, I remember the day when the kids from a new family came into the school. I remember the older girl's name – it was Rose Wicks (shades of Steinbeck). There were about five Wicks who filed in after the rest of us had settled down to our work. The kids were poor – and when you say "poor" in rural Wisconsin, you mean it. Their hair wasn't combed – it seemed straight, unwashed, uncut, kind of sandy. I don't think the boys wore t-shirts; they just had well-worn shirts on over their bare torsos. They all seemed dirty. They smelled. You didn't want to get too near them. The kids made fun of them during recess and there was a fight. I remember Rose trying to protect her younger siblings. I expect that I also joined in on the teasing – but I also remember that if I did, I knew it was wrong. They were gone in a few weeks.

After my grandparents lost the farm (we were the typical rural, working-class, extended family), my nuclear family moved to a house a mile and a half outside Richland Center, Wisconsin, population 4,000. As I approached junior high age, the major social class difference was between town and country. I used to ride my bike into town to play in the park, and I learned about the wealthier kids in town. I became friends with several and eventually fell in love with one of them. They were clearly the more popular kids, which set them apart from the rest of us. I also learned about the kids on the other side of the tracks. Like a true straddler,[27] I was friends with a few of them, too.

One thing is worth noting: because Richland Center was a small town, which minimizes social class differences, we all seemed to share the same language. I wasn't fully aware of the linguistic differences between myself and my middle-class peers until I got to graduate school at the University of Wisconsin. There I experienced the common cross-over's fear of mumble-speak. I knew we were being evaluated in our seminars on the basis of our contributions to the discussions, which really meant on how we were displaying our cultural and linguistic capital. I worried about being able to speak in complete sentences. I would spend so much time rehearsing my comment that I wasn't able to keep track of what was going on, so that when the professor finally called on me with my hand vestigially raised, whatever mess came out of my mouth was clearly irrelevant to the conversation. In a strange way, this might correspond to Bourdieu's notion of hysterisis, the lag effect.[28] By the time working-class students hit the target, it has moved elsewhere.

---

[26] Richard Rodriguez, *Hunger of Memory: The Education of Richard Rodriguez* (New York: Bantam Books, 1982).

[27] Lubrano's term.

[28] Bourdieu, *Distinctions*, 142.

My ragged professional trajectory is not unusual for working-class academics. Some working-class academics are very smart, and they shoot to the front of the class – probably more quickly than their middle-class counterparts, who were born to privilege. But the rest of us start late, we pick up speed late, and we end late – which is why we are known as latecomers (the flipside of being a true beginner). I have been painfully aware of my latecomer status since I began work on my PhD at age 40 after having taught high school English for thirteen years. It would take a book to describe the different permutations I have gone through and self-doubts I have entertained in my struggle to gain middle-class acceptability. I of course didn't know that's what I was looking for, but that's what it was. In the early stages, I just wanted to be liked. I mistook membership in the popular group of kids for being liked – and, although I shudder to be so crass, membership in that group meant distancing myself from the distinctly rural, working-class kids I had grown up with. I didn't know at the time that meant distancing myself from my family as well.

I achieved this distancing by becoming one of the better students. I belong firmly in the middle of the working-class academic trope of being a voracious reader, stimulated by my mother, who knew that reading was a way out of the social class into which she had married – her father had been working-class and her mother from the vaguely intellectual fraction of the middle class. I learned early on that reading was my escape from my father, who always wanted me to be holding the wrenches while he fixed the car. He would come into the house and yell, "Where's that Irvie?!" and I would be lying on my bed and reading something like *The Count of Monte Cristo* – the first book I remember as truly transporting me into another world. My father would be one word away from violence if he caught me reading on a Saturday afternoon. I thought then that a perfect life would be to be a writer whose other world magically unfolded as he or she wrote, who would be reading the words for the first time as they flowed from the pen. I tried to imagine what it would be like to have the words come out faster than you could think them. You wouldn't know the scenes until they appeared on the page. Later I read Jack London's description of being caught up in a "white hot sheet of flame." I didn't have those words for it, but that's what I meant.

I am sixty-one years old now, and I can say that I have for most of my adult life been pursuing that flame. It has come to me now and then when the words roll out beneath my fingers, but it happens only when I forget that I am writing with a purpose and audience in mind. It happens when I write to figure something out and I don't have to worry about pages or time. But then, inevitably, as now, I am jerked back into the real world when I remember that I should be adding publications to my name – which is the academic's way of being liked.

So let me return to my theme. I am making some connections here: these connections are the web that constitute my life as a working-class academic, one who learned how to use his unflame-like writing to escape his working-class origin, which my paragraphs above reveal as the classic oedipal desire to overturn the rule of my father (I'll skip the bit about being in my mother's bed). The central thread is the link between literacy and social class. My father represents the working-class ethos. He doesn't like words. He is authoritarian. He values manual labor and distrusts the intellectual class – which is really the part of my mother that he intensely dislikes. In his working-class world, people who labor don't have time to read and write. Reading and writing represent the world he distrusts and even hates, the world of people who don't have to work for a living. Extrapolating from Bourdieu's thesis, you could say the difference between the working and middle classes is the difference between words (symbolic goods) and labor.

I wanted to get into the world of words. I disguised my motivations with a funhouse of false gestures, but at the core of my life has lain this escape from my working-class origins through literacy; one could call it white, middle-class, male literacy. The urge to read and write – which is fundamentally an urge to read and write within the frame of middle-class discourse – may well be identifiable with and inseparable from the desire to escape our working-class origins. This is why so many of our narratives feature the "I-was-different" trope, the one that has us so often in the library. In a way, my father was right: by hanging around the library, I was trying to get out of work. I was in effect learning how to stage myself.

Perhaps because this escape is a core motivation, it is unacceptable. Consequently, I have staged myself within a variety of more acceptable social narratives, starting with variations on the search for truth. I have travelled though a more general knowledge-search narrative, to the dedicated-teacher narrative, which leads almost ineluctably for working-class academics to the social justice one. I do not mean to make light of any of these stories we tell about ourselves, but neither do I (in this essay which is flirting with the off-stage me) want to deny the complications of having been a working-class kid who used literacy as a means of escaping his social class origin. Steinbeck said a novelist is just a well-paid liar. I don't think academics are all that different. What's most remarkable is the way we can make up stories about ourselves and forget we told them.

Selected Bibliography

Adair, Vivyan C., and Sandra L. Dahlberg, ed. *Reclaiming Class: Women, Poverty, and the Promise of Higher Education in America*. Philadelphia: Temple UP, 2003.

Bartolomé, Lilia. *The Misteaching of Academic Discourses: The Politics of Language in the Classroom*. Boulder CO: Westview Press, 1998.

Berger, Peter, and Thomas Luckmann. *The Social Construction of Reality*. New York: Anchor Books, 1967.

Bernstein, Basil. *Class, Codes, and Control*, vol I. London: Routledge & Kegan Paul, 1971.

Bourdieu, Pierre. *Language and Symbolic Power*. Ed. John B. Thompson. Transl. Gino Raymond and Matthew Adamson. Cambridge, MA: Havard UP, 1991.

Bourdieu, Pierre. *Distinction: A Social Critique of the Judgement of Taste*. Trans. Richard Nice. Cambridge MA: Harvard UP, 1984.

Bowles, Hebert, and Samuel Gintis. *Schooling in Capitalist America*. New York: Basic Books, 1976.

Brice Heath, Shirley. *Ways with Words: Language, Life, and Work in Communities and Classrooms*. New York: Cambridge UP, 1983.

Black, Laurel Johnson. "Stupid Rich Bastards." *This Fine Place So Far from Home: Voices of Academics from the Working Class*. Eds. Dews, C. L. Barney, and Carolyn Leste Law. Philadelphia: Temple UP, 1995. 13-25.

Gee, James Paul. "Learning Language as a Matter of Learning Social Languages within Discourses." *Language Learning and Teacher Education: A Sociocultural Approach*. Ed. Margaret R. Hawkins. Clevedon UK: Multilingual Matters, 2004. 13-31.

_____.*Social Linguistics and Literacies*, 2d ed. Bristol PA: Taylor & Francis, 1996.

Giroux, Henry. *Border Crossing: Cultural Workers and the Politics of Education*. New York: Routledge, 1991.

Kohn, Melvin L., and Carmi Schooler. "Stratification, Occupation, and Orientation." *Work and Personality: An Inquiry into the Impact of Social Stratification*. Eds. Melvin L. Kohn and Carmi Schooler. Norwood NJ: Ablex, 1983. 5-33.

Lakoff, George. *Women, Fire, and Dangerous Things: What Categories Reveal About the Mind*. Chicago: U of Chicago Press, 1987.

Lareau, Annette. *Unequal Childhoods: Class, Race, and Family Life*. Berkeley, CA: U of California Press, 2003.

Linkon, Sherry Lee, ed. *Teaching Working Class*. Amherst, MA: U of Massachusetts Press, 1999.

Lubrano, Alfred. *Limbo: Blue-Collar Roots, White Collar Dreams*. Hoboken, N.J.: John Wiley & Sons, Inc., 2004.

Rosch, Eleanor. "Principles of Categorization." *Cognition and Categorization*. Eds. Eleanor Rosch and Barbara Lloyd. Hillsdale NJ: Lawrence Erlbaum Associates, 1978. 25-49.

Rose, Mike. *Lives on the Boundary: The Struggles and Achievements of America's Underprepared* New York: Penguin Books, 1990.

Rodriguez, Richard. *Hunger of Memory: the Education of Richard Rodriguez*. New York: Bantam Books, 1982.

Ryan, Jake, and Charles Sackrey, eds. *Strangers in Paradise: Academics from the Working Class*. Boston: South End Press, 1984.

Shephard, Alan, John McMillan, and Gary Tate, eds. *Coming to Class: Pedagogy and the Social Class of Teachers*. Portsmouth, NH: Boynton/Cook, 1998.

Shevin, David, and Larry Smith, eds. *Getting by: Stories of Working Lives*. Huron, Ohio: Bottom Dog Press, 1996.

Welsch, Kathleen A., ed. *Those Winter Sundays: Female Academics and Their Working-Class Parents*. Lanham, MD: UP of America, 2005.

Willis, Paul E. *Learning to Labor: How Working-Class Kids Get Working-Class Jobs*. Westmead, England: Saxon House, 1977.

Wittgenstein, Ludwig. *Philosophical Investigations*. New York: Macmillan. 1953.

Zandy, Janet, and Larry Smith, eds. *Writing Work: Writers on Working-Class Writing*. Huron, OH: Bottom Dog Press, 1999.

Class Distinctions: Mapping Poverty on the Contemporary US Class Landscape

Vivyan C. Adair (Hamilton College)*

In arguing for more finely nuanced and inclusive understandings of class in the contemporary United States, I write as a feminist "poverty class scholar" articulating an identity, experience, marginality, and concomitant consciousness and epistemology distinct from those of working class and more traditional, middle class and elite scholars and academics. Much has been written about the need to authorize the experiences and perspectives of the working class, whose voices are all too easily subsumed under the universalizing mantle of the middle and elite classes.[1] As Michelle Tokarczyk notes, the working class suffers "irrevocable losses" as they are silenced "by the singular middle class voice of the academy."[2]

Yet, it is also the case that both in and out of academe, representations of working class identity are juxtaposed against and thus reinforce the "otherness" of poor women who are positioned as boundary markers, demarcating the unacceptable and illegal "others" of the working class. Concomitantly in claiming to speak for and then neglecting these differences, working class scholarship allows for the co-optation, erasure and mis-representation of the experiences and perspectives of the poor. Ultimately, I argue that only by acknowledging, exposing, and critiquing the differential impact of class on poor women's lives can we begin to understand the complex operations of class in the contemporary U.S.

Missing from Class

November 30, 1999, dawned overcast and gray as demonstrators marched toward the long-awaited World Trade Organization's opening ceremonies at the historic Paramount Theater in Seattle, Washington. By mid-day upwards of 50,000 labor union members and supporters had joined with tens of thousands of impassioned demonstrators of every ilk, as Capital Hill residents cheered and a portable CD player blared out the late Seattleite Jimi Hendrix's rendition of *The Star Spangled Banner*. As the world watched, steelworkers, machinists,

---

* This essay appeared in *Sociology*, 39:5, 2005, 817-834. It is reprinted here on permission of Sage Publications Ltd. from Vivyan Adair, "US Working Class/Poverty Divides." (Copyright BSA Publications Ltd, 2005).
[1] See Michelle Tokarczyk and Elizabeth Fay, *Working Class Women in the Academy: Laborers in the Knowledge Factory* (Amherst: University of Massachusetts Press, 1993), Jake Ryan and Charles Sackrey, *Strangers in Paradise: Academics from the Working-Class* (New York: University Press of America, 1996), and C.L. Barney Dews and Carolyn Leste Law, *This Fine Place So Far from Home: Voices of Academics from the Working Class* (Philadelphia: Temple University Press, 1995).
[2] Tokarczyk, *Working Class Women in the Academy*, 5.

service employees and tradesmen walked and protested through the streets of
Seattle arm in arm. Taxi drivers struck for the day and Longshoremen shut
down docks along the west coast of the United States in a show of unity. The
"WTO, Battle in Seattle" had begun in earnest. The next day labor leader Brian
McWilliams addressed a pre-march rally in a packed stadium telling the crowd,

> There will be no business as usual today [...] demonstrating to the corporate
> CEOs that the global economy will not run without the consent of the workers
> everywhere [...]The interests of working people transcend international
> boundaries.[3]

In steadfast solidarity, a very small but vocal band of welfare recipient and
rights activists, made up of women of different races, ethnicities, sexualities and
ages, many with children in tow, joined the protest. However, it quickly became
very apparent to us that we were not necessarily viewed as "sisters in struggle,"
that indeed we were less than welcome on these streets teeming with proud and
defiant workers. One group of steelworkers reading our "Poor Women and
Children Fight Back" sign, suggested in rather pornographic terms that we had
no right to walk with "real workers" since we were more suited to other "walking occupations." A team of telephone line-men behind them similarly insisted
that we "go back to the *projects* to finish watching *Oprah*." As the angry men
surrounded us, one warned me personally that I had better "get off [my] ass and
get a real job," if I expected to earn *his* support. While I held firm, a friend and
colleague was groped by a large man sporting a steelworker's hat. Although at
one level the WTO protests were a remarkable show of workers' unity on the
larger world stage, to many the event also highlighted the degree to which even
self-defined locations on the contemporary American class landscape are sites
of heated contestation.

What was at stake in this unfortunate and momentary public clash of class
markings was the right of poor women to call themselves members of the working class. Ironically, in other venues US working class academics claim and co-
opt the experiences of poor women as their own, even as nascent "poverty class
academics" attempt to articulate and leverage a distinct class positionality.
These gaps are palpable and resonant although little addressed in contemporary
US class studies.

Class theorist Michael Zweig does attempt to address this lacuna in *Working Class Majority: America's Best Kept Secret.*[4] Here he argues that the US
working class is quite broad and that the poor should be considered an integral
part of the working class because they do work and always have worked. Zweig
adds that because "poverty happens to the working class," and because position-

---

[3] *Seattle Post Intelligencer*, "Demonstrators Colorful, Peaceful, and Purposeful,"
http://seattlepi.nwsource.com/local/note01.shtml (Consulted September 25, 2004.)
[4] Michael Zweig, *The Working Class Majority: America's Best Kept Secret* (Ithaca, New York: ILR
Press, 2000).

ing the poor as the underclass separates them and "prohibits coalition work among all working people ... giving voice and power to the poor requires giving voice and power to the working class, bringing into focus its reality in a class-conflicted society." His point is that "the ability to carry our combined grievances to the capitalist requires the power of an organized, united working class."[5]

US working class scholars exercise Zweig's perspective, claiming to consider representation and analysis of the poor, in particular the new working poor of the welfare class. For example, the Center for Working-Class Studies at Youngstown State University ("the first center of its kind in the United States devoted to the study of working class life and culture") purports to value interdisciplinary work that considers intersections of class with race, gender and sexuality, creating an inclusive vision of the working class that could include members of the working poor and welfare class. Yet this center focuses almost exclusively on working-class experience and culture as they are related to "labor organizing, the economy and politics, and the meaning of work...in a shifting global economy." As a result, projects at Youngstown center around industry and economics, attempting to provide an understanding of "workers consciousnesses," "the labor community," the "mobilization of workers," "migrations of industrial workers," labor history, and even sculpting and filmmaking representing "the plight of the industrial working class."[6] There is not a hungry child, a homeless single mother, a punitive welfare policy, or a child-care issue in sight.

Similarly, at the biennial *How Class Works Conference* at SUNY Stony brook, organizer Zweig promises a focus on "the lived experiences of class [...] that are rooted in and illuminate social realities." Rather, the overwhelmingly white and heterosexual conference participants deliver thoughtful investigations of mechanics and newspaper strikes and union work, workplace autonomy, globalization, and the economics and politics of war. Rather than addressing the class politics that lead to a shameful lack of medical care or food for poor families, they consider workplace policies on medical insurance, the practice of medicine as labor, and Bourdieu-ian working class consumption patterns; rather than debating issues of punitive welfare policy and prohibitions concerning higher education for poor single mothers, they puzzle over questions of intellectual work, academic labor and the dilemmas of "scholarship boys" who don't quite fit in.[7] Despite optimistic proclamations to the contrary, it is clear that US working class academic praxis most often centers on the lives and experiences of blue color, white, and heterosexual industrial male workers.

---

[5] Ibid, 78–79.

[6] Youngstown State University, *The Center for Working-Class Studies at Youngstown State University*, www.as.ysu.edu (Consulted November 10, 2005)

[7] SUNY Stony Brook, "How Class Works, 2006 Conference," https://naples.cc.sunysb.edu/CAS/wcm.nsf/pages/conference. (Consulted January 12, 2006.)

Most class theorists maintain that "working class" is a designation premised on distinctions that are a matter of income, assets, power, cultural distinctions, and prestige.[8] By coupling the experiences of blue color workers with those of poor women and their children, they juxtapose an allegedly unified "working class" experience against that of members of the middle and elite classes. In the act of claiming to speak for and then neglecting the unique experiences and expressions of lower-income women of all races who work both inside and outside of their homes, a sub-set of the "working class" – including unwaged home workers, women on welfare, low-wage service and domestic workers and undocumented women and men engaged in non-union day labor – are co-opted, erased and rendered silent.

Additionally, as British sociologist and class theorist Diane Reay points out, "even contemporary research which argues for the inclusion of women in classifications of social class works exclusively with women as employees in the labour market." Further, and crucially, she argues that a singular focus "based on male labour market participation…overlooks the complexity inherent in the relationships between gender and social class" and results in an "over simplification of what class constitutes."[9] This leads to virulent forms of misrecognition and exclusions that "overlook the complexity inherent in the relationship between gender and social class…the public and the private, the family and labour market." Leon Fink adds that "in these male work centered labor history narratives, questions of gender relations are likely to be forsaken for more publicly dramatic points of conflict," and we forgo "tougher, more self-critical [and productive] angles of analyses."[10]

Other theorists imagine and position the lives and perspectives of the poor as a part of the spectrum of working class experience.[11] Indeed, class in the US is relational, and the connections and distinctions among members of the middle, elite and working classes could be (and sometimes are) represented by a synecdoche or singular US class archetype.[12] A continuum of class analysis could include a range of experiences running from the profoundly and generationally impoverished to the relatively secure, propertied and "respectable" working class, or for that matter through to the middle class and on to the wealthiest, most privileged, powerful and elite in our nation. Inhabitants on this class spectrum are bound by common relationships to identity development

---

[8] See Zweig, *The Working Class Majority*, and Stanley Aronowitz, *How Class Works: Power and Social Movement* (New Haven, CT: Yale University Press, 2003).

[9] Diane Reay, "Rethinking Social Class: Qualitative Perspectives on Class and Gender," *Sociology*, 32:2, 1998, 259-75.

[10] Leon Fink, *In Search of the Working Class: Essays in American Labor History and Political Culture* (Chicago: University of Illinois Press, 1994) 3.

[11] Louis Alvarez and Andres Kolker, *People Like Us: Social Class in America* (New York: Center for New American Media and the Corporation for Public Broadcasting, 2001)

[12] Sarah Mondale and Sarah Patton, *School: The Story of American Public Education* (Boston: Beacon Press, 2001).

through deeply entrenched ideologies of citizenship, nation, freedom, progress, ownership, family, sacrifice and duty. However, there are obvious dangers inherent in this methodology; indeed this is one of the mechanisms through which our appreciation of class difference is leveled and erased in the US.

By positioning poor women and children within larger class matrixes, the question of who speaks for, who represents and who symbolizes the identities, experiences, and perspectives of those embedded in the struggle against capital, emerges as central. In "The Unhappy Marriage of Marxism and Feminism," Heidi Hartman pointed out that like the marriage of husband and wife sanctioned in English common law, Marxism acts to subsume the perspectives and material realities exposed through Feminist analysis. She claims that in this unhappy union Marxism and Feminism become one, and that one is Marxism. One could extend Hartman's metaphor to say that in class studies today we proclaim that "the working class and the poor are one, and that one is the working class." Like Hartmann I would suggest that, "either we need a healthier marriage or we need a divorce."[13]

The most obvious differences between the working class and the poor rest on questions of income, resources, and power. In the United States today the poorest families are headed by single mothers: In 2004 women earned about seventy-six percent of what men were paid for comparable full-time work; single mother incomes sufficed as family incomes; often for every dollar a single mother earned she incurred childcare costs (in terms of money and risk) often leading to a zero sum gain; single mothers – and low-income women in general – were less able to secure lucrative college, professional, technical and trade credentials; and simply put, one income was often half (or less) that of two.[14]

The US Census Bureau indicated that over seventy-six percent of the single parent families in the United States were headed by single mothers, and the median annual income for these households was $29,001 in 2003. This income is approximately 200% of the poverty line, precisely the artificial figure intended to demarcate the boundary between a liveable and an unsustainable family wage in the US.[15] (The median income for families headed by single fathers with no female present in 2003 was $41, 711). A full one-third of single mother families had $10,000 or less a year to live on; 3.4 percent of them lived on less than $5,000 per year; and a single mother with two children who was able to qualify for and receive welfare, supported her family on under $7,000 per year in cash grants and food stamps, somehow surviving on less than one half of the

---

[13] Heidi Hartman, "The Unhappy Marriage of Marxism and Feminism," in *Women and Revolution,* ed. Lydia Sargent, (Boston: South End Press, 1981) 97-115.
[14] "National Compensation Survey: Occupational Wages in the US," *US Bureau of Labor Statistics,* http://www.bls.gov/ (Consulted January 15, 2005).
[15] In the United States most federally funded "poverty programs" set "200% or less of the poverty level" as the requirement for enrolment and receipt of benefits. http://www.statecoverage.net/schlp.htm (Consulted January 15, 2006).

official poverty threshold for a family of three in that same year. Unmarried
mothers and single mothers of color are disproportionately represented among
the poor, at the bottom rung (the fifth quintile) of the income latter, while married, white men and women are over-represented in the highest quintiles of family income distribution charts. The median income for US families with married
parents in 2003 was $61,254, and the average "blue collar" working class popu-
lation – composed most often of married, or once married, working class men,
women and their children – earned a median family income that enabled them
to live well above the poverty line in the same year.[16]

Specifically, in the three counties surrounding Seattle – the home of the
1999 WTO class battles – in 2004 nearly 300,000 people lived in poverty although at least one of their family members worked full-time. These are cash-
iers, janitors, maids, childcare, food service, and grounds workers making between six and eleven dollars an hour or about $12,000 - $15,000 per year.[17] In
stark contrast, the labor union workers, pipe-fitters, electricians, machinists, and
longshoreman who proudly marched in the WTO protests had individual annual
incomes of $40,120 - $80,920 in 2004.[18]

Two representatives of the "working class" in Seattle were recently highlighted in a series of articles in the *Seattle Post-Intelligencer* entitled "The
Other View from the Top: Hard work, Hard Times." Narciza Pineda is a single
mother and a janitor who "scrubs and polishes the floors and toilets at [the
Space Needle] Seattle's most visible symbol of progress" for $10.75 per hour.
Taking home about $15,000 per year, Pineda and her three children barely sur-
vive, living in a "dented white trailer beyond the safety net of a nearby driving
range and a block from the city's household hazardous materials waste dump."
The rented trailer her family lives in has one bed for four people and the bath-
room is missing its door. Pineda regularly runs out of food for her children, is
habitually ill, and drives an unreliable and broken down car so that she can
work all night leaving her children alone and unprotected.[19] Although Pineda
works full-time she and her children are poor and share distinct experiences and
understandings of poverty with others who constitute a common consciousness
and a class.

Another article in the series similarly highlights the plight of a solid member of the working class, Rob Anderson, a white "family man" who lost a job as
an electrician at age 47. Prior to his lay-off in 2000, Anderson, who had worked
at Totem Electric in Tacoma, Washington, was making $60,000 per year. Al-

---

[16] Carmen de Navas Walt and Robert Cleveland, "Income in the United States 2003: Current Population Reports, Consumer Income," *US Census Bureau*, http://www.census.gov/prod/2003pubs/p60-
221.pdf (Consulted January 11, 2005)
[17] Heather Foster, Paul Nygan and Phuong Cat Le, "Hard Work, Hard Times," *Seattle Post Intelligencer*, sec. A11, February 10, 2005.
[18] *National Compensation Survey*. http://www.bls.gov/ (Consulted January 15, 2006).
[19] Foster, "Hard Work Hard Times," A11.

though impoverished during the layoff, Anderson had accrued almost $40,000 in savings that allowed him to weather the storm and to keep his house, his car, and to attend classes related to his trade credentials. By 2005, Anderson enjoyed a salary of $68,000 as a union electrician with a contracting firm. He and his wife have a family wage that should approach $100,000 in 2005.[20] In this salary range most US working class families have some health care, savings and insurance. They own their own homes, eat regular meals and pay their electric and heating bills. Many take occasional vacations, send at least some of their children to college, and will have a modest income in retirement.[21] It is difficult to imagine the utility of a "working class" demarcation that covers such a wide range of incomes and benefits, much less one that attempts to locate a broad spectrum of experiences including both Anderson who lives well above the poverty level and Pineda and others who are barely able – and some who are unable – to even subsist.

I hasten to point out that for many class theorists, economic conditions and their immediate implications constitute just one – sometimes misleading – aspect of social class distinction. Reay points out in "Re-thinking social class; qualitative perspectives on class and gender," that class is more than income, that it is rather "a complicated mixture of the material, the discursive, psychological predispositions and sociological dispositions" that are "played out in interaction with others in social fields."[22] US class theorist Donna Langston also notes in "Tired of Playing Monopoly?" that "class is more than just the amount of money you have: it is also the presence of economic security" and determines life chances and choices. She adds:

> As a result of the class you are born into and raised in, class is your understanding of the world and where you fit in; it is composed of ideas, behavior, attitudes, values and language; class is how you think, feel, act, look, dress, talk, move, walk…We experience class at every level of our lives. Class affects what we perceive as and what we have available to us as choices…class doesn't wash out in the rinse water.[23]

Indeed, an enormous and irresolvable income disparity represents only the most superficial distinction between the poor and the working classes in the US; it is rather the lived, bodily, psychological and social manifestations of such disparity that are most compelling. Mary Federman reflected in *Monthly Labor Review* that whereas 77.6% of working families own a home as few as 24.63% of

---

[20] Carol Smith, "The Other View from the Top: The Working Poor," *Seattle Post Intelligencer Special Report*, sec. A1, February 10, 2005.

[21] Peter Schochet and Anu Rangaragjan, "Characteristics of Low Wage Workers and Their Labor Market Experience," *Mathematica Policy Research Inc,* http://www.mathematica-mpr.com (Consulted January 10, 2005).

[22] Reay, "Rethinking Social Class," 259.

[23] Donna Langston, "Tired of Playing Monopoly?" in *Race, Class and Gender: An Anthology*, eds Margaret Anderson and Patricia Hill Collins (Hayworth, CA: Wadsworth Press 2003) 141.

poor single parent headed families in the US do so.[24] Similarly, poor American families are far less likely to have health insurance, a phone, or a car. They are significantly more likely to experience eviction, discontinuation of gas or electric service, lack of food, infant mortality, violent crime, domestic abuse, and crowded and/or unsafe living conditions.[25] In this sense the economics of class are tied to its material and psychological manifestations for poor women. Material class distinctions become imprimaturs, producing, marking, mutilating and fixing the bodies of poor women and their being and value in the world, in ways that distinguish them from the working, middle and elite classes in the US.

Michel Foucault refers to human bodies as "dense transference point[s] of power." Reading poverty through Foucault's theories of bodily inscription, in "Branded with Infamy: Inscriptions of Poverty and Class in the United States" I examined the means by which, unlike members of "higher classes:"

> Poor women and children of all races in the United States today are multiply marked with signs of both discipline and punishment that cannot be erased or effaced. They are systematically produced through both twentieth-century forces of socialization and discipline and eighteenth-century exhibitions of public mutilation. In addition to coming into being as disciplined and docile bodies, poor single mothers and their children are physically inscribed, punished, and displayed as dangerous and pathological other…These are more than metaphoric and self-patrolling marks of discipline. Rather, on myriad levels poor women and their children, like the 'deviants' publicly punished in Foucault's scenes of torture, are marked, mutilated, and made to bear and transmit signs in a public spectacle that brands the victim with infamy.[26]

My own life provides further evidence of these very specific and not so "hidden injuries of class."[27] I was raised by a poor, single, white mother who struggled to keep her four children sheltered, clothed, and fed. As a result poverty was written onto and into our senses of being as children at the level of private and public thought and body.

What I recall most vividly about being a child in a profoundly poor family was that we were constantly ill and hurt, and because we could not afford medical attention, illnesses and accidents spiraled into more dangerous conditions that became both a part of who we were and "written" proof that we were of no value in the world. Despite my mother's most valiant efforts to protect us, at an early age my siblings and I were stooped, bore scares that never healed prop-

---

[24] Mary Federman, "What Does it Mean to be Poor in America?," *Monthly Labor Review*, 119:9, 1996, 32-42.

[25] Katherine Edin and Laura Lein, *Making Ends Meet: How Single Mothers Survive Welfare and Low-Wage Work* (New York: Russel Sage Foundation, 1997).

[26] Vivyan C. Adair, "Branded with Infamy: Inscriptions of Poverty and Class in the United States," *Signs: Journal of Women in Culture and Society*, 27:2, 451-72.

[27] Richard Sennett and Johnathan Cobb, *The Hidden Injuries of Class* (New York: Vintage Books, 1972).

erly, and limped with feet mangled by ill-fitting, used Salvation Army shoes. When my frail, four year old sister's forehead was split open by a car door slammed in frustration, my mother was forced to sew the angry wound together on her own, leaving a mark of our inability to afford medical attention, of our physical and metaphoric "lack," on her very forehead. Our dirty and tattered clothing; posture that clearly reflected guilt, shame and lack of a sense of entitlement; scars and bodily dis-ease; and sheer hunger marked us as Others among our more fortunate working class neighbors and colleagues. When throughout elementary school we were sent to the office for mandatory and very public yearly check-ups, after privately testing the hearing and eyesight of working class children, the school nurse sucked air through her teeth as she donned surgical gloves to publicly check the hair of poor children for lice.

Other students and even our working class teachers read us as "trailer trash," as unworthy, laughable, and dangerous. They laughed at our "ugly shoes," our crooked and ill-serviced teeth, and the way we stank. In class we were excoriated for our inability to concentrate in school, our "refusal" to come to class prepared with proper school supplies, and our unethical behavior when we tried to take more than our allocated share of "free lunch." The daughters of working class parents in our school wore inexpensive twin-sets and matching knee socks from the Sears catalogue, lived in modest homes with mothers and with fathers who worked on their older cars on weekends, went bowling with their cousins. We were paraded in front of these working class students shamed and humiliated in our ragged and ill-fitting hand-me-downs, our very bodies signalling our Otherness while representing and testing the limits of working class identity and "deservedness."

If as children, our dishevelled and broken bodies were produced as signs of inferiority and undeservedness, as adults our mutilated bodies are read as signs of inner pathology and indecency as we are punished and then read as proof of the need for further discipline and punishment. When as a poor single mother my already bad teeth started to rot, and I was out of my head with pain, my choices as a welfare recipient, dependent upon state medical coupons, were either to let my teeth fall out or to have them pulled out, leaving me toothless. In order to pay our rent and to put shoes on my daughter's tiny feet I sold my blood at plasma clinics on a monthly basis until I was rejected as a "donor" because I had become so anaemic. One good friend sold her ovum to a fertility clinic in a painful and potentially damaging process. Others exposed themselves to danger and disease by selling their bodies for sex in order to feed and clothe their babies.

In the US the bodies of poor women and children are scarred and mutilated by state mandated material deprivation and public exhibition. Our broken bodies are positioned as spectacles, as patrolling images used to socialize and con-

trol bodies within the body politic.[28] As Loic Wacquant has pointed out, programs targeted toward the poor in the US have increasingly been "turned into
instruments of surveillance and control" allowing the state to materially mark
the poor as signs of pathology and "criminalize poverty via the punitive con-
tainment of the poor."[29] As a result, poor women and children are taught to read
our abject bodies as the site of our own punishment and erasure.[30] In this excess
of meaning the space between private body and public sign is often collapsed.

I am committed to not reducing experiences of poverty to those of our
markings; indeed my own community of origin resisted and was also of course
a source of strength, vision, beauty and wisdom. My point is also not that members of the working class do not suffer class inscription and concomitant oppression, for I know that they do. Rather I hope to illustrate that A) poor women
and children are positioned, develop, and resist differently than do the working
class on myriad levels, B) increasingly the articulation of working class identity
is juxtaposed against and thus reinforces the "otherness" of poor women who
are positioned as boundary markers, denoting the unacceptable and illegal "others" of the working class, and C) at the same time in claiming to speak for and
then neglecting these differences, representations of the working class allow for
the co-optation, erasure and mis-representation of poor women and children.[31]
Beverly Skeggs notion that "we need to shift perspective, therefore from recognition and think instead about who is being made invisible and who is empathi-
cally denied in the process of recognition" seems apropos and long overdue in
the case of poor women vis-à-vis articulations of working class identity and
value in the contemporary US.[32]

Speaking of the Working Class

These material, psychological and social distinctions are intimately associated
with disparate representations and (de)valuations of the poor and the working
class. In the US poor women are imagined – and then as a result punished and

---

[28] Vivyan Adair and Sandra Dahlberg, eds., *Reclaiming Class: Women, Poverty and the Promise of
Higher Education* (Philadelphia: Temple University Press, 2003).

[29] Loic Wacquant, "Urban Marginality in the Coming Millennium," *Urban Studies*, 36:10, 1999,
1639-47.

[30] As I have argued in "Branded with Infamy: Inscriptions of Poverty and Class in the United States"
welfare reform programs such as "Bride-fare" "Tidy-fare" and "Work-fare" are designed to socialize
others by exposing and publicly punishing and marking "misfits" whose bodies are read as proof of
their refusal or inability to capitulate to capitalist, racist and heterosexist values and mores.

[31] Sandra Dahlberg concurs, adding that: "cultural differences and chances for opportunities are as
distinct between the working class and the poverty class as those that distinguish the middle class
from the upper class. While recognizing the similarities, explorations of working-class and poverty-
class experience and theory must be disjoined and examined separately to challenge negatively essen-
tialized portrayals and perceptions distinctly applied to each." See her "Survival in a Not So Brave
New World" in *Relcaiming Class*, 71.

[32] Beverly Skeggs, *Class, Self, Culture* (London: Routledge, 2004) 13.

disciplined – as single mothers who are marked by race, lack male authority and values, make bad choices, engage in pathological behaviors, and are a threat to our nation and indeed our own children. At the same time the working class is most often imagined as unmarked in terms of race and as consisting of families with male heads of household, who although "rough," work diligently and embody and enjoy independence, legal heterosexuality, autonomy, logic and order. Although not "polished," elite or privileged – and as a result not viewed as "natural" academics, leaders, or intellectuals – in the service of hegemony, members of the working class are valued as the "bedrock" of a democratic and capitalist culture.

Public descriptions and analysis of "the great unwashed" are regularly juxtaposed against these alleged values of the working class. Lillian Rubin's best selling *Worlds of Pain: Life in the Working Class Family*, presents us with representations of the working class that position them as fragile and yet normative in the contemporary US.[33] Here Rubin introduces us to "decent, clean, honest and hard working families" who constitute the American working classes. Attempting to evoke pathos, Rubin reminds us that members of the working class "[play] by the rules of the game," that they "try hard, work hard, [marry], obey the law and [teach] their children to do the same."[34] Even though these good citizens are workers and consumers – collecting goods, homes, appliances, campers, trucks, and boats – the "good life allude[s] them." What Rubin laments is not hunger, homelessness, public scorn and "otherness," but the fact that for her fifty working class families "wages were increasing but not as fast as prices," "life was hard, bills kept coming," "there was little free time to enjoy prized possessions," and thus the working class finds itself "running – always running to keep from falling by the wayside." [35]

The fear of "falling" into the alleged chaos of poverty looms large for these white, married and working class families. Rubin adds:

> [As a nation] we knew plenty about the poor families, the dependent families, the delinquent families who made the headlines, who crowd the welfare roles, who tap public resources. But we knew almost nothing of the 40 million American workers [...] employed in blue-collar jobs, most of them steady workers living in stable families, most of them asking for nothing and getting nothing from the government programs.[36]

These "ordinary, fiercely independent and decent working class Americans" are similarly heralded in an article in the *Wall Street Journal*, that focuses on the "hard work, no-nonsense attitudes, honesty, integrity, and a commitment to spouse, children, church and community" of the working class in the United

---

[33] Lillian Rubin, *Worlds of Pain: Life in the Working Class Family* (New York: Basic Books, 1992).
[34] Ibid, 14.
[35] Ibid, 14.
[36] Ibid, 18.

States today.[37] In a backhanded sort of way, even class historian Stanley Aronowitz recognizes that "by invoking the phrase 'working families,' the labor movement ... places itself on the side of one of the icons of conservative culture, the nuclear family, with all of its religious, homophobic, and exclusionary connotations."[38]

In pointed contrast, in public rhetoric poor single mothers are portrayed as "lazy due to years of government programming" "illogical...out of control" and "crazed trying to meet [their] own selfish needs."[39] These narratives representing poor women as dangerous parasites who have somehow violated the mandates of capitalism and heterosexism, invariably compare "unmarried mothers, misfits and spongers who are idle" to "legitimate and moral members of the working class who follow the rules, sacrifice and work"[40] and contrast "never married mothers who stay at home watching Jerry Springer"[41] to those "decent, married families [sic] who work hard everyday."[42] Outside of and against the circumscribed value and normalization of the working class, poor single mothers are constructed as what Giorgio Agamben calls "homo sacer," people with no value, the "enemy within."[43]

As a result, policies that connect poor mothers to the public sphere of the workplace are construed as narratives of rehabilitation that transform dangerous – sexualized and racialized – poor women's bodies into those of the relatively unmarked working class, safely neutralized under the covertures of work and marriage. For example, Heather MacDonald analyzes "work first" programs that "only [begin] with the moral reconstruction of the inner city" and culminate with a "restructuring [of] the lives of those women who are poor." This is a movement, she reminds us, from "moral weakness, irresponsibility and illegitimacy" to "the hard work and straightforward worker mentality of mainstream American society."[44]

In this logic it is work and marriage that redeem working class women and a rupture of patriarchal control, both inside and outside of the home that marks and condemns poor, unmarried mothers. To fail to recognize these differences in and through which the poor and working class are diametrically imagined, constructed, represented and materially and bodily maintained, even in the service of working class solidarity and important coalition work, is to erase the ex-

---

[37] Gary McDougal, "The Missing Half of the Welfare Debate," *The Wall Street Journal*, sec. L23, September 6, 1995.

[38] Aronowitz, *How Class Works*, 20.

[39] Heather MacDonald, "Love, Honor and Get off the Dole," *Daily News*, June 9, 2002, *Manhattan Institute*, http://manhattan-institute.org (Consulted March 4, 2005).

[40] Ibid

[41] George Gilder, "Welfare Fraud Today," *American Spectator*, sec. B6, September 5, 1995.

[42] Ruy Teixeira, "It's the White Working Class, Stupid," *Center for American Progress, Public Opinion Watch*, http://www.americanprogress.org (Consulted January 10, 2005).

[43] Qtd. in Skeggs, *Class, Self, Culture*, 178.

[44] Heather MacDonald, "Work=Slavery?" *New York Post*, sec.3, November 4, 2002.

perience and perspective, and as Zweig himself notes, the dignity and authority of the poor. Poor women and children struggle to wrest the same human dignity and articulate sense of self from the narrative of the working class, as do members of the working class from those who would seek to incorporate them into universalizing models of middle class identity.

Poverty Class in Academe

Many women born into poverty in the US become poor mothers. Those of us who somehow no longer experience the hardships of economic poverty identify our community and culture as emerging from the experience of poverty and remain grounded in that identity as surely as members of the working class or middle class maintain their own class identities and allegiances despite economic fluctuations. Poor women who have somehow – against all odds – made it to the academy and gone on to become scholars, are trebly distanced from working class, middle class, and elite scholars and scholarship. We view higher education and its structure, culture, and policies from the vantage point of poverty.

Our scholarship is shaped by our vision of poverty as it is read through our own experiences, perspectives and subsequent understandings of the processes of identity development as class intersects with gender, race, sexuality, disability and a range of salient identity markers. Our perceptions of the world, our notions of family and community, our frameworks, indeed our very epistemologies and methodologies come out of these experiences, connect us to each other, and are reinforced, shaped, and patrolled by our difference in the world. As such, I argue, we represent a class. We are members of the poverty class and in the academy some of us are beginning to work with our allies to struggle and engage with and through the development of "poverty class scholarship."

Both under and against the mantle of working class pedagogy, methodology, theory and praxis, poverty class scholars attempt to illuminate and theorize the specific mechanisms and processes through which the experiences, identities, perspectives and consciousness of individuals who were poor as children and/or as parents are articulated and maintained. By striving to theorize class from experience outward, poverty class scholars articulate particular standpoints that are fluid and contested, and that move both within and against the category of the working class, as well as the larger rubric of class in the US. Examining class as it is developed, lived and resisted in, through, and with our very bodies, we argue that although poor single mothers and their children share similarities and opportunities for solidarity with the working class, at a very fundamental level, the differences between us are literally "written on the body."

US working class scholars have well articulated the anomie and sense of dislocation they have experienced in the halls of higher education. Jake Ryan and Charles Sackrey's *Strangers in Paradise: Academics from the Working-*

Class,[45] explores working class scholars' experiences of anxiety, insecurity, and internalized contradiction. In this collection – made up of essays by twenty two white men and two white women – contributors explore their senses of anomie in academia while emphasizing their working class values of integrity, hard work and commitments to religion, marriage, family and education. These images are set against the raced, classed, gendered and sexed spectre of lower and lesser "others." In *Working Class Women in the Academy: Laborers in the Knowledge Factory*,[46] published three years before *Strangers in Paradise,* Tokarczyk and Elizabeth Fay had explored similar themes of dislocation and alienation. Contributors to this fine collection reflected their experiences of lack of support, guilt, self-doubt, erasure and exploitation in the academy.

Tellingly, none of the contributors to either collection described experiences of homelessness, lack of food, being left to fend for themselves while parents worked, the material costs of going without medical or dental care, or the pain and humiliation of public vilification; certainly none of these contributors themselves reflected experiences of working, caring for children and trying to keep a family intact, and fending off public assaults while earning educational degrees. The interpretation of experiences of poverty are simply absent from the texts. These omissions represent boundaries; to borrow from Reay, stories of working class identity and resistance in these collections are "fantasies which, in classic post-colonial terms, trap the colonized in the fantasies of the colonizer and which therefore play right into the hands of prevailing relations of power by silencing other actual or potential speaking positions."[47]

Similarly, in C.L. Barney Dews and Carolyn Leste Law's collection, *This Fine Place So Far from Home: Voices of Academics from the Working Class*, contributors evocatively described the psychological pain of embodying the "oxymoronic phrase: working class academic."[48] Again, working class contributors to this collection decried their sense of loss, conflict, and dislocation in academe as working class academics. These men and women had been raised by frugal, plain spoken, strong willed, decidedly father-centered, and legally married parents who although distanced from their children's academic lives provided security, a no-nonsense love of books, and a well tutored work ethic to their growing children. With two parents and usually one income, life was difficult but tolerable for these "honorable" members of the working class. These are powerful and poignant stories that press for a hearing; they are not however, the stories of poverty class academics. Indeed, the archetype of the lazy, illogical, over-sexed and illegal poor woman and her "brood of children" are precisely what these decent, hardworking and yet alienated children of the working class are implicitly juxtaposed against in these narratives. As Rita Felski ac-

---

[45] See fn. 1 for reference.
[46] Ibid.
[47] Reay, "Rethinking Social Class," 263.
[48] See fn. 1 for reference.

knowledges, a semiotics of "order and respectability" marking the working class is set against (and thus dependent upon) "sexualized images of lower-class women's bodies."[49]

The handful of US poverty class academics who survive and attempt to speak, certainly have similarly profound, complex, and raw feelings about the prices they paid, and continue to pay, for accessing higher education.[50] However, again at the level of the body and in terms of public representation and vilification (as both products and producers of the body), poverty class scholars share a very different experience, perspective, methodology, epistemology, and pain. Added to the general malaise expressed by working-class scholars is the very materiality of our lives. For example, I had come to academe as a thirty-four year old, undergraduate, unmarried mother who had dropped out of school. My body had been indelibly marked by poverty, I had a fragile child and too few resources, I came with medical and dental injuries and ailments that had not been properly cared for, and I moved with a posture that reflected my fear of taking up space, resources, or time. Those signs were read and reinscribed by many of my professors, colleagues and supervisors as proof of the mistakes I had made and would presumably make again. My Otherness was continuously inscribed on and read from my body. Perhaps as a result, my work and scholarship were often framed as suspect, and my body, my child and our material needs, were read as pathological in a paradigm that pitted the allegedly chaotic body of the poor woman against an archetype of independent, autonomous, ordered scholarship and class identity.

In this model working class students can be read as being mobile and able to "progress." Indeed, in the US our entire national narrative is based on the premise of upward mobility through "work and sacrifice." To the degree that their presence can reinforce the myth and absolve the privileged members of the academy of guilt, working class students are read as deserving, albeit "unrefined." This is not so with poverty class students who are seen as illegitimate and as de-historicized, de-contextualized, dangerous and static "Others" who refuse transformation.

As a result, I learned to pretend that I was a divorcée rather than an unmarried mother; that I did not have a child at home; that I was not frantic trying to sell my blood so that I could secure food and books; that I was not awake at nights worrying about the insurmountable debt I was accruing or the physical and mental stability of my child. Like most poor women I knew who tried to survive in academe, I learned to pass as a humble member of the working class. The more I passed, the more I was rewarded, and yet I was reminded on almost a daily basis that the truth of who I was, was simply unspeakable. In the proc-

---

[49] Rita Felski, "Nothing to Declare: Identity, Shame and the Lower Middle Class," *PMLA*, 115:1, 2000, 33-45.

[50] Adair and Dahlberg, *Reclaiming Class*, 6.

ess, my experiences and the perspectives and theories that grew out of them, were made ob-scene and invisible. I was disgraced and silenced.

These overwhelming, debilitating judgments and tropes proliferate in the academy. My own profound sense of dislocation as a poor, working, single mother student was exacerbated in classes where I became both the subject and the object of investigation. I recall one particularly painful experience of liminality where in my class, students and teacher alike were lamenting and laughing at the inability of the poor to ever come to political consciousness. One student, the proud daughter of working class parents as I recall, pointed out how poor single mothers were "too busy breeding and eating Cheetoes" to fight for political equity at labor rallies. As the class chuckled with amused agreement, I felt myself ripped in two. I was laughing with my new working class colleagues about their reading of my own experience, my own people, my own body. In the bitterness of that moment I knew that I was homeless.

Similarly, in "Not by Myself Alone: Upward Bound with Family and Friends," Deborah Megivern, a poor white woman responsible for a family of three, recalls an overwhelming sense of alienation and resentment that arose in her classrooms. She remembers:

> Fellow students expressed extremely negative and stereotypical views of poor people, and I was too afraid to challenge their thinking. An economics professor assigned the works of writers such as Charles Murray...we were assigned an essay titled "What's So Bad About Being Poor?" which romanticizes poverty. Years of hardship had left me numb and virtually unable to cry, but reading this essay caused weeks of internal wrenching and waterless tears.[51]

Megivern's "classes on poverty were particularly challenging," as working and middle class students "who had never gone hungry were essentially discussing my family, my friends, even me, as though we were all objects."[52] Like Megivern, Tonya Mitchell, an African American student and single mother recalls, in "If I Survive, It Will Be Despite Welfare Reform," that in her community college classes "poverty bashing was delivered as academic gospel." She clarifies:

> In one sociology class, the professor opened the discussion by telling the class ridiculous anecdotes about lazy poor women sitting at home collecting welfare checks so they could buy color television sets... while the rest of us take care of families or work for a living. He had no proof for these allegations, no foundation on which to generalize his obscene little stories. But he did encourage the other students to join in with their own ideas of the outrageous misdeeds that the poor inflict on our country.[53]

---

[51] Deborah Megivern, "Not by Myself Alone: Upward Bound with Family and Friends," in *Reclaiming Class*, 128.
[52] Ibid, 129.
[53] Tonya Mitchell, "If I Survive it will be Despite Welfare Reform," in *Reclaiming Class*, 128.

These stories highlight the ways in which many poor women of all races continue to be publicly censored in and out of the academy.[54] The effects of poverty bashing, however, are even more widespread and damaging. Because the bodies of poor women are positioned and read as racially and sexually pathological in law and public policy, we are increasingly prevented from entering into and surviving in institutions of higher education.[55] Reading our bodies as aberrant and untrustworthy in the academy prevents those few of us who are able to make it to college from ever coming to voice. Finally, the pressure to redefine ourselves as working class prevents many of us from ever finding or developing that "measure of power over [our] lives" that Zweig refers to as "a full realistic self-identity [as] a basic requirement for human dignity."[56]

When as a hopeful feminist class scholar I enrolled in courses so that I might begin to explore the complex operations of race, gender, sexuality, and class – representing with pin-point precision the systemic devaluation of my life and those of my own people – I was stunned to find that my experiences and perspectives as a poor woman were rejected as irrelevant, peripheral and unwelcome. When I was drawn to working class literature courses in the hope of engaging in finely nuanced understandings of identity and representation, I was similarly disenfranchised. What I found were largely unmitigated and often pat, stereotypical portrayals of the alleged brutality of the lower classes and voyeuristic and obscene portraits of "trailer trash." But, occasionally I also found and celebrated beautiful and resonant representations of the dignity of decent, hard-working and "legitimate" blue-color families. Still, my life and the struggles of my people were nowhere in sight. When I excitedly enrolled in Labor Studies courses I was thrilled to learn about an important history of unions and activism, but in classes devoted to poverty, I was greeted with faceless calculations and "objective assessments" of the "despondency and rage…the unstoppable downward spiral of deterioration…of urban hellholes rife with deprivation, immorality and violence where only the outcasts of society would consider living."[57] Nowhere did I encounter even a glimpse or a fragmentary sense of the deeply rooted, multifaceted and sometimes even ambiguous pain and power of my own community, of my own gendered, raced, sexed *and* classed "human condition."

---

[54] Vivyan C. Adair, "Poverty and the (Broken) Promise of Higher Education," *Harvard Educational Review*, 71:2, 217-39.

[55] Skeggs adds that "the ability to claim and promote an 'identity' is often based on access to sites of representation such as higher education" (123). While it has always been extremely difficult for poor single mothers to complete college degrees, recent federal welfare legislation has made it increasingly difficult, and now nearly impossible, to do so. An alarming reduction of the numbers of poor single mothers who are able to enroll, let alone complete, college programs, means that poor women are denied access to the tools of constructing and disseminating representations of their own senses of class experience.

[56] Zweig, *Working Class Majority*, 5.

[57] Wacquant, "Urban Marginality," 1644.

As a graduate student and junior scholar I sought out the advice of feminist and working class professors, seeking support and guidance in my exploration of literary and cultural representations of poor women. More often than not I was patronized and dismissed. One of my favorite professors chided me by claiming that my "identity platform was weak" and that I had nothing "new to offer since all students and certainly all graduate students were or have been poor at some point in their lives." She later confided in me that when she and her husband bought their first condominium as graduate students, they suffered through eating nothing but beans for a week! One Marxist scholar insisted that I *was* working class, and that the stories I sought out were simply "aberrations" of an otherwise proud and dignified working class history.[58]

These experiences underscore my sense that questions of voice and authority are central to a multi-faceted and rigorous understanding of the operations of class in the United States, both in and out of the academy. bell hooks and Mary Childers in their seminal "A Conversation about Race and Class" remind us that when poor students are not allowed to speak their own truths, even in courses designed to interrogate categories of "race, class and gender," they are "suppressed in the tale of identity and development."[59] A notable lack of representations of the experiences, perspectives and burgeoning theories of poor women – even embedded in the supposed safety and inclusion of working class studies – erases many of the complexities of class as it is actually lived, while simultaneously prohibiting first-hand poverty class analyses of the American condition, to the bane of assiduous class scholars and students.

An inclusive vision of class in the US would allow for a careful and respectful examination of identity formations at the multiple and shifting intersections of experiences of race, gender, sexuality and class embodied nowhere more forcefully and urgently than on the body of the poor woman. Ultimately, I want to expand Skegg's pivotal challenge to class theorists, by calling for both a "wider and deeper" and a more complex, more inclusive and even a more contradictory conceptualization and decoding of what it means to be working class in the US. For, as she posits,

> class formation is dynamic, produced through conflict and fought out at the level of the symbolic. To ignore this is to work uncritically with categories produced through this struggle, which always exist in the interest of power. Class must always be a site of continual struggle and refiguring precisely because it

---

[58] Eventually, with the assistance, support and generous encouragement of Professors Sydney J. Kaplan, Joycelyn Moody, Gail Stygail, and George Dillon I was able to write a dissertation on this topic, which has since been published.
[59] bell hooks and Mary Childers, "A Conversation about Race and Class," in *Conflicts in Feminism*, eds., Marianne Hirsch, Evelyn Fox Keller (New York: Routledge, 1990) 60-81.

represents the interests of particular groups.[60]

Fink adds that our desire for "connectedness" should not "come at the expense of conceptual fields missing altogether from the main narrative of working class studies."[61] By developing theories that help us to understand and critique the impact of differential access to economic, social and cultural resources on a range of women's lives, without claiming an incontestable authenticity or epistemic privilege, and by recognizing the multiplicity and contradictions of identity and community formation, we can begin in earnest to explore rather than overlook the operations of class as it is lived, theorized and contested in contemporary society.

Selected Bibliography

Adair, Vivyan C. *From 'Good Ma' to 'Welfare Queen': A Genealogy of the Poor Woman in American Literature, Photography and Culture.* New York: Garland Publishing, 2000.

Adair, Vivyan C. "Poverty and the (Broken) Promise of Higher Education." *Harvard Educational Review* 71:2 (2001): 217–39.

Adair, Vivyan C. "Branded with Infamy: Inscriptions of Poverty and Class in the United States." *Signs: Journal of Women in Culture and Society* 27:2 (2002): 451–72.

Adair, Vivyan C. and Sandra Dahlberg. *Reclaiming Class: Women, Poverty and the Promise of Higher Education in America.* Philadelphia: Temple University Press, 2003.

Alvarez, Louis and Andrew Kolker. *People Like Us: Social Class in America.* New York: Center for New American Media and The Corporation for Public Broadcasting, 2001.

Aronowitz, Stanley. *How Class Works: Power and Social Movement.* New Haven: Yale University Press, 2003.

Center for Working Class Studies. Youngstown State University, 2005. URL: http://www.as.ysu.edu (Consulted November 10, 2004).

Dahlberg, Sandra L. "Survival in a Not So Brave New World." *Reclaiming Class: Women, Poverty, and the Promise of Higher Education in America.* Eds. Vivyan C. Adair and Sandra L. Dahlberg. Philadelphia: Temple University Press, 2003. 67–84.

"Demonstrators Colorful, Peaceful, and Purposeful," *Seattle Post Intelligencer,* 1 December 1999.

---

[60] Beverly Skeggs "Classifying Practices: Representation, Capital and Recognition," in *Class Matters: Working Class Women's Perspectives on Social Class*, eds. Pat Mahony and Christine Zmroczk , (New York: Taylor and Francis, 1997) 5.

[61] Fink, *In Search of the Working Class*, 42.

URL: http://seattlepi.nwsource.com/local/note01.shtml (Consulted September 25, 2004).

Edin, Katherin and Laura Lein. *Making Ends Meet: How Single Mothers Survive Welfare and Low-Wage Work*. New York: Russell Sage Foundation Publication, 1997.

Federman, Mary. "What Does it Mean to be Poor in America?" *Monthly Labor Review* 119:9 (1996): 32-42.

Felski, Rita. "Nothing to Declare: Identity, Shame and the Lower Middle Class," *PMLA* 115:1 (2000): 33-45.

Foster, Heather, Paul Nyhan and Phuong Cat Le. "Hard Work, Hard Times." *Seattle Post Intelligencer*, 10 February 2005: A5, A8, A9.

Gilder, George. "Welfare Fraud Today." *American Spectator*, 5 September 1995: B6.

Hartman, Heidi. "The Unhappy Marriage of Marxism and Feminism: Towards a More Progressive Union." *Women and Revolution*. Ed. Lydia Sargent. Boston, MA: South End Press, 1981. 97–111.

Jackson, Laura Riding. *The Telling. The Collected Works of Laura Riding Jackson*. Tallahassee, FL: University of Florida Press, 1973.

MacDonald, Heather. "Love, Honor and Get off The Dole." *Daily News* 9 June 2002a, URL: http://www.manhattan-institute.org (Consulted March 4, 2005.)

MacDonald, Heather. "Work = Slavery?" *New York Post*, 4 November 2002b.

McDougal, Gary. "The Missing Half of the Welfare Debate." *The Wall Street Journal*, 6 September 1995: L23.

Megivern, Deborah. "Not by Myself Alone: Upward Bound with Family and Friends." *Reclaiming Class: Women, Poverty and the Promise of Higher Education in America*. Eds. Vivyan Adair and Sandra Dahlberg. Philadelphia, PA: Temple University Press, 2003. 119–30.

Mitchell, Tonya. "If I Survive it will be Despite Welfare Reform." *Reclaiming Class: Women, Poverty and the Promise of Higher Education in America*. Eds. Vivyan Adair and Sandra Dahlberg. Philadelphia, PA: Temple University Press, 2003. 113–18.

Mondale, Sarah and Sarah Patton. *School: The Story of American Public Education*. Boston, MA: Beacon Press, 2001.

Morely, Louise. "A Class of One's Own: Women, Social Class and the Academy." *'Class Matters': Working Class Women's Perspective on Social Class*. Eds. Pat Mahony and Christine Zmroczek. London: Taylor and Francis, 1997. 109–22.

National Compensation Survey: Occupational Wages in the US, US Bureau of Labor Statistics 2004, URL: http://www.bls.gov/ (Consulted January 15, 2005.)

Reay, Diane. "Rethinking Social Class: Qualitative Perspective on Class and Gender." *Sociology* 32:2 (1998): 259–75.

Rubin, Lillian. *Worlds of Pain: Life in the Working Class Family*. New York: Basic Books, 1992.

Ryan, Jake and Charles Sackrey, eds. *Strangers in Paradise: Academics from the Working-Class*. New York: University Press of America, 1996.

Schochet, Peter and Anu Rangaragjan. "Characteristics of Low Wage Workers and Their Labor Market Experience." Mathematica Policy Research Inc. Washington, DC, 2004.URL: http://www.mathematica-mpr.com (Consulted January 10, 2005.)

Sennett, Richard and Jonathan Cobb. *The Hidden Injuries of Class*. New York: Vintage Books, 1972.

Skeggs, Beverly. "Classifying Practices: Representation, Capital and Recognition." *Class Matters: Working Class Women's Perspective on Social Class*. Eds. Pat Mahony and Christine Zmroczek. New York: Taylor and Francis, 1997. 123–39.

Skeggs, Beverly. *Class, Self, Culture*. London: Routledge, 2004.

Smith, Carol. "The Other View from the Top: The Working Poor. PI Special Report: Hard Work, Hard Times." *Seattle Post Intelligencer*, 10 February 2005: A1and A8.

Teixeira, Ruy. "It's the White Working Class, Stupid." Center for American Progress. Public Opinion Watch, 2005.
URL: http://www.americanprogress.org (Consulted January 10, 2005.)

Tokarczyk, Michelle and Elizabeth Fay. *Working Class Women in the Academy: Laborers in the Knowledge Factory*. Amherst, MA: University of Massachusetts Press, 1993.

Wacquant, Loïc. "Urban Marginality in the Coming Millennium." *Urban Studies* 36:10 (1999): 1639-47.

Walt, Carmen De Navas, Robert Cleveland and Bruce Webster Jr. "Income in the United States 2003: Current Population Reports, Consumer Income." US Census Bureau, 2004.
URL: http://www.census.gov/prod/2003pubs/p60-221.pdf
(Consulted January 11, 2005.)

Zweig, Michael. *The Working Class Majority: America's Best Kept Secret*. Ithaca, NY: ILR Press, 2000.

Notes on Contributors

Vivyan C. Adair, Ph.D., is the Elihu Root Endowed Peace Fund Chair and Associate Professor of Womens' Studies and the founder and Director of the ACCESS Project at Hamilton College (serving welfare eligible student parents as they access higher education and income stability). She is the Co-editor of *Reclaiming Class: Women, Poverty and the Promise of Higher Education in America* (Temple University Press, 2003) and the author of *From Good Ma to Welfare Queen: A Genealogy of the Poor Woman in American Literature, Photography, and Culture* (Garland 2000) and articles in *Signs: Journal of Women in Culture and Society, Harvard Educational Review, Sociology (UK), Labor Studies in Working-Class History of the Americas, Pedagogy, The AAUW's On Campus with Women* and *Feminist Studies*.

Rosalie Murphy Baum is associate professor of English at the University of South Florida in Tampa. She is author of more than twenty articles and book chapters on early, 19th-century, and modern American literature; is editor of the Parkman Dexter Howe *Sarah Orne Jewett Collection* and of the first edition of *Contemporary Poets of the English Language*; and is co-editor of the Norton edition of *The Blithedale Romance*. In 1996 she was awarded the University's Jerome Krivanek Distinguished Teacher Award.

Kevin M. Cahill is Associate Professor of Philosophy at the University of Bergen, Norway. His research interests are in the history of Analytic Philosophy, rationality and culture, and the relationship between Analytic and Continental Philosophy. Cahill is currently working on a project with the title *Skepticism and the Human Condition*.

Malini Cadambi is a Sociology and Historical Studies Ph.D. student at the New School for Social Research. Her research areas include the sociology of work, U.S. labor history, and immigration and diaspora studies. She is also a Senior Researcher for the Service Employees International Union 1199 United Healthcare Workers East in New York City.

Evan Matthew Daniel is an archivist at the Tamiment Institute Library/Rober F. Wagner Labor Archives, New York University and a Ph.D. candidate in the departments of history and political science at the New School for Social Research. His research interests include the intellectual, social and political history of Cuba, Spain and the United States with an emphasis on empire and revolution, class, race, and immigration. He is presently writing his dissertation on the transnational work culture and anarchist ideology of Cuban cigar makers in Havana, South Florida and New York City in the mid-late nineteenth century.

Lene M. Johannessen is associate professor in the English department, University of Bergen, Norway. She teaches and researches on American, Chicano, Postcolonial literatures and cultures, theories of language, politics and identity. She has published several essays in these areas, and a book on Chicano literature is forthcoming. The current book project is "The Architectonics of Memory in Exile and Migration."

Marina Moskowitz is a Senior Lecturer in History and American Studies at the University of Glasgow. She is the author of *Standard of Living: The Measure of the Middle Class in Modern America* (Baltimore, 2004). She has held fellowships at the Library of Congress, the Smithsonian Institution, and the Warren Center at Harvard University.

Jason C. Myers is Associate Professor of Political Science at California State University, Stanislaus and has also lectured at the University of Cape Town. He is the author of several articles dealing with concepts of ideology, legitimacy, and historical materialism.

Tom Nesbit is Associate Dean of Continuing Studies at Simon Fraser University in Vancouver, Canada. A former trade union official, his academic interests include adult and post-secondary education, labour studies, workers' and workplace education, and the intersections of social class and higher education.

Kenneth Oldfield was raised by his grandmother. She had a grade-school education and worked as a cook in a "greasy spoon" restaurant. After hearing that Harvard is "the West Liberty State College [WLSC] of the Northeast," Ken took his undergraduate degree from WLSC, in the hills of northern West Virginia. Oldfield is an emeritus professor of public administration at the University of Illinois at Springfield. He has published articles on various topics including property tax administration, Graduate Record Examination predictive validity, the Office of Economic Opportunity, personnel selection and orientation, community college funding disparities, property-assessment uniformity measures, tax increment financing, the human genome project, graduate internships, social class based affirmative action for students and professors, the philosophy of science, and the sociology of knowledge.

Irvin Peckham is an associate professor at Louisiana State University, where he directs the University Writing Program. He has published articles in *Composition Studies, Computers and Writing, English Journal, WPA Journal, Pedagogy*, and in several collections of essays. His interests are in social class reproduction and writing assessment – the former because thats what he likes and the latter because that's what he does.

Masood A. Raja is Assistant Professor of Postcolonial Literature and Theory in the Department of English at Kent State University, Ohio. His critical essays have been published in the *South Asian Review*, *Digest of Middle East Studies*, *Caribbean Studies* and *Mosaic*. He has also contributed chapters to two anthologies and has written biographical introductions for two Pakistani poets for *The Encyclopedia of World Poetry*.

Stephen Routh has a PhD in Political Science from University of California, Davis. He is currently Associate Professor of Political Science with the Department of Politics and Public Administration at California State University, Stanislaus, in Turlock, California. Routh's research focuses on American national institutions – Presidency, Congress, Supreme Court, Judicial Politics, and Constitutional Law. His publications have appeared in *Annual Review of Political Science*, *Political Research Quarterly*, and *The Social Science Journal*.

Omar Swartz (Ph.D., Purdue University, 1995; J.D., Duke University, 2001, *magna cum laude*) is an Assistant Professor in the Department of Communication at the University of Colorado Denver and Health Sciences Center. Dr. Swartz is the author of *In Defense of Partisan Criticism* (2005); *The View From On The Road: The Rhetorical Vision of Jack Kerouac* (1999); *The Rise of Rhetoric and its Intersections with Contemporary Critical Thought* (1998); and *Conducting Socially Responsible Research: Critical Theory, Neo-Pragmatism, and Rhetorical Inquiry* (1997). In addition, Dr. Swartz is the editor of *Social Justice and Communication Scholarship* (2006) and the author more than 60 essays, book chapters, and reviews.

Wuming Zhao comes from China. Her main research interest is the representation of gender and class in American, Chinese, and Japanese popular culture, especially films. She worked in the Foreign Film Studies Department at China Film Association and is presently a Ph.D. candidate in the Graduate School of American Studies, Doshisha University.

Transnational and Transatlantic American Studies
edited by Mita Banerjee (Siegen), Kornelia Freitag (Bochum), Walter Grünzweig (Dortmund), Randi Gunzenhäuser (Dortmund), Rüdiger Kunow (Potsdam), Wilfried Raussert (Bielefeld), Michael Wala (Bochum)

Walter Grünzweig
The United States in Global Contexts
American Studies after 9/11 and Iraq
The momentous events since September 11, 2001, both challenged the field of American Studies and opened up new opportunities for research, teaching, and activism. This book presents more than 160 short contributions by Americanists and Non-Americanists from around the world in an essayistic brainstorm that brings together many questions asked about "America" and American Studies in the age of globalization. Die einschneidenden Veränderungen seit dem 11. September 2001 stellen für die Amerikanistik eine große Herausforderung dar, eröffnen aber auch neue Wege zu Forschung, Lehre und politischem Engagement. Die mehr als 160 Kurzbeiträge von Amerikanist/innen und Nicht-Amerikanist/innen aus vielen Teilen der Welt sind ein essayistischer brainstorm, der wichtige Fragen zu „Amerika" und zur Amerikanistik im Zeitalter der Globalisierung zusammenführt.
Bd. 1, 2004, 184 S., 19,90 €, br.,
ISBN 3-8258-8262-4

Aija Poikāne-Daumke
African Diasporas
Afro-German Literature in the Context of the African American Experience
This book investigates the development of Afro-German literature in the context of the African American experience and shows the decisive role of literature for the emergence of the Afro-German Movement. Various Afro-German literary and cultural initiatives, which began in the 1980s, arose as a response to the experience of being marginalized – to the point of invisibility – within a dominant Eurocentric culture that could not bring the notions of „Black" and „German" together in a meaningful way. The book is a significant contribution to the understanding of German literature as multi-ethnic and of the the transatlantic networks operating in the African Diasporas.
Aija Poikane-Daumke graduated from the University of Latvia where she received her BA and MA degrees in education and English philology. She discovered her interest in Black literature and culture in the course of her high school year Cleveland, Ohio. In 2002, she was awarded a scholarship by the German Academic Exchange Service (DAAD) and pursued her doctoral thesis in American Studies at Universität Dortmund. In Dortmund, she taught several seminars on Afro-German and African American literature. Currently, she is engaged in a project on East European immigrant narratives in the US after WW II.
Bd. 2, 2006, 144 S., 24,90 €, br.,
ISBN 3-8258-9612-9

African Connections in Post-Colonial Theory and Literatures
edited by Ulrike Auga, Ulrike Kistner, Rita Schäfer, David Attwell

Ulrike Ernst
From Anti-Apartheid to African Renaissance
Interviews with South African Writers and Critics on Cultural Politics Beyond the Cultural Struggle
The focus of this collection is the cultural and literary policy of the tripartite alliance (ANC, SACP, COSATU) after its denouncement of 'culture as a weapon'. Three shifts are noted between 1990 – 2000: the end of apartheid, the alliance's accession to power, and the change of presidency from Nelson Mandela to Thabo Mbeki, including the adoption of a

LIT Verlag Berlin – Hamburg – London – Münster – Wien – Zürich
Fresnostr. 2 48159 Münster
Tel.: 0251 – 62 032 22 – Fax: 0251 – 23 19 72
e-Mail: vertrieb@lit-verlag.de – http://www.lit-verlag.de

neo-liberal macro-economic policy. The investigation stresses the importance of the role of writers and intellectuals in political and societal transformation processes that have a tendency to destroy the agency that initially set them in motion. Startling revelations are being made, which highlight the emptiness of much Rainbow Nation sloganeering.

Bd. 1, 2nd edition, 2004, 208 S., 20,90 €, br., ISBN 3-8258-5804-9

Ulrike Kistner
Commissioning and Contesting Post-Apartheid's Human Rights
HIV/AIDS – Racism – Truth and Reconciliation
The essays compiled in this book take issue with some of the directions of human rights politics in the immediate post-apartheid period. They look at the relationship between different sets of rights within the political contestations in South Africa. To the terms of social struggles for rights and justice, this book brings perspectives from narrative, psychoanalysis, political philosophy, and medical history; and from the history of national liberation struggles, nationalism and citizenship.
Bd. 2, 2003, 216 S., 25,90 €, br., ISBN 3-8258-6202-x

Rita Schäfer
Im Schatten der Apartheid
Frauen-Rechtsorganisationen und geschlechtsspezifische Gewalt in Südafrika
Mit dem Ende der Apartheid änderte sich die Ausrichtung der südafrikanischen Frauen-Rechtsorganisationen: Sie waren sie bis dahin Teil der Befreiungsbewegung und hatten die besondere Problemlage von Frauen dem Kampf gegen das Apartheid-Regime untergeordnet. Nach der politischen Wende 1994 forderten sie die Verankerung von Frauenrechten in der neuen Verfassung. Nun arbeiten sie mit der ANC-Regierung zusammen, um die Rechtsrealität von Frauen zu verbessern und die Gewalt zu reduzieren. Denn Vergewaltigungen und häusliche Gewalt verhindern die Umsetzung der nun geltenden Gleichheitsgrundsätze. Diese Studie analysiert, inwieweit Frauen-Rechtsorganisationen gesellschaftliche Veränderungen in Südafrika mitgestalten. In umfassender Weise beleuchtet sie die historischen Hintergründe und kulturellen Legitimationen unterschiedlicher Gewaltformen. Auf breiter empirischer Basis dokumentiert sie die Arbeit von Frauen-Rechtsorganisationen in verschiedenen Landesteilen. Das Buch eröffnet neue Perspektiven für die *Gender-*, Gewalt- und Rechtsforschung in Afrika.
Bd. 3, 2005, 496 S., 29,90 €, br., ISBN 3-8258-8676-x

Contributions to Asian American Literary Studies
edited by Rocío G. Davis (University of Navarre) and Sämi Ludwig (Université de Haute-Alsace Mulhouse)

Rocío G. Davis; Sämi Ludwig (Eds.)
Asian American Literature in the International Context
Readings on Fiction, Poetry, and Performance
In their different and yet complementary perspectives, all of the essays in *Asian American Literature in the International Context: Readings on Fiction, Poetry, and Performance* reiterate the universal lesson of pluralism. They are divided into sections that deal with biraciality and biculturality, interethnic negotiations, poetic creations, narrative experiments, and (re)constructing self. The wide variety of approaches reflects the contributors' training in different cultures and across cultures. It showcases refreshing new perspectives in reading that combine the views of literary scholars from three different continents. This collection creates a space for discussion and commentary, of heightened appreciation and increased creativity, a forum that turns the discipline of Asian American Studies into a truly intercultural debate.
vol. 1, 2002, 272 pp., 25,90 €, br., ISBN-DE 3-8258-5710-7, ISBN-CH 3-03735-137-3

LIT Verlag Berlin – Hamburg – London – Münster – Wien – Zürich
Fresnostr. 2 48159 Münster
Tel.: 0251 – 62 032 22 – Fax: 0251 – 23 19 72
e-Mail: vertrieb@lit-verlag.de – http://www.lit-verlag.de

Alicia Otano
Speaking the Past
Child Perspective in the Asian American "Bildungsroman"
Child perspective is a symbolic narrative strategy that designs multilayered possibilities for meaning in ethnic writing. This book positions Asian American bildungsromane in the context of American writing about children, reading them through the lens of their narrators ,– the oftentimes dual child/adult perspective ,– to examine how narrative point of view nuances and shapes issues of personal, ethnic, and national positioning. This approach privileges the authors' narrative choices and engagement with genre, revealing how these critical writerly decisions construct texts that signify on multiple levels, and dialogue productively with ofher texts. Their interpretation and creative negotiation of the key elements of narrative perspective lead us to uncover aspects which are constitutive of the successful manipulation of narrative voice. The texts analyzed in this study, by Gus Lee, Cecilia Manguerra Brainard, Heinz Insu Fenkl, Lois-Ann Yamanaka, and Fiona Cheong, demonstrate the flexibility of this narrative technique, and its usefulness as a critical tool though which important thematic issues ,– family, race, culture, war, assimilation, and language ,– may be deployed. Reading the way Asian American texts manipulate child perspective positions these texts within developing critical paradigms and allows us to examine the manner in which they influence the development of American literature and the theory that reads it.
Bd. 2, 2004, 184 S., 19,90 €, br.,
ISBN 3-8258-7748-5

Begoña Simal; Elisabetta Marino (eds.)
Transnational, National, and Personal Voices
New Perspectives on Asian American and Asian Diasporic Women Writers
The growing heterogeneity of Asian American and Asian diasporic voices has also given rise to variegated theoretical approaches to these literatures. This book attempts to encompass both the increasing awareness of diasporic and transnational issues, and more "traditional" analyses of Asian American culture and literature. Thus, the articles in this collection range from investigations into the politics of literary and cinematic representation, to "digging" into the past through "literary archeology", or analyzing how "consequential" bodies can be in recent literature by Asian American and Asian diasporic women writers. The book closes with an interview with critic and writer Shirley Lim, where she insightfully deals with these "transnational, national, and personal" issues.
Bd. 3, 2005, 264 S., 29,90 €, br.,
ISBN 3-8258-8278-0

Rocío G. Davis; Jaume Aurell; Ana Beatriz Delgado (Eds.)
Ethnic Life Writing and Histories
Genres, Performance, and Culture
This collection focuses on how literary creativity and historical inscriptions produce texts that require nuanced readings of forms of life writing. These reflections support the use of life writing as an interpretative frame for historical information, validating it for historical discourse as the act of telling and writing one's story affirms as it performs identity. Our approach is based on a methodology that connects genre studies and historiography, to arrive at conclusions about the writing of the history of globalization, immigration, racial and ethnic negotiation.
Bd. 4, 2007, 256 S., 24,90 €, br.,
ISBN 978-3-8258-0257-8

Anglistik / Amerikanistik

Jörg Rademacher (Hrsg./Ed.)
Modernism and the Individual Talent/Moderne und besondere Begabung
Re-Canonizing Ford Madox Ford (Hueffer)/Zur Re-Kanonisierung von Ford Madox Ford (Hüffer). Symposium Münster June/Juni 1999
Bd. 6, 2002, 224 S., 25,90 €, br.,
ISBN 3-8258-4311-4

LIT Verlag Berlin – Hamburg – London – Münster – Wien – Zürich
Fresnostr. 2 48159 Münster
Tel.: 0251 – 62 032 22 – Fax: 0251 – 23 19 72
e-Mail: vertrieb@lit-verlag.de – http://www.lit-verlag.de

Ulrike Ernst
From Anti-Apartheid to African Re-naissance
Interviews with South African Writers
and Critics on Cultural Politics Beyond
the Cultural Struggle
Bd. 7, 2002, 208 S., 20,90 €, br.,
ISBN 3-8258-5804-9

Andreas Lienkamp; Wolfgang Werth;
Christian Berkemeier (Hg.)
"As strange as the world"
Annäherungen an das Werk des Erzählers
und Filmemachers Paul Auster
Bd. 8, 2002, 170 S., 20,90 €, br.,
ISBN 3-8258-6046-9

Victor Grove
Hamlet
Das Drama des modernen Menschen
Bd. 10, 2003, 248 S., 30,90 €, br.,
ISBN 3-8258-6224-0

Birgit Lahaye
Pirating History
Die Darstellung des haitianischen Unab-hängigkeitskampfes in der Erzählliteratur
Bd. 12, 2003, 288 S., 29,90 €, br.,
ISBN 3-8258-6718-8

Radhouan Ben Amara
The Fragmentation of the Proper Na-me and The Crisis of Degree
Deconstructing King Lear
Bd. 13, 2004, 144 S., 20,90 €, br.,
ISBN 3-8258-6736-6

Heike Haase
Oscar für alle – Die Darstellung Oscar Wildes in biofiktionaler Literatur
Bd. 16, 2004, 280 S., 29,90 €, br.,
ISBN 3-8258-6985-7

Martin J. Meyer
Tolkien als religiöser Sub-Creator
Bd. 17, 2004, 376 S., 29,90 €, gb.,
ISBN 3-8258-7200-9

Sabine Kozdon
Memory in Samuel Beckett's Plays
A Psychological Approach
Bd. 18, 2006, 344 S., 29,90 €, br.,
ISBN 3-8258-7255-6

Victor Grove
Hamlet – The Drama of Modern Man
Bd. 19, 2004, 208 S., 24,90 €, br.,
ISBN 3-8258-7455-9

Heike Michaelis
Darwinismus und literarischer Diskurs in England am Beispiel von George Eliot und Thomas Hardy
Darwins Evolutionstheorie stellt eine der be-deutendsten Zäsuren in der Geistesgeschichte
der Neuzeit dar. Sein Werk löste Reaktionen
in allen wissenschaftlichen Disziplinen aus,
doch in der englischen Literatur sind bisher
kaum Spuren Darwinscher Theoreme aufge-zeigt worden. Das vorliegende Werk setzt sich
mit der Adaption evolutionärer Modelle in
Werken von George Eliot und Thomas Hardy
auseinander und zeigt anhand der Analyse
ausgewählter Romane auf, in welch enger
Symbiose sich Literatur und Evolutionstheo-rie tatsächlich befinden.
Bd. 20, 2004, 280 S., 24,90 €, br.,
ISBN 3-8258-7720-5

Stefanie Krämer
Das Motiv des Fegefeuers bei Samuel Beckett
Seit dem Mittelalter ist das Fegefeuer ein be-liebtes Motiv in der Literatur. Dabei lassen
sich mit dem Bild der Wanderung in diesem
Reich zwischen Tod und Auferstehung so-wie der Frage nach Läuterung und Erlösung
immer wieder zwei Leitmotive erkennen.
Samuel Beckett greift diese Motive auf. Ei-ne Analyse seiner Werke und Manuskripte
zeigt, wie der Autor die unterschiedlichsten
Quellen nutzt, um ein Spannungsverhältnis
zwischen christlichen Motiven und biblischen
Zitaten einerseits und Agnostizismus anderer-

LIT Verlag Berlin – Hamburg – London – Münster – Wien – Zürich
Fresnostr. 2 48159 Münster
Tel.: 0251 – 62 032 22 – Fax: 0251 – 23 19 72
e-Mail: vertrieb@lit-verlag.de – http://www.lit-verlag.de

seits herzustellen, so daß ein gänzlich neues Fegefeuermotiv entsteht.

Bd. 21, 2004, 208 S., 19,90 €, br.,
ISBN 3-8258-7747-7

Eva-Marie Herlitzius
A comparative analysis of the South African and German reception of Nadine Gordimer's, André Brink's and J. M. Coetzee's works
The canonical academic status as well as the immense commercial success of a small selection of 'white' South African authors such as Nadine Gordimer, André Brink and especially the latest Nobel Prize winner J. M. Coetzee raise many questions. How did their images as 'representative' South African writers influence national and international understandings of the country South Africa? And how does the publishing media contribute to the construction and communication of South Africa as a cultural product? How do readers of different social and geographical locations react to the ways multi-national publishing companies promote their international best-sellers?
Bd. 22, 2005, 392 S., 32,90 €, br.,
ISBN 3-8258-8349-3

Maria Moss
Höhlenein- und Ausgänge: Wirklichkeitsbewältigung in der zeitgenössischen Literatur Nordamerikas
Was kommt nach der Postmoderne, die sich – besonders in der amerikanischen Literatur – mittlerweile als literarische Tradition erschöpft hat? Um diese Frage beantworten zu können, die auch immer eine Frage nach den Befindlichkeiten einer ganzen Epoche ist, analysiert die Literaturwissenschaftlerin Maria Moss die zeitgenössische nordamerikanische Literatur (1980 bis Anfang des 21. Jahrhunderts) anhand eines anthropologischen Musters, welches aus der Mythostheorie des Philosophen Hans Blumenberg entwickelt ist. Blumenberg hat in seinen Schriften – besonders in *Arbeit am Mythos* und *Höhlenausgänge* – ein Muster der Weltbewältigung entworfen, welches den Individualisierungstendenzen und dem Bedeutungsschwund unserer Zeit entgegenwirkt. Das anthropologische Muster bezeichnet Formen der Realitätsbewältigung, deren kreative Auslegung die Rückkehr mimetischer Vorstellungen – weniger als Bestätigung des Bekannten, sondern vor allem als Bewältigung des Unbekannten – in ausgewählten Texten der zeitgenössischen nordamerikanischen Literatur verdeutlichen und verstehen hilft.
Bd. 24, 2006, 248 S., 24,90 €, br.,
ISBN 3-8258-9521-1

Anahita Teymourian-Pesch
Amerikaner in der Fremde – Humor als Überwindungsstrategie
Ideal und Wirklichkeit widersprechen einander oftmals. Ist das Dasein des Menschen deshalb notwendig tragisch? Der Text untersucht, wie mit dieser existenzphilosophischen Frage in Literatur umgegangen wird. These ist, daß es durch ein humorvolles Ethos gelingt, die fundamentalen Widersprüche des Daseins zu versöhnen und Krisen zu überwinden. Welt und Leben werden nicht als Orte des Scheiterns erlebt, sondern als soziales Abenteuer erfahren. Ideal und Realität bleiben erhalten.
Bd. 25, Herbst 2007, 280 S., 24,90 €, gb.,
ISBN 3-8258-9659-5

Nicola Birkner
AIDS Narratives
Die literarische Imagination von Krankheit
Bd. 26, 2006, 328 S., 24,90 €, br.,
ISBN 3-8258-9935-7

LIT Verlag Berlin – Hamburg – London – Münster – Wien – Zürich
Fresnostr. 2 48159 Münster
Tel.: 0251 – 62 032 22 – Fax: 0251 – 23 19 72
e-Mail: vertrieb@lit-verlag.de – http://www.lit-verlag.de